D0936488

PRAISE FOR *GANGS AND THE MILITARY*

"Carter F. Smith breaks down the theory, types, and definition of gangs, bikers, and terrorists and how they impact the community and workforce. He offers a fascinating historical analysis of gangs through the nation's war years, illuminating how gang culture, in some form, has plagued government authorities since the post–Revolutionary War era in much the same manner that they plague investigators and communities today. *Gangs and the Military: Gangsters, Bikers, and Terrorists with Military Training* has greatly expanded the knowledge of gang investigators with this seminal work. It is a gem!" —**Ron Stallworth,** SGT, Ret., former gang intelligence coordinator, Utah Department of Public Safety

"For anyone interested in understanding the insidious nature of criminal gang and extremist infiltration of the armed forces in America, *Gangs and the Military* is a must-read. The author not only provides a comprehensive and thorough examination of the history of gangs in the U.S., but also sets forth clearly articulated evidence of the infiltration of the gangster mentality and its associated criminal influence within our nation's military branches." —**Christopher Grant**, national Native American gang specialist

"Smith spotted the problem of gang members with military training years ago; here is the evidence! The book is well researched, very comprehensive, and proven. A useful contribution. Well done!" —**Simon Harding,** lecturer at Middlesex University; author of *The Street Casino: Survival in Violent Street Gangs*

"This is a very fascinating and eye-opening book! The interesting part of gang investigations is that there are always new things to learn. Gangs are not a new phenomenon, and this book helps highlight that. This problem is not going away, and hopefully this book will help awaken some who still hide their heads in the sand and hope that gangs will just go away." —**Jim Quick,** president, Tennessee Gang Investigators Association

"Smith has provided an excellent examination of issues often missed and more often misunderstood. He provides the reader with a fantastic historical perspective, which offers a wonderful lead into an analysis of the issues of military training and service for gang members. These are extremely important cautionary notes that the reader should take the time to examine in detail before considering the consequences of having military-trained gang members moving back to civilian communities. In this book, Smith looks at some of the key questions arising from gang studies in the twenty-first century." —**Andy Bain,** PhD, director of criminal justice studies, University of Mount Union, Ohio; co-author of *Outlaw Motorcycle Gangs: A Theoretical Perspective*

"Smith has created a book that is exceptional for those in law enforcement, military, and in the civilian community. His extensive knowledge in the field of gangs shines through in his literature and teachings. The information contained in this book covers a wide variety of topics, from a historical introduction to early gangs to showing how various wars have impacted and changed the gang culture, as well as updated information on modern-day street gangs. This well-written book is a definite must-read!" —**Dave Harris,** Boise Police Department Gang Unit; vice president, Northwest Gang Investigators Association

Gangs and the Military

Gangsters, Bikers, and Terrorists with Military Training

Carter F. Smith

ROWMAN & LITTLEFIELD
Lanham • Boulder • New York • London

ST. JOHN THE BAPTIST PARISH LIBRARY
2920 NEW HIGHWAY 51
LAPLACE, LOUISIANA 70068

Published by Rowman & Littlefield
A wholly owned subsidiary of The Rowman & Littlefield Publishing Group, Inc.
4501 Forbes Boulevard, Suite 200, Lanham, Maryland 20706
www.rowman.com

Unit A, Whitacre Mews, 26-34 Stannary Street, London SE11 4AB

Copyright © 2017 by Rowman & Littlefield

All rights reserved. No part of this book may be reproduced in any form or by
any electronic or mechanical means, including information storage and retrieval
systems, without written permission from the publisher, except by a reviewer who
may quote passages in a review.

British Library Cataloguing in Publication Information Available

Library of Congress Cataloging-in-Publication Data
Names: Smith, Carter F., author.
Title: Gangs and the United States military : veterans and active duty
    military veterans in street gangs, biker gangs, and domestic terrorist
    groups / Carter F. Smith.
Description: Lanham : Rowman & Littlefield, [2017] | Includes index. |
    Description based on print version record and CIP data provided by
    publisher; resource not viewed.
Identifiers: LCCN 2017006831 (print) | LCCN 2017013374 (ebook) | ISBN
    9781442275171 (electronic) | ISBN 9781442275164 (cloth : alk. paper)
Subjects: LCSH: Gang members—United States. | Veterans—United States. |
    Soldiers—United States.
Classification: LCC HV6439.U5 (ebook) | LCC HV6439.U5 S613 2017 (print) | DDC
    364.106/6086970973—dc23
LC record available at https://lccn.loc.gov/2017006831

♾™ The paper used in this publication meets the minimum requirements of
American National Standard for Information Sciences—Permanence of Paper
for Printed Library Materials, ANSI/NISO Z39.48-1992.

Printed in the United States of America

Contents

Foreword

The U.S. military has a long history of serving America by protecting the country's citizens. Specialized and modernized training, a military style of discipline, and a focus on national and international security has allowed America's fighting forces to become the most formidable, well-trained military in the world.

Many young men and women have honored the millions of civilians with their military service. But that is the point. The ranks of our military have come from society. Even with all the discipline and leadership, the ranks of our military still represent a slice of America's general population.

Along with that cohort comes the issues and problems associated with society in general, albeit probably at a lower rate; but nevertheless they exist. This book examines those issues and offers some simple, yet effective strategies in dealing with gangs within our military. I know there have been media and news specials highlighting certain instances where gang members are also active duty military members. It is easy to suggest that gangs in the U.S. military are a severe and present danger. In fact, they are not. However, they do, and continue to disrupt commands to the contrary, prey on children of active duty members and typically do not abandon, or give up, their gang affiliation while on active duty.

Gangs have even made their presence known on overseas military bases and on board military vessels. Interestingly, in 2007, a Pentagon official commented that gangs are in the military, but gang members are 1 percent, or less, of the total military population. That would work out to approximately 10,000 gang members. That would be equal to the size of one of our largest military bases.

Not surprisingly, some gang experts believe the general U.S. gang population is most likely less than 1 percent of the general U.S. population. You see, the military represents a small segment of society. So, issues affecting the general population will also affect the military population.

This is nothing to be ashamed of or deny . . . people are people and they will have personal and family issues whether they are active duty or civilians. So let us examine in a candid manner, without the influence of the media, the gang issue in the U.S. military. It is still the finest, best trained, and most advanced military service in the world.

Al Valdez, PhD, Professor
University of California, Irvine
School of Social Sciences
Retired Supervising Investigator
Orange County District Attorney's Office
Santa Ana, California

Preface

I joined the U.S. Army in 1978. My main reason for joining (no joke) was to see why the police officers treated me and my juvenile-delinquent friends the way they did. I told the recruiter that I wanted to be in the Military Police (MP), and after attending basic training at Fort McClellan, Alabama, I was assigned to the 66th MP Battalion in Karlsruhe, Germany. I progressed from rookie to patrolman to desk clerk to desk sergeant and found I loved the job, so I chose to stay for five years. I learned a lot about police work from my leaders and the local Polizei. I spent a few years working on the drug investigations team, where I learned a lot about how to talk to "normal" people. I loved the experience most of the time I was in Germany, but all good things come to an end. I delayed the end of my tour in Germany by re-enlisting, but in 1984 the Army chose to send me to my next duty assignment—Fort Campbell, Kentucky.

When I arrived at Fort Campbell, I worked on the drug investigations team. It was supervised by the CID and there were a handful of MP Investigations folks, like me, on the team. After working several very interesting and successful drug cases, I returned to general MP investigations. I thought I was finished working with CID (I liked the investigations but wasn't too keen on the bureaucracy), but when I received orders to report back to Germany, I went looking for ways to avoid doing so (I had tried to stay while I was there, and I am not a fan of moving, to put it lightly). Applying for CID seemed the most effective way, and I signed on as a Special Agent in 1986. In 1990, I transferred (briefly) to Korea and returned to Fort Campbell. Did I mention that I am not a fan of moving?

Beginning in the early 1990s, many of the more inquisitive Military Police Investigators (MPI) and Criminal Investigations (CID) Agents in the Army began seeing indicators that groups of individuals were engaging in coordinated criminal (gang) activity. At Fort Campbell, Kentucky, we hadn't seen anything like that before, but having learned to maintain relationships with police officers in other locations (and having kept up with current events), we knew what we had discovered. The problem, as we saw it, was that gangs had infiltrated our small, relatively private, military community.

On one occasion, I was working with an MPI investigator on multiple car break-ins in some parking lots on the installation. We had determined that the sheer number of incidents, with some distinct differences in methods, indicated there were multiple coordinated offenders. Our suspicions were verified when we caught two of the culprits. They told us they were members of a local gang.

Not long afterward, we encountered several male military family members who were also claiming to be part of a gang. We just started looking for gang indicators, and as we learned what they were and we realized the more you get out and talk to people in the community, the more you see them earlier. If you are nice to them and ask them for help, most members of the community will either contact you and tell you what they saw (or tell you when you see them again and ask).

We were never out shaking the bushes looking for work; we were just responding to a problem that we saw in a way that seemed natural for us. This was all just a grassroots effort by a small handful of MPI Investigators and CID Special Agents. This wasn't the Special Agent-in-Charge (SAC) saying, "*I think we have a gang problem. You guys better go find out what's going on. Here's all the resources you ever thought about needing.*" When working in grassroots mode, we actually spent a lot of our personal time, the time we would've used to go home earlier, doing this additional stuff. I don't mean we worked covertly, I mean we realized we had given the Army the amount and level of work that they paid us for, and we could take a little bit of our own time to explore something work-related that we were interested in. It's funny that we had doubters about the existence of gang members in the military back then! Who would spend a lot of their own time chasing down rabbit holes that aren't likely to have rabbits in them? If you didn't see a rabbit go into that rabbit hole, it's usually just best to fill it in, rather than see if it's coming back! When we tried to reach out to more experienced gang investigators, we often served as an impromptu office joke. But we had arrested criminals who claimed to be gang members, so what were we to do?

Some of the military supervisors (both CID and those of the soldiers identified) responded with a "prove it" or a "oh they're wannabes" or "oh that's nice" response. We realized that what it all boiled down to was that no one likes investigating conspiracy cases. They just wanted criminal information and evidence for their cases in a simple and uncomplicated way. They didn't want anything that took a long time to investigate or prosecute. We realized we were seeing the shift into denial mode.

At one point, we started putting the word "gang" on our initial report. We said it was a "gang of youths" and we were corrected immediately by the folks in Washington, D.C. We were told "do not use that word in the initial report," as those were not "proven" gang members. We agreed begrudgingly and decided to make up our own term to see if they would let that slide. We settled on reporting in our initial and subsequent reports that, for example, a "witness reported a Group of Primarily Black Juveniles (GPBJs) in the area . . ." *or* the patrol observed a "Group of Primarily White Juveniles (GPWJs) flee the scene upon their arrival. . . ." Before you judge the selections, recall that I am talking about the 1990s. Many gangs were organized and aligned by race and ethnicity back then. Yes, there was a hint of subtle "in your face" attitude, but that's what you get when you tell someone that something they see regularly doesn't exist, right?

We spent a lot of time training military leadership on gang indicators. What we learned was that we needed to first educate our community, and second, investigate what was happening in our community. At first we didn't know what we were going to do with it, so we just collected all the information and followed up when we saw more indicators. We included a lot of the information in our briefings and we'd see some graffiti and try to translate it, and then include it in our briefings. We couldn't have planned a better grassroots effort in my opinion, because whenever we'd get a visit from our next higher command, we'd give them a briefing on what we were doing and soon they were asking for updates and including our information in their own briefings. Soon afterward, we were being asked to send someone to several installations as well as civilian locations to brief folks on "Gangs in the Military."

From its inception in June of 1997, until it ceased continuous operation about four years later, the Gang-Extremist Team at Fort Campbell provided federal, state, and military briefings to thousands of people. We got the first conviction for distribution of extremist literature in the Department of Defense and had a lot of proactive work prior to 9/11. We organized and presented the first Military Gang/Extremist Training Conference in February 1998. We assisted local law enforcement agencies with implementation of gang programs and a focus on hate crimes investigation. And when I retired, I handed the team off to a quite capable agent. And then 9/11 happened.

I went to law school after retiring, not knowing what I was going to do with a law degree other than getting one. After graduation, I ended up working in the business world in the Nashville area until I found myself back in Fort Campbell working at Army CID as a civilian. I contacted the folks with whom I had "entrusted" all the gang and extremist information, briefings, and so on before I retired in 1999. Sadly, most had not added much to the collection, but it gave me a place to start. I found some willing collaborators and got back into the intelligence collection mode. It helped that I had been hired as the Criminal Intelligence Manager.

I stayed at Fort Campbell from 2004–2006, until I realized that I was not making enough of a difference in the community. It didn't have anything to do with the (continued) lack of interest that the Army displayed for this topic. Nor did it have much of anything to do with the impression I got that the Command was heading in a direction I did not agree with. The driving force was that I felt a strong calling to change careers and become a part of the higher education of tomorrow's leaders. I began working full time at Middle Tennessee State University (my law degree qualified me for that) while pursuing a PhD.

It was while on the PhD track that a new direction for my investigations (research) was identified. Not only did I no longer have the inside track (not directly, anyway) on what was going on in the military criminal investigations world, but I also realized that the problem had evolved—likely long before I recognized it. The bigger problem was with gang members with military training who had left the military. With my connections with civilian law enforcement, I could take a different approach to examine the issue. Research on military-trained gang members in the civilian community had begun.

My dissertation was on (not surprisingly) military-trained gang members and most of the academic publications I have written since then have been on that same general topic, too. I have been able to stay relevant (with current information) because when I visit various gang investigator and police conferences, I talk with law enforcement and military folks and ask for their insight. Recently, I started doing so in a more organized fashion, the results of which you will see later in the book.

While I may not call this my life's work, I hope it's clear that I do find the topic important. It's so important to me that I delayed quite a few larger projects to get this book done. As you will see, the biggest problems with gangsters, bikers, and domestic terrorists in the military began in the early 1990s. I doubt that they will end by the time you read this book, but I am confident that I will see less ahead than I have behind. I do hope you enjoy the read!

Acknowledgments

I extend a special thanks to those who investigated and researched this topic before, while, and since I have. As is often the case, those who investigate activities before anyone else does are considered something akin to an overly curious lunatic while they are doing it and an unparalleled visionary once everyone else catches on and wants to know what they learned. Folks like Johnny Welch, George Knox, and Karen McMaster examined the periphery and foundation of what we see today while others were focused elsewhere. Investigators like Hunter Glass, Richard Valdemar, Scott Barfield, Jeff Stoleson, Al Valdez, Bob Stasch, John Bowman, and Carl Dewyer challenged the status quo to varying degrees and ensured that the dangerousness of military-trained gang members was not overlooked as isolated incidents.

There are many others cited throughout the book that helped put all the pieces together and many continue to do so. I am most thankful to Steve Chancellor, friend, supervisor, and mentor (not necessarily in that order), for fighting the onslaught of naysayers as we addressed a very dangerous and very real threat, and thankful to Tim Zimmerman, Chuck Clapper, and Tony Valdes for giving me the opportunity to learn what this phenomenon was all about. Thomas (T.J.) Leyden (and men like him) helped us understand some of what we were investigating by sharing his past as a neo-Nazi both in and out of the Marine Corps.

I am very thankful to my wife, Sharmyn, for encouraging my "diversion" from the rigors of my other passions. I tremendously appreciate the confidence of Kathryn Knigge, editor with Rowman and Littlefield, for enabling the reprioritization of this book at "just the right time," my anonymous reviewers, without whom the manuscript would have remained underdeveloped, and the amazing and irreplaceable Rowman & Littlefield editing and publishing machine that transformed the digital manuscript into the book you are now holding. Finally, I thank my preliminary manuscript reviewer, Mitzie (GG) Forrest-Thompson, for her painstaking analysis of each and every word, line, paragraph, and page of the early manuscript. We all need a second set of eyes on our writing, and she provided a quite capable set to look after mine.

Acronyms

AFB	Air Force Base
AFOSI	Air Force Office of Special Investigation
AR	Army Regulation
ATF/BATF/ BATFE	Bureau of Alcohol, Tobacco, Firearms, and Explosives
ATP	Army Techniques Publication
ATTP	Army Tactics, Techniques, and Procedures
CID	Criminal Investigations Division
CRIMINTEL	Criminal Intelligence
D.A.R.E.	Drug Abuse Resistance Education
DE	Domestic Extremist
DEA	Drug Enforcement Administration
DOC	Department of Corrections
DoD	Department of Defense
DoDI	Department of Defense Instruction
DTE	Domestic Terrorist and/or Extremist
FBI	Federal Bureau of Investigation
FM	Field Manual
GAO	Government Accounting Office
GDEATA	Gang and Domestic Extremist Activity Threat Assessment
GREAT	Gang Resistance Education and Training
IACP	International Association of Chiefs of Police
IOMGIA	International Outlaw Motorcycle Gang Investigators' Association
LE	Law Enforcement
LEO	Law Enforcement Officer
LER	Law Enforcement Report

MCIO	Military Criminal Investigative Organizations
MGPQ	Military Gang Perception Questionnaire
MP	Military Police
MPI	Military Police Investigations
MS-13	Mara Salvatrucha
MTGM	Military-Trained Gang Member
NCIS	Naval Criminal Investigative Service
NGC	National Gang Center
NGIC	National Gang Intelligence Center
NYGC	National Youth Gang Center
RICO	Racketeer Influenced and Corrupt Organizations Act
RISS	Regional Intelligence Sharing System
ROI	Report of Investigation
SAC	Special Agent-In-Charge
SHARP	Skinheads Against Racial Prejudice
SPLC	Southern Poverty Law Center
STG	Security Threat Groups
SWAT	Special Weapons and Tactics
TNGIA	Tennessee Gang Investigators' Association
UCMJ	Uniform Code of Military Justice

Chapter One

The History of Gangs and the Military Connection

In December 1992, members of the Cedar Block Pirus, a Blood gang originally from Los Angeles, California, murdered a father and his three children, all military dependents, in Tacoma, Washington. The Pirus, assisted by two Fort Lewis, Washington, soldiers, killed Mr. Allen King Sr. and his three children at the King's residence on Fort Lewis. The soldiers drove the gang members to King's home, drove the gang members to a motel, and disposed of evidence of the crime.[1] Mr. King and his children were hacked to death because the gang members believed King had reported them for operating a crack house in Tacoma. Sergeant (SGT) Lisa A. King, Mr. King's wife, was on duty in South Korea at the time.[2] King's death was one of the first military-connected gang-related murders in recent history. The activities of the subjects demonstrated how the presence of gang members in the military community can otherwise endanger law-abiding citizens. It also demonstrated the extent to which criminal street gang members are willing to conceal their activities and instill fear in the community. There will be more about the King murders in chapter 2.

Traditionally, or perhaps historically, gang membership has been considered more of an advanced form of juvenile delinquency. Gang problems have typically been treated as issues with youngsters from lower on the socioeconomic scale, often coming from broken homes, poverty, and an environment that provides little in the way of nurturing, encouragement, or an opportunity to improve. Unlike the gang members of the past, most gang members in the last half century have been African American or Latino (Hispanic), and they often have had limited formal education. Like most gang members of the past, most gang members in the last quarter century have been adults. Most communities have been or at least felt immune to most gang problems, especially military communities, and the average citizen has had little chance

1

to encounter gangs or gang members. Nonetheless, the continued increase in military-trained gang members being released from the military without restriction threatens to make our gang members more sophisticated and our communities less safe.

This book is about the intersection of gang life and military service. Military-trained gang members have come from every wartime period for the United States—from the Revolutionary War to the conflicts we are presently engaging in! It is important to note that when we talk about gang members, we typically mean not only street gang members but also outlaw bikers and domestic terrorists. With that said, you will see that there are significantly more street gang members than there are of the other types, though some might like to believe otherwise. A military-trained gang member (MTGM) is defined as a member of a street gang, prison gang, outlaw motorcycle gang, or domestic terrorist group who appears to have received military training either directly or indirectly.[3] We will expound on that definition later in this chapter.

This book is about gang members both in and out of the military. You will see the negative effect of these gang members in military units and the increased level of dangerousness they bring to both the military and civilian communities both while they are in the military and when they enter the ranks of our nation's veterans. I will also share some things about my experience first investigating, and now researching, a topic that many find incredible, as I did in the preface. If you skipped over the preface, please take a moment to go back and read it, as it will put a lot of the book in context. Some have even claimed that the problem does not exist, yet as you will see, MTGMs have existed for as long as the United States.

We will begin the adventure with the history of gangs up to the 1900s, an overview of the types of gangs we will be examining to make sure we lock in on some of the terms, and then an assessment of potential threats that MTGMs bring to the community. In chapters 2 and 3, we will continue to examine the growth of MTGMs throughout history and identify several variations of the government response. I will also point out a few of the turning points for both gang members and gang investigators with respect to the military environment and how it limited (or didn't) the freedom of MTGMs.

In chapter 4, we will identify and examine some of the traditional ways that community leaders try to prevent, or limit, the effects that the presence of these gangs has on their citizens. In chapter 5, we will look at over twenty-five years of investigations conducted on gang members serving in the military and evaluate some of the research conducted around the United States on the perceptions that police and corrections officers assigned as gang investigators have reported regarding MTGMs in their jurisdictions. We will wrap up with chapter 6 by assessing the actual threat posed by gangs with military training, both in and out of the military and examine some solutions that I feel should be considered. In each chapter I will highlight several connections between gangs and the military as well as the impact of gangs on other government functions.

In this first chapter, we will look at the history of gangs in Western culture and the emergence not long afterward of military-trained gang members. We will then examine some definitions for gangs, consider the different types of gangs and evaluate the effect of a gang presence in the community and in the workplace. While this book was written for both academic and general interest readers, the layout is not as staunchly academic as some readers might expect. This chapter contains the first part of what would be considered the literature review (or history) of the topic(s), as well as some definitions and focused application of gang theory. As we head out on this adventure, prepare to see many similarities between the early gangs and those we see today. There are excellent examples of history repeating itself, and I have found it very beneficial to heed the advice of George Santayana, philosopher, poet, and novelist, who observed, "Those who cannot remember the past are condemned to repeat it." Many communities repeat past mistakes when it comes to gangs. My hope is that we can limit some of the serious mistakes with the following insight and information.

EARLY GANGS

Among the earliest recorded gangs were the criminal groups in London identified by Henry Fielding, a writer who became a barrister (lawyer), and served as a justice of the peace and later a magistrate. Fielding is best known in police and criminal justice circles as the founder of London's first police force, the Bow Street Runners. In his writings, Fielding predicted with surety that public safety in London would be replaced with anarchy.[4] Geoffrey Pearson, a British scholar of street crime and violence, suggested that Fielding's concern may have been with the organized gangs running the streets of London since the early 1600s. Identifying themselves with names like Mohocks, Circling Boys, Roaring Boys, and Bravadoes, those gangs terrorized their communities by breaking windows, assaulting those engaged in policing the community, and attacking travelers and old women.[5] They also fought among themselves, wearing colored ribbons to distinguish themselves from their adversaries, not unlike the practice of contemporary gangs that choose gang colors to distinguish themselves.

In the early years of the United States, most urban neighborhoods were (and often still are) divided by ethnic groups (Italian, Jewish, Irish, German,

Polish, etc.). The Northeast United States was settled first, and the growth of the new country progressed mostly westward and southward. The cities of New York and Chicago were the primary cities (and largest) that influenced the evolution of gangs and the community responses to them. It is appropriate, then, that our study is initially focused on those cities.

Most of the first settlers in the New World were from England and the Netherlands and were coming to North America to better their lot in life. Writer and biographer James Haskins noted that a lot of the first settlers were lower-class citizens who were poor, and one of the ways they could improve their status was through criminal activity.[6] Whether as the perpetrators or victims, immigrants were part of a culture that was quite demanding and the criminality of a few often increased the demands on the many. Such a lifestyle may have toughened the settlers to allow them to survive the early years in the new country, but many of the settlers did not survive. Thus, the new and growing community was forced to provide orphanages for their children.

In the orphanages, by the time the boys reached twelve to fourteen years old, they were apprenticed to a craftsman to learn a trade. Haskins reported that as part of this process, the orphans became a social class of their own and many were alienated by their communities.[7] Though the apprenticeships were arranged for good purposes, they often fell short of their goals. While their delinquent activity would not likely be considered gang activity, at least when compared to the contemporary definitions, many of the young, homeless boys were a major source of trouble.

Haskins noted the first organization to qualify as a gang in the colonies was the group run by Ebenezer Mackintosh, a man from Boston. Mackintosh led a group of men called the South Enders, the frequent winners of the annual brawl with the North Enders. Mackintosh was a shoemaker, in his late twenties when he led the South Enders gang around 1764. Each year on November 5, known as Guy Fawkes Day or Pope's Day, the two groups fought over each other's effigies of the Pope, which were burned by the winners. The gang became so bold as to loot the homes of several government officials in their protest of the Stamp Act of 1765 (remember learning about "No taxation without representation"?), and MacIntosh became a powerful figure in the community.[8] After the tax protests, Mackintosh was known as the South Enders' "Captain General," a term used by the militia of the time to denote supreme authority of an area or command.[9]

Luc Sante, a writer who studied the experiences of the lower classes and urban life in early New York City, found the first street gangs in New York appeared a few years later, around 1783 following the American Revolution. He noted the gangs emerged in the eastern US cities, which had conditions conducive to gang formation and growth, mostly created by the many waves of immigration and urban overcrowding.[10] In New York, the gangs emerged from an area that was previously swampland but was developed to make room for the growing population. The Five Points area was on the outskirts of town during the early years of the Republic. It was a wilderness surrounding a large lake referred to as the Collect, according to Herbert Asbury.[11]

Sante observed gangs of that time were not always criminal organizations when they started and they were often formed around a trade. Also, many neighborhoods started groups to counter the delinquency and criminal activity they experienced, and youth and young adults often naturally grouped together to represent and protect their neighborhood. Many were respected butchers, mechanics, carpenters, and shipyard workers, while only a few were gamblers and tavern workers. The members of those "respected" groups did engage in violence, though, often protecting something or someone in the neighborhoods they represented. Like the gangs of today, the early gangs often aligned themselves along racial lines. White gangs like the Smith's Vly gang, the Bowery Boys, and the Broadway Boys had geographic foundations like many contemporary gangs, too, as did the African American gangs known as the Fly Boys and Long Bridge Boys.[12] Their typical arsenal of weapons consisted of stones and slung (not sling) shots, a predecessor to the blackjack.[13] Although you may not need the reminder, the presence of gangs at the time was particularly bothersome in New York because New York served as the nation's capital from March 1789 until July 1790.

The First Military-Trained Gang Members

Clearly the first criminal groups that were led by men with military training were river or inland pirates in the 1790s. Their leaders had military training and experience, so the members of the gang received military training, and the group operated as a gang, not too different from how a gang operates today. The river pirates conducted ambushes, assaults, thefts, and robberies of both travelers and merchants on the rivers. Perhaps the biggest difference between those gangs and contemporary gangs was the mode of transportation. Today's gang members typically travel by automobile, which had not yet been invented, while the river pirates of the 1790s travelled in boats.

The river pirates were especially concentrated around Red Banks, Kentucky, near Evansville, Indiana, in the northwestern part of Kentucky near the state border with Illinois. They preyed on travelers and merchants shipping their products from areas in the Northeast, like Pittsburgh, to the Gulf of Mexico and all points between. Red Banks, now known as Henderson, was located near the intersection of the Cumberland River, which heads south into Kentucky and Tennessee, and the Ohio River, which heads west to connect to the Mississippi.

The leader of one group of river pirates, Samuel Mason, received his military training as a militia captain in the American Revolution. He joined the Ohio County Militia, part of the Virginia State Forces, in January 1777. The earliest record of his military life was in May of 1777. Mason and his militia unit pursued some Indians (Native Americans) who had robbed and killed a family near Pittsburgh. Mason and his men "gallantly followed the murderers" and frightened them so badly that the expedition was regarded a success.[14] Mason was given command of Fort Henry, in what is now known as West Virginia. He was badly wounded later in 1777, when a band of Indians from several eastern tribes ambushed a rescue party during an attack.[15] Mason, responding to a false report that there were six Indians near the fort, proceeded with fourteen men to attack them. He soon discovered that he had been trapped by several hundred Indians and was unable to retreat.[16] All his men were massacred, as was a group that tried to come to their aid. Of the twenty-eight soldiers who took part in the battle only five escaped, including Captain Mason, who "after being severely wounded, concealed himself behind a fallen tree until the Indians withdrew."[17]

Mason ultimately left the military and searched for a new career. In the 1790s, he settled at Red Banks and chose river piracy as his new profession. The travelers of that time often used flatboats and keelboats to travel up and down the river. The flatboat era covered the period from the 1780s to 1820.[18] River pirates had the advantage over travelers as they used small watercraft like canoes on dark nights for sudden attacks and escapes. Flatboats were typically built not more than 20 feet wide to successfully navigate the river and ranged from 20 to 100 feet in length. There were no motors, and they were guided by oars and poles while using the current of the river for propulsion. While the use of sails or pulling the boat with horses walking along the bank were alternative methods, neither was appropriate for the larger rivers used by the travelers of that time. The first commercial steam-powered paddleboat was not available until 1807.

In 1797, Mason moved his headquarters to a well-known landmark known as Cave-in-Rock, on the Illinois side of the Ohio River across from northwestern Kentucky. According to Otto Rothert, the cave looked like a crypt, bewildering those who entered.[19] It was carved out of limestone by the river and weather over a period of many years. The mouth appeared semi-elliptical, measuring about fifty-five feet wide at the base. The cave was about one hundred and sixty feet deep and almost uniformly forty feet wide.[20] At the time Mason and his crew, known as the Mason gang, were based there, several tall trees grew in front of the mouth of the cave, partially concealing it.

Mason, like other criminals of past and present, took on aliases to avoid capture and identification.[21] Period researcher and historian Robert M. Coates

Cave-in-Rock, currently part of the Illinois State Park System. Samuel Mason and other river pirates along the Ohio and Mississippi Rivers used the cave as a headquarters in the late 1790s and early 1800s. Source: *Shutterstock*

found that Mason also went by the name Bully Wilson, although some historians have suggested that Mason and Wilson were not the same person. Among the tricks Mason used to lure unsuspecting river travelers to stop at Cave-in-Rock was a prominent sign which read, "Wilson's Liquor Vault and House for Entertainment."[22] Mason's gang included two of his sons and any other men he could persuade to engage in river piracy with him. The gang welcomed riverboat travelers, distracting them while other gang members examined their possessions for anything of value. If they found something they wanted, they robbed the visitors as they left the docks. Other strategies included offering to assist in piloting a boat through the shallow parts of the river. Once aboard, the pirates would run the boat aground to facilitate their crimes. If their offer of assistance was declined, they often chased the boat and killed all aboard.[23]

In the summer of 1799, the Mason gang was forced to leave Cave-in-Rock when they were attacked by a group of vigilante bounty hunters.[24] The gang moved their criminal operations downriver to the territory known as Spanish Louisiana. They became land pirates (highwaymen) on the Natchez Trace, robbing and killing travelers who traversed the 440 miles of wilderness that extends along a ridgeline between Nashville in Tennessee and Natchez in the Mississippi Territory (about eighty-five miles north of Baton

Rouge, Louisiana). The Trace was also called "The Devil's Backbone" during that era both due to the rough traveling conditions and the danger of encountering murderous groups like the Mason gang along the way. Tennessee volunteers in the United States Army (preceding the existence of the Army Corps of Engineers) did some work to improve the Trace as a thoroughfare shortly after 1800.

Kathy Weiser reported that Mason was given the nickname "Wolfman" about that same time. Coates observed that Mason had a tooth out of place, only coverable by his lip with some effort.[25] It may have also been because he had grown his hair and beard long and adopted a more "wild" look as a land pirate than when he made his living as a river pirate.[26] Coates also noted that Mason was a large man—about 200 pounds and "portly pompous."[27]

Coincidentally, among Mason's later victims on the Trace was a party of Kentucky boatmen returning home. The Trace was often used for returning overland travel by folks who had taken a boat down the Mississippi River, as it was much more difficult to travel upriver in a boat than it was to travel over land. The boatmen had just eaten supper and were putting out pickets (lookouts) before retiring for the night. In going to their positions one of the pickets stepped on one of Mason's men who was hidden in the grass. The man jumped up, yelled, and fired his gun. The Kentuckians panicked and ran off while Mason's gang stole everything from their camp.[28]

Otto Rothert observed that Mason had been called "a striking example of a lawless man receiving his just reward."[29] The reward he received was perhaps best demonstrated in January 1803, when Spanish officials arrested Mason and many of the men with him after they caught up with him in southeastern Missouri. The Spanish court found him guilty. While being transported to New Orleans, where he was to be turned over to the American governor in the Mississippi Territory, Mason escaped.[30] But the justice system of that time was not finished with him yet, and the $2,500 reward offered for his capture motivated two of his fellow criminals to bring in Mason's head in September 1803. Whether they killed Mason or he died from wounds he received during his escape from the Spanish was unknown. Fittingly, instead of being paid the reward, the two river pirates that betrayed him were recognized, arrested, tried in federal court, and found guilty of river piracy.[31]

Mason had a rival, or contemporary, who may also have had military training. Former Colonel Fluger also led a gang of river pirates. Colonel Fluger, also spelled Fleuger, or Pfleuger, was born in Rockingham County, New Hampshire.[32] By age twenty-four he was said to be a militia colonel, and not long afterward, he was imprisoned for indebtedness. Upon his release from prison, he headed west.[33] Fluger put together a criminal gang of river pirates that operated near Fort Massac, near Metropolis, Illinois, about

50 miles further west than Cave-in-Rock. Fort Massac was designed to protect military and commercial interests in the Ohio Valley, on the Ohio River, and also on the Mississippi.[34]

Colonel Fluger shortened his family name and used the alias Plug.[35] The core group of his gang included his girlfriend, known as Pluggy, and a trusted friend called "Nine Eyes," in addition to however many fellow criminals they could enlist from time to time.[36] The gang's signature strategy involved Colonel Plug secreting himself aboard a flatboat that had been docked by its owners overnight. Once aboard, he would remove the caulk from between the planks or bore holes in the boat's bottom, carefully plugging the holes to keep the boat from sinking.[37] Once enough caulk was removed or holes were bored and unplugged, the boat would begin to sink. Colonel Plug's gang would then appear to rescue those aboard, but would only salvage the valuable contents and Plug.[38] Colonel Plug's gang of pirates traveled up and down the Ohio and Mississippi Rivers, stealing from warehouses and robbing travelers.[39]

The gang's scheme served them well, except for the time when they descended on a decoy boat. When they went to rob the boat of its contents, they found an overwhelming number of attackers below deck. Much of Colonel Plug's gang was killed, and Plug himself was tied to a tree and beaten. He was rescued by Pluggy before being bitten by "a fog of mosquitos."[40] While admittedly a solid part of southern Illinois and western Kentucky folklore, no sources have been located regarding his military service. Researcher J. W. Allen even speculated that Plug may have received the title of Colonel while in Kentucky, as the Commonwealth was (and is) of the practice of bestowing such honorary titles on noteworthy residents without requiring actual military service.[41] It is also a possibility that the folktales of Plug and his gang may have been based on the activities of Mason, with a fabricated ending to match the embellished story. The era of the river pirates continued a bit longer than either Mason or Plug, although most of the larger gangs of river pirates had discontinued their operations by 1825, according to Asbury's research.[42]

The river pirates, generally, were depicted in two mass-produced and readily available films. The first was the 1956 Walt Disney movie *Davey Crockett and the River Pirates*, which was filmed in and around the cave and depicted the context of the gangs' operations. It showed the Mason gang attempting to lure Crockett and legendary river man Mike Fink and their respective keelboats to shore pretending to be women who were interested in their company. The Mason gang was also shown to be impersonating Indians as they attacked river boats. Colonel Plug was depicted as a traveling banjo-playing peddler in a tavern, and Plug and Mason were shown as collaborators. *How the West was Won*, a 1962 production by Metro-Goldwyn-Mayer (MGM), documented the westward expansion of the United States in the nineteenth century. One of the earlier scenes shows a group of river pirates welcoming travelers in and then attacking and robbing them.

The Evolution of the Early Gangs

During the early 1800s, the Five Points area of New York was a relatively peaceful place requiring little in the way of law enforcement. By the early 1820s, though, the character began to change as the older buildings began to crumble or sink into the poorly drained ground.[43] Asbury observed that families that lived there often chose to move to nicer areas and their run-down living quarters were likely to be occupied by former negro slaves and Irishmen.

The gangs were drawn to the vice and crime in the area, increasingly filling the saloons, dance halls, and speakeasies in Five Points. The speakeasies were sometimes referred to as green-grocery speakeasies, as they had racks of vegetables on display outside the store. But all the business was in the back room, out of which the shopkeepers sold alcohol at prices much lower than the saloons. Gangs like the Forty Thieves, the Chichesters, the Plug Uglies, the Roach Guards, and the Dead Rabbits frequented the area, and by 1840, the area had earned the title of "the most dismal slum section in America."[44]

With the evolution of those gangs, they took on more of a hierarchical, quasi-military structure, much like contemporary gangs. In addition to the police force, other local government functions were threatened by gangs in the Five Points area as early as the early 1850s. Author Tyler Anbinder found that one of the local gangs had taken a fire engine and beat some of the firefighters before running off.[45] It was perhaps no coincidence that many firemen of the time were brawlers, and often acquainted with local gangs and gang members, but the reported events were attacks on the fire department itself, not just the firefighters who were also gang members.

And there was an early military connection to the firefighters, too. As the country had not yet formed a standing army, the young nation depended on volunteer militias in the event of attack. Some of the firefighters joined those local militias to acquire military training, especially target proficiency, to help them aim the hoses at fires.[46] Anbinder reported many of the firefighters also banded together in organizations that were both gang-like and political in nature, further blurring the lines between government-provided service organizations and the members of criminal gangs.

The Bowery district in New York, formerly a farming area outside the city and the location of the first Young Men's Christian Association (YMCA), was located just east of Five Points. In the mid-1800s, the Bowery was home to several infamous gangs of its own, including its namesake the Bowery Boys, the Atlantic Guards, and the American Guards.[47] While the gangs in the Bowery engaged in typical gang-like debauchery, they had some admirable moments, too. On one occasion, the Bowery Boys defended the police from attack by the Mulberry Boys from the Five Points area. The first time it happened was in the Bowery district, but they did it again in the area of Five Points. The Bowery Boys also proved themselves to be superior marksmen, shooting with pistols and rifles at the Mulberry Boys who were attempting to conceal themselves behind barricades. Feuds between the gangs from Five Points and those from the Bowery (often the Dead Rabbits versus the Bowery Boys) were legendary, and often supported by the other gangs from both areas.[48] The potential level of dangerousness of those gangs was different than before, too, as it was not until the 1840s that widespread individual ownership of guns became possible. That was the year Samuel Colt created a revolver that could be aimed. It was a significant adaption of the revolving flintlock pistol of the time.

Asbury noted there were some juvenile gangsters as well, many as young as eight, who adopted supporting roles and emulated the adult gang members. The Little Dead Rabbits were one such group, and the younger males often emulated the older gang members in both appearance and behavior. Groups of juveniles represented the other gangs, too, with membership in the Forty Little Thieves, the Little Plug Uglies, and the Little Roach Guards. Asbury found that changes in the activity of welfare agencies, housing conditions, policing, and education affected the juvenile gangs.

Sante identified a different type of gang along the waterfront. Gangs with names like the Daybreak Boys, Buckaroos, Hookers, and Slaughter Housers typically mugged, and otherwise victimized, the shipping patrons in the East River area.[49] The typical method was to lure the unsuspecting sailor or other victim to a place under a window, where a co-conspirator would dump ashes on the victim, causing enough of a diversion to allow the gang to attack him. In addition to muggings, robberies, and murders, the gangs often robbed ships, like the earlier river pirates along the Ohio and Mississippi Rivers, amassing tens of thousands of dollars in stolen property in a short period.

Near the West Side docks, the Charleston Street Gang robbed nearby houses and stole ships from the docks. The leader of that gang, Sadie the Goat, fancied herself a pirate; she flew the Jolly Roger on the mast of stolen ships, directed her gang to conduct kidnappings, and made captives walk the plank.[50] Sadie and the rest of the gang were ultimately defeated by a group of farmers from Hudson Valley. But they weren't the only gang operating in that area. Asbury found that at one point, there were about fifty gangs comprised of 450 river pirates in the Fourth Ward, according to the chief of police.[51]

In Chicago, the gangs were not nearly so organized prior to the 1850s. There were only nine members of nighttime law enforcement (watch) in the city (one for each district), by mid-century. Crimes of violence were commonplace then, but their perpetrators were described as bands of boys and men acting in response to the suffering of their families, as the economic shift of the time had resulted in significant unemployment. While there was little in the way of documentation, it appeared the formation of gangs in Chicago roughly paralleled, in chronology and foundation, those in New York. In his research of the city's gang history, Asbury found no record of criminal activity in Chicago until 1833.[52] That made sense, since Chicago's first charter election wasn't until 1837. Asbury found that thousands of criminals descended on Chicago from all over the country, lured by the easy money available in such a boomtown.[53]

Military-Trained Gang Members from East to West

The Hounds of newly named San Francisco (the city was named Yerbe Buena—meaning "good herb"—until January 1847) appeared to be the first Domestic Terrorist Extremist group comprised mostly of military-trained gang members. It might seem strange to trace the history of military gangs to the West Coast, since California did not become a state until September 9, 1850, but the region was instrumental to the expansion of U.S. interests. The area had just been acquired by the United States from Mexico in 1848, the same year gold was discovered there.

Due to the gold rush, many sea captains lost control of their crews, leaving them no way to offload their cargo upon arriving at the San Francisco port. The problem was quite overwhelming, and in a very short time, thousands of seamen quit as soon as their ships arrived, leaving 400 ships abandoned in the harbor, many full of cargo. The sailors who had abandoned their responsibilities went unchallenged for the most part, as the city of San Francisco had no official police force.[54] Instead, private police were employed to protect individual establishments and sometimes entire neighborhoods. That was a challenge, as they had no official sanction or authority, and the population was increasing rapidly. In mid-1847, a tally of the citizens revealed just over 450 residents.[55] While there was a significant growth the following year, with a final count of 1,000 residents, nothing could have predicted the explosive growth to more than 25,000 San Franciscans by 1849.[56]

Without adequate local law enforcement, several businessmen contracted with a group of recently discharged army veterans to return runaway sailors at $25 a head.[57] Most of the veterans had arrived in San Francisco as early as as military recruits from New York. They were members of Colonel Jonathan

Stevenson's regiment of volunteers, brought in to fight against Mexico in the Mexican-American War (April 1846–February 1848).[58] Originally, the plan was that after the war they would settle in California. When the peace treaty with Mexico was ratified, the regiment was released from August to October 1848.[59] About sixty of the former soldiers, many of whom had been members or associates of the Bowery and Five Points gangs in New York, formed the group that was hired by local businessmen to round up the sailors.

Those loosely organized veterans and former gang members transformed into the Hounds. San Francisco historian Zoeth Skinner Eldredge noted subtly that the "rough element was largely represented," and there was little doubt the former New York gang members had formed "a considerable portion of the organized band of desperadoes known as Hounds."[60] It was also observed that, even back then, the gang member mindset trumped military discipline. There were many complaints of insubordination and disorder while the unit was still intact, apparently because the officers had little control over the former gangsters.[61] Not all the regiment's soldiers ended up as criminals, though, and many of the veterans (especially the officers) attained positions of wealth and influence.[62]

The organization of Hounds formed to "protect American citizens against Spanish-speaking foreigners," during the Gold Rush. Bear in mind that the discovery of gold excited not only the locals (of which there were few), but people from all over the world. Before many from the Atlantic side of the North American continent or treasure-seekers from Europe could set up gold-mining operations, San Francisco was "overrun with such men from the various countries and ports on the Pacific."[63] Initially, the Hounds simply practiced military drills and demanded order in the city. Ultimately, they became a nativist or anti-foreigner gang and attacked Chilenos (people from Chile) as well as Peruvians and Mexicans who had traveled to California as part of the Gold Rush, claiming their motivation for beating and stabbing their victims was patriotism. Although not one of the contemporary classifications for Domestic Terrorist Extremists (DTE), the Hounds were considered nationalists. Contemporary nationalism typically advocates a racial definition of national identity, so the closest DTEs for the Hounds would have been the white supremacists, whom we will examine later in the book.

By 1849, members of the Hounds became bolder, increasing their attacks, adopting the name of San Francisco Society of Regulators and demanding that all San Franciscans pay them for protecting the city in their self-appointed role of law enforcement.[64] Often they would order drinks at a bar and instead of paying their tab before leaving, would suggest the bartender collect their debt from the city. They often beat and robbed business owners and citizens who failed to respect (and avoid) them. The group was notorious for their "gross acts of pillage upon public and private property," according to Eldredge.[65]

Sam Roberts, described by historian Rand Richards as an illiterate boatman, was in charge of the group, at least at the end of their reign.[66] He was also a former member of the New York Volunteer Regiment. Roberts prompted the end of his reign with a fit of jealousy.[67] He had become infatuated with a Chilean prostitute, and when he found her one day in the company of a German man, Roberts "beat him senseless with a wooden plank."[68] He then cut the unconscious man in the face with a spur, inciting those around him to challenge his (Roberts') manliness. That night, Roberts and the Hounds caused a lot of damage in town, shooting off guns and threatening people indiscriminately.

Eventually, the responsible citizens began "taking back" their city as two hundred and thirty men were appointed as special deputies and ordered to arrest the gang members.[69] While few were killed during the Hounds' rampage, the destruction perturbed many a citizen, and a crowd of over 400 volunteer-vigilantes seized them.[70] The Hounds scattered, and only about twenty members, including their leader, Roberts, were captured. Roberts and eight others were convicted, but there was no record of him actually serving his sentence. Richards suspected it was due to his political connections or limitations of the criminal justice system at the time.[71] Other members of the Hounds escaped, all apparently ceased their criminal behavior, and many fled the city. California requested to join the United States on December 3, 1849, and was accepted on September 9, 1850.

The Effect of the Civil War on Gangs

The inter-gang fighting continued in New York until the Draft Riots of 1863. The Draft Riots were fueled by the public outcry in response to the Conscription Act passed by Congress in April of that year to draft men to fight in the ongoing Civil War. President Abraham Lincoln announced the draft would begin in New York on July 11, only six months after the Emancipation Proclamation, which freed the slaves in the Confederency, had taken effect on January 1, 1863. One of the biggest motivators for the rioters was the clause that exempted men from the draft if they paid the government three hundred dollars (about $5,500 in today's dollars).[72]

Asbury learned that although little preparation was made for protection of the military representatives sent to begin the draft, as soon as the first protesters formed, the mayor and police commissioner asked for support from the National Guard.[73] The rioters' targets initially included only military and governmental buildings, but before long the protests turned into a race riot, with white rioters attacking African Americans throughout the city. The involvement of the gangs brought unrestricted violence and mayhem, and the police often found the need to summon assistance from the National Guard or Regular Army.[74] Sometimes, military artillery was used to stop the gangs, but more often they departed when confronted by the infantrymen's muskets. The draft was reinstated the following month.

The Draft Riots changed the landscape of street politics in New York, strengthening the ranks of some gangs and empowering the leadership in others. The gangs also branched out in other ways. Asbury noted that following the Civil War, New York experienced an increase in the number of juvenile gang members.[75]

U. E. Perkins found white street gangs had been documented in Chicago since the 1860s.[76] Not long after that, the gangs started demonstrating some type of military-like organization. Chicago crime historian Richard Lindberg found that following the Civil War, gangs in early Chicago made use of the first military-style home-invasions, though there was no record of any of them in military service. After spending a considerable time surveilling a home, they concealed their faces with boot polish and entered during the night.[77] Many a social gathering and house party was interrupted by those gang members.

As was seen in New York, the first gangs in Chicago were almost exclusively made up of immigrants. Many groups, including Irish, Italians, Jews, and Poles, formed community support groups that evolved into gangs between 1880 and 1920. Like the early gangs in New York, many of those gangs may have had connections to service organizations like fire departments.[78] They used group names like "Fire Kings," likely named after Engine Company No. 1, known as Fire King. Those groups of young men hosted social events and competed against each other both professionally and personally, often fighting as groups in the streets. As the firefighters organized under local government authority, like the early gangs in New York, the gang-like organizations of Chicago shifted their headquarters elsewhere, such as the saloon known as the Limerick House, the home base of one of the gangs of that period.[79]

By the 1860s, the Irish and German gang members had developed a reputation for violence. Some of the Irish gang members, like those known as the Dukies and the Shielders, operated around the stockyards. Among their money-making pastimes were gambling and robbing employees of the stockyards leaving work. They also terrorized the German, Jewish, and Polish immigrants who settled in the neighborhoods nearby.[80] Chicago saw an influx of African American gangs following the Civil War, as many sought to escape the punishing and limiting laws in the South. Gang researcher James C. "Buddy" Howell found that a lot of them were similarly marginalized by the racially restrictive covenants on real estate, and by the racist attitudes and actions of the established white gangs in the area.[81]

Dr. Frederíck M. Thrasher reported the first recorded gang in Chicago was in 1867. The gang, he said, was comprised of about a dozen young men, aged seventeen to twenty-two years old. They were unemployed, and spent time gambling with cards and robbed other citizens on payday, often disposing of their bodies in a nearby creek.[82]

The end of the Civil War (in May of 1865) saw large-scale criminal activity of a small handful of military veterans who had trouble returning to a peaceful society.[83] The James brothers, for example, began a life of crime after serving as guerillas, known as bushwhackers, for the Confederate forces. In 1866, Jesse and Frank James began robbing banks, and they received the admiration of many citizens due to their personality and flair.[84] The motivation for their crimes was unique, though. When they committed the first organized bank robbery in America, their motivation was not wealth, but politics.

The first bank they robbed, the Clay County Savings Association in Liberty, Missouri, was a symbol of oppression to the James brothers.[85] Their allegiance was with the South, and the bank's founders were supporters of the North. That robbery was intended as revenge in their minds. Many of their future crimes, attacks on banks and railroads especially, were also attacks on what they considered symbols of the evil Union government.

For sixteen years, the Jameses and their compatriots committed eleven bank robberies in five states, twelve train robberies, four stagecoach holdups, and the robberies of a paymaster in Alabama and a state fair box office in

The James brothers robbing a Missouri train, 1870s. Jesse and Frank James were Confederate guerillas during the Civil War. Source: *Shutterstock*

Missouri.[86] Retired FBI agent Jerry Clark and veteran journalist Ed Palattella reported that their haul was estimated at $350,000, worth over $6 million in today's dollars. Not only did the James' robberies provide a new standard and example for successful bank robberies, their proficiency in public relations provided an example for criminals and terrorists far into the future. Jesse wrote letters engaging the local newspaper, in which he denied involvement in the crimes. They even found a champion in a former Confederate major turned newspaper editor. John Edwards often praised the James gang as heroes, and saw Jesse as the Rebel Savior.[87]

Some Americans saw the James brothers as modern-day Robin Hoods—heroes who took from the rich and gave to the poor. They were not heroes, though, they were brutal criminals. After they murdered two innocent men during an 1881 train robbery, the state of Missouri offered a reward of $5,000 each for their capture. Shortly thereafter, Jesse was shot by one of his own gang members for the reward money, and Frank turned himself in a few months later. After an unsuccessful attempt by prosecutors to convince juries in three separate trials that Frank was a criminal, he was declared a free man.[88] For the next thirty years, he worked as a race starter at county fairs, a theater doorman, and a star attraction in traveling theater companies before retiring to his family's farm in Missouri.

The period following the Civil War also gave birth to one of the most notorious groups which are still classified as Domestic Terrorist Extremists today. Six young Confederate veterans returned home to Pulaski, Tennessee, after the war. It wasn't long before they found their hometown, along with much of the South, in a bad way both economically and socially. With little promise of a job or much of anything to do, they bored easily. They decided to start an exclusive club that would stand for purity, preservation of the home, and protection of the orphans of Confederate soldiers.[89] They chose colors to represent their group – white for purity, and red for the blood they were prepared to shed to defend the helpless. Their uniforms were simple and consisted of sheets and pillowcases.

The process by which this group, the Ku Klux Klan, was formed was not unlike the process that started other gangs with military connections. In fact, according to James Haskins, whites in the South felt a lot like the immigrants and African Americans in the North following the Civil War.[90] During that period of Reconstruction, the South was occupied and governed by the Union, and those committed citizens were forced to watch as their communities were occupied by the intruders from the North and the recently freed Black slaves. The Klan represented justice to many in the South, and without a central authority, there was little the government could do to limit the group's activities.[91]

MODERN DAY CRIMINAL GROUPS

We will look at more of the historical perspectives of criminal groups in the coming chapters. Before we get too far into the history of gangs and military-trained gang members, we need to make sure we are talking about the same thing with the terms used throughout the book. So, let's look at the three types of gangs currently distinguished and investigated by the military: street gangs, Outlaw Motorcycle Gangs, and Domestic Terrorist Extremists. Note that until recently, the military identified all three groups as "gangs." Thus, in earlier years the groups were treated similarly. When researchers or investigators call a group a gang they can typically mean any of the groups we are examining. If not otherwise clarified or indicated by context, the reader should consider the same.

Street Gangs Defined and Explained

A concise and agreed-upon definition has yet to be found in the study of gangs, though most scholars agree a gang is a group of three or more individuals who form a loosely organized group, with one of the primary purposes of that group being the continued commission of criminal acts. Street gangs vary greatly in size, geography, criminal sophistication, modus operandi, and their impact on the community or communities. Well-known youth gang researcher Walter Miller observed that gangs were by nature violent and engaged in illegal activity, had identifiable leadership, and a structured organization.[92] In his "Working Definition," gang scholar John Hagedorn proposed that gangs were street organizations of either socially excluded or alienated elements of a dominant racial, ethnic, or religious group. He noted that gangs sometimes evolved into political, ethnic, or religious groups, and that at times political or military forms devolved into gangs, concerned mainly with criminal ventures.[93] But neither of those definitions seemed to focus on the adult criminal gang member who serves in the military.

For the purposes of military prohibitions and investigations, street gangs are (1) an association of three or more individuals; (2) whose members collectively identify themselves by adopting a group identity which they use to create an atmosphere of fear or intimidation frequently by employing one or more of the following: a common name, slogan, identifying sign, symbol, tattoo or other physical marking, style or color of clothing, hairstyle, hand sign, or graffiti; (3) the association's purpose, in part, is to engage in criminal activity and the association uses violence or intimidation to further its criminal objectives; (4) its members engage in criminal activity, or acts of juvenile delinquency that if committed by an adult would be crimes; (5) with the intent to enhance or preserve the association's power, reputation, or economic resources.[94] There is much diversity in street gang membership, and all races and ethnic backgrounds are included. As we will see in future chapters, though, most contemporary street gang members are African American or Hispanic.

African American Street Gangs

Today, there are four primary organizations (nations) under which most traditionally African American gangs unite: Crips, Bloods, Folk, and People.[95] The Crips and Bloods originated in Los Angeles and have branched out across the nation. Many of their sets were established strategically by foundational Los Angeles–area gangs, but others were started without such a connection by individuals with little or no previous gang experience. Some of the more well-known Crip affiliates include the Grape Street Crips, Rollin 60's Neighborhood Crips, Rollin' 30s Harlem Crips, and Shoreline Crips. Blood affiliates include the Bounty Hunter Bloods, Nine Trey Gangsters, Pirus, Sex Money Murda, and United Blood Nation, among others.

The Folk and People gang nations originated in Chicago, with groups like the Gangster Disciples and Vice Lords representing each nation, respectively. Other Folk-affiliated gangs include the Black Disciples, La Raza, Latin Disciples, Simon City Royals, and Spanish Cobras. People gangs include the Black P. Stones, Latin Kings, Gaylords, Mickey Cobras, Four Corner Hustlers, and Almighty Saints. Chicago-based gangs tend to be more organized than Los Angeles-based gangs and have strong leadership structures. Folk and People gangs are international in their presence. The Nations often have an alliance of some kind between the individual gangs that comprise them, and typically show solidarity to each other during conflict.[96] Most African American gang members, while they retain their street gang allegiance, typically associate with the Black Guerilla Family (BGF) prison gang when in prison. The BGF was originally a political group founded at San Quentin State Prison, in Marin County, California in 1966 by former Black Panther members intent on eradicating racism, maintaining dignity in prison, and overthrowing the U.S. government.

Hispanic Street Gangs

Hispanic-American gangs often unite under the Sureño or Norteño organizations depending on the locations of their hometowns. The dividing line is around Bakersfield, California.[97] The term "Sureño" means Southerner in Spanish. Sureños align with the Mexican Mafia in prison. Even though Sureños were established in 1968, the term was not used until the 1970s because of the continued conflict between the Mexican Mafia and Nuestra Familia in California's prison system. Norteños means Northerners in Spanish. The Norteños align with the Nuestra Familia while in prison. Norteños may refer to Northern California as Norte.

The Mexican Mafia was formed in 1957 by street gang members from different Los Angeles neighborhoods that were incarcerated in the Deuel Vocational Institution, a California Youth Authority facility. The contemporary Mexican Mafia is the controlling organization for almost every Hispanic gang and gang member in Southern California. Sureños, including Mara Salvatrucha (MS-13) and Florencia 13, use the number 13 to show allegiance to the Mexican Mafia. M is the 13th letter of the alphabet. Members of almost all related Hispanic gangs are obliged to carry out orders from made (affirmed) Mexican Mafia members. The order is best understood with the assumption that since most gang members are involved in criminal activity, there is a likelihood that they will at some point be incarcerated. The Mexican Mafia has control in many jails and prisons. The Mexican Mafia has an alliance with the Aryan Brotherhood, a white supremacist prison gang.

Nuestra Familia is the criminal organization of choice for incarcerated Hispanic gang members from Northern California. Nuestra Familia was organized in California correctional facilities in 1968. After the Mexican Mafia formed in 1957, Hispanics affiliated with Northern California gangs looked for a way to protect themselves and their interests. While members of the Norteños gang are affiliated with Nuestra Familia, being a member of Nuestra Familia does not signify association as a Norteño. The Nuestra Familia gang influences much of the criminal activity of Norteño gang members in California much like the Mexican Mafia does with their affiliated gangs. Norteños use the number 14 which represents the fourteenth letter of the alphabet. Nuestra Familia has a loose alliance with the Black Guerilla Family prison gang.

One of the more familiar Hispanic gangs that does not have primarily Mexican heritage is the Latin Kings. While there are several variations of the current name of the gang, its roots date to 1943. It developed in the Puerto Rican community in Chicago. Membership comes predominately from Latino neighborhoods in Chicago, New York City, and other cities; the U.S. territory of Puerto Rico: and countries such as Peru, Mexico, and Spain.

Street Gang Types

Researchers Nikki Ruble and William Turner found there were at least three distinct types of gangs. The first is referred to as a social gang, a relatively stable organization of individuals that "hangs out" at a specific location.[98] Social gangs are not very likely to participate in criminal activity and will commit physical violence only if attacked or retaliating against attackers. The organization stays together because there is a mutual attraction between its members, rather than a need for protection.[99] Social gang members tend to represent the average citizen in the community more than the other types of gangs.

The second type of gang is the delinquent gang. That type is often organized around monetary gain from illegal activity.[100] Survival of the gang and its members depends on each member's competence and support for each other. The third gang type identified by Ruble and Turner is the violent gang.[101] The primary purpose of the gang is to commit violent activities to acquire power and personal satisfaction.[102] Those gangs tend to have a quasi-military hierarchy, and members often overestimate the importance, size, and power of their group. The gang is prone to intragroup violence, and members may be verbally or physically violent with each other.[103]

In addition to the varied types of gangs, there are different evolutions or levels of gangs, as defined by the term Third Generation Gangs. The term comes from analysis conducted by Los Angeles Sheriff's Department Lieutenant John P. Sullivan and Dr. Robert J. Bunker, expert and consultant with the National Law Enforcement and Corrections Technology Center—West.[104] Third Generation Gangs are a representative minority of street gang organizations, but this minority is growing and is a significant threat to the safety, security, and future of our communities.

First Generation Gangs are those considered primarily turf gangs. Some turf gangs evolve into drug gangs or entrepreneurial organizations with a market-orientation, thus filling the Second Generation. Some Second Generation Gangs find the need or desire to enhance their position, and ultimately transition to the Third Generation. Gangs in the Third Generation include those with a mix of political and mercenary elements who operate or are at least capable of operating in the global community.

Three factors determine a gang's (and many organization's) evolutionary potential: Politicization, Internationalization, and Sophistication. Politicization is often seen in organizations and communities that respond to external stimuli with which they do not agree. Many of the gangs we looked at in the first part of the 1800s developed in response to class distinction, bias, and racism.[105] Street gangs are known for reacting to social pressures, and national and international events.[106]

Internationalization for organizational purposes occurs when the vision of the organization's leadership outgrows the geographic restrictions of its current operation. Gangs have responded to trends towards globalization by transforming their focus to sophisticated criminal activity that is unrestricted by national and international borders. Sophistication occurs in the natural transformation of an organization that follows Bruce Tuckman's five-stage model for group development in his theory of group dynamics: forming, storming, norming, performing, and adjourning.[107] It can be the result of continued politicization and internationalization. It requires a unified organization with clearly defined goals.

First Generation Gangs are traditional street gangs with a turf orientation, meaning they claim geographic territories as their own.[108] They operate at the lower end of extreme societal violence, and their organization has a loose leadership structure.[109] Those gangs focus their attention on turf protection and gang loyalty within their immediate area. They are largely opportunistic in activity and local in scope, and are, for the most part, limited in political scope and sophistication.[110] First Generation Gangs are the Mom and Pop stores of the gang world.

Second Generation Gangs are engaged in business, are entrepreneurial, and are usually engaged in drug trafficking and distribution or are in some way drug-centered.[111] They are known to protect their markets and frequently use violence to control their competition. They have a broader, market focused, sometimes overtly political agenda, and operate in a broader spatial or geographic area. Their operations sometimes involve multi-state and even international areas.[112] They tend to have centralized leadership and sophisticated operations for market protection.[113] That places them in the center of the range of politicization, internationalization, and sophistication. Second Generation gangs are the city-wide or regional multiple-location businesses of the gang world.

Third Generation Gangs have evolved (and usually clearly defined) political aims.[114] They operate, or aspire to operate, globally. Third Generation Gangs use their sophistication to garner power, aid financial acquisition, and engage in mercenary-type activities. Most Third Generation Gangs have been primarily mercenary in orientation; yet, in some cases they have sought to further their own political and social objectives.[115]

As with any growing or large corporation looking to expand its footprint, gangs who qualify in the Third Generation will have several members who appear to be in the First and Second Generations. It is the middle management and leadership of these gangs who have the shared vision, the organizational skills, and the technological awareness to qualify the gang as a Third Generation Gang. Third Generation Gangs are the General Electrics, Apples, and General Motors' of the gang world. Although they may come from humble backgrounds, their focus is on growth and, in many cases, domination. Their goals do not include placing second to another gang.

Potential North American Third Generation Gangs include: the 18th Street Gang, MS-13, the Gangster Disciples, and the Vice Lords.[116] It is important to note the relationship each of these gangs has with at least one other Third Generation Gang. The 18th Street and MS-13, based out of Central America (with ties to Los Angeles) are long-time rivals, as are the Gangster Disciples and the Vice Lords, both based out of and originating from Chicago.

Not all gangs qualify for the Second and Third Generation classifications, as profit-making enterprises intent on expanding outside of their neighborhoods and cities. Researchers Jerome Skolnick, Elizabeth Navarro, and Roger Rabb distinguished between cultural gangs (more like those in the First Generation described by Sullivan and Bunker), and entrepreneurial gangs (more qualified to fill the Second or Third Generation models).[117] Cultural gangs, originating from local neighborhoods, are much more common than entrepreneurial gangs, despite efforts by some in law enforcement and elsewhere in the community to make all gangs look entrepreneurial and desirous of growth.[118] Nonetheless, gangs currently operating as First Generation Gangs have the potential to evolve into the Second and Third Generation Gangs, especially if they implement management and organizational techniques in conjunction with a comprehensive vision of expansion.

Each of these organizations has a clearly defined hierarchy. In addition to a hierarchy, gangs have peripheral associates—either in preparation for membership or engaging in activity that falls short of complete membership and maintain contacts with individuals outside of their organizations who are engaged in similar, usually illicit, activity.[119] Gang members come from all walks of life, represent a variety of household incomes and often have stable households (aside from the existence of a gang member in them). Gang members are individuals from many ethnicities, races, and nationalities. Gangs have evolved to become what the Office of Juvenile Justice and Delinquency Prevention referred to (in 2000) as "an increasingly significant social policy issue."[120]

Outlaw Motorcycle Gangs Defined

Outlaw Motorcycle Gangs (OMGs) are ongoing organizations whose members use their motorcycle clubs as conduits for criminal enterprises. OMGs are highly structured criminal organizations whose members engage in criminal activities such as violent crime, weapons trafficking, and drug trafficking. OMGs range in size from single chapters with five or six members to hundreds of chapters with thousands of members worldwide.[121] OMGs differ from street gangs primarily in their demographics and typical mode of transportation, although for criminal enhancements, they may be prosecuted under laws designed for street gangs. OMGs are associations or groups of three or more persons with a common interest or activity characterized by the commission of, or involvement in, a pattern of criminal conduct. Members must typically possess and be able to operate a motorcycle to achieve and maintain membership within the group.[122] Most OMG members are older, white, and male. There are OMG members of other races, but they are predominately white. Their preferred mode of transportation is the motorcycle, supplemented by a variety of four- (and more) wheeled vehicles.

The U.S. Department of Justice defines OMGs the same as street gangs. As of May 8, 2015, the definition was (1) an association of three or more individuals; (2) whose members collectively identify themselves by adopting a group identity which they use to create an atmosphere of fear or intimidation frequently by employing one or more of the following: a common name, slogan, identifying sign, symbol, tattoo or other physical marking, style or color of clothing, hairstyle, hand sign or graffiti; (3) the association's purpose, in part, is to engage in criminal activity and the association uses violence or intimidation to further its criminal objectives; (4) its members engage in criminal activity, or acts of juvenile delinquency that if committed by an adult would be crimes; (5) with the intent to enhance or preserve the association's power, reputation, or economic resources; (6) the association may also possess some of the following characteristics: (a) the members employ rules for joining and operating within the association; (b) the members meet on a recurring basis; (c) the association provides physical protection of its members from other criminals and gangs; (d) the association seeks to exercise control over a particular location or region, or it may simply defend its perceived interests against rivals; or (e) the association has an identifiable structure.[123]

OMGs should be contrasted with motorcycle clubs, which are groups of individuals whose primary interest and activities involve motorcycles. Motorcycle clubs vary in their objectives and organizations and are often organized around a brand or make, or around a type of riding (e.g., touring). Some of the more well-known (or oldest) clubs include the Yonkers Motorcycle Club, the Pasadena Motorcycle Club, and the Patriot Guard Riders. Motorcycle clubs are not considered OMGs.

The largest OMGs are the Hells Angels, Pagans, Vagos, Sons of Silence, Outlaws, Bandidos, and Mongols.[124] All are classified as "one percent" (1%) clubs. The term originated following a riot that occurred on July 4, 1947, when the president of the American Motorcycle Association released a statement. He said that 99 percent of the motorcycle-riding public was honest, law-abiding citizens, and only 1 percent constituted troublemakers. OMGs have evolved since the middle of the twentieth century from barroom brawlers to sophisticated criminals. OMGs have spread internationally and today they are a global phenomenon.[125]

The largest African American motorcycle gangs, the Chosen Few, Hell's Lovers, Outcasts, Sin City Deciples (*sic*),[126] Thunderguards, and Wheels of Soul have a males-only membership policy. African American motorcycle gang violence has historically involved assaults and homicides, which have been directed against smaller motorcycle group members.[127] Although there does not appear to be a formal alliance, some African American Outlaw Motorcycle Clubs have formed informal alliances when advantageous.[128]

Domestic Terrorists and Extremists Defined

The U.S. Code defines Domestic Extremists as those who engage in activities known as domestic terrorism, that—(A) involve acts dangerous to human life that are a violation of the criminal laws of the U.S. or of any State; (B) appear to be intended—(i) to intimidate or coerce a civilian population; (ii) to influence the policy of a government by intimidation or coercion; or (iii) to affect the conduct of a government by mass destruction, assassination, or kidnapping; and (C) occur primarily within the territorial jurisdiction of the U.S.[129]

The U.S. Department of Homeland Security (DHS) has defined domestic terrorism as any act of violence that is dangerous to human life or potentially destructive of critical infrastructure or key resources committed by a group or individual based and operating entirely within the United States or its territories without direction or inspiration from a foreign terrorist group.[130] Domestic terrorism typically defines those actions that appear to be intended to intimidate or coerce a civilian population, to influence the policy of a government by intimidation or coercion, or to affect the conduct of a government by mass destruction, assassination, or kidnapping. A domestic terrorist differs from a homegrown violent extremist in that the former is not inspired by and does not take direction from a foreign terrorist group or other foreign power.[131]

Domestic terrorism includes acts within the territorial United States that are dangerous to human life, violate federal or state criminal laws, have no actual connection to international terrorists and appear to be intended to intimidate or coerce a civilian population, influence domestic government policy through intimidation or coercion, or affect the conduct of our government by mass destruction, assassination, or kidnapping. Domestic terrorism cases often involve firearms, arson, or explosive offenses; crimes relating to fraud; and threats and hoaxes.[132]

The U.S. Departments of Defense, Homeland Security, and Justice typically use the terms extremist and terrorist interchangeably, likely because they all use the U.S. Code definition. It appears there may be a need for distinguishing between terrorists and extremists. Extremism has been defined as a radical expression of one's political values. It is a precursor to terrorism, used by terrorists to justify their violent behavior.[133] Violent extremism occurs when individuals or groups openly express their ideological beliefs through violence or a call for violence.[134] The content and the style of one's beliefs are basic elements for defining extremism, which is characterized not only by what one believes, but also in how they express their beliefs. Beliefs alone do not make one an extremist.[135] Organized crime and terrorism researcher Jerome Bjelopera suggested that using the term extremist allows prosecutors, policymakers, and investigators to discuss terrorist-like activity without having to label the activity as terrorism.[136]

Domestic terrorist groups that are operating or which operated in the past include the following:

- **Animal rights extremists** who are against people, businesses, or government entities perceived to be exploiting or abusing animals. Animal rights extremists attack those they believe are linked to the abuse of animals. Typical targets include the fur industry, companies and individuals involved in animal research, and businesses that ship animals.
- **Environmental rights extremists** who are against people, businesses, or government entities destroying, degrading, or exploiting the natural environment. Environmental extremists target those they believe are destroying the environment, such as businesses and individuals involved in construction or automobile sales.
- **Anti-abortion extremists** who are against the providers of abortion-related services, their employees, and their facilities in support of the belief that the practice of abortion should end. Anti-abortion extremists have targeted women's reproductive clinics and the health care professionals and staff who work in these facilities, including doctors, nurses, receptionists, and even security guards.
- **Lone offenders** are individuals who appear to be motivated by one or more extremist ideologies and, operating alone, support or engage in acts of violence in furtherance of that ideology or ideologies. Typically, assassins and school-attackers have been classified as lone offenders, or lone wolves. Some white supremacist leaders have encouraged lone wolf tactics to lessen the risk of law enforcement attention. The lone wolf concept can be traced to Louis Beam, a former Klansman, who coined the term "leaderless resistance" and advocated using clandestine cells driven by ideology with no traceable direction from group leaders.
- **Anarchist extremists** who say they believe that all forms of capitalism and corporate globalization should be opposed and that governing

institutions are unnecessary and harmful to society. Anarchist extremists usually target symbols of capitalism they believe to be the cause of all problems in society—such as large corporations, government organizations, and police agencies.

- **Militia extremists** who profess belief that the government is deliberately stripping Americans of their freedoms and is attempting to establish a totalitarian regime. Militia extremists mainly target those they believe could violate their constitutional rights, such as police officers and judges.
- **Sovereign citizen extremists** who claim belief that the legitimacy of U.S. citizenship should be rejected; almost all forms of established government, authority, and institutions are illegitimate; and that they are immune from federal, state, and local laws. Sovereign citizen extremists usually target members of the government—including judges, police officers, and tax officials.
- **Black supremacist extremists** who claim they oppose racial integration and/or support efforts to eliminate non-Black people and Jewish people. Supremacist extremists often believe that the U.S. government is hurting the country or secretly planning to destroy it.
- **Racist skinhead extremists** and **white supremacist extremists** both claim belief that Caucasians are intellectually and morally superior to other races and that the government is controlled by Jews.[137] These extremists typically believe that the U.S. government is hurting the country or secretly planning to destroy it. White supremacy extremists target the federal government and racial, ethnic, and religious minorities. Their methods have included murder, threats, and bombings.

The FBI has added the word *violent* in their public descriptions of some of these groups.[138] Because of the multiple and potentially confusing uses of the terms *terrorist* and *extremists*, in addition to other qualifiers that may or may not be used consistently by all U.S. government entities, unless inappropriate based on definition or context, we will use the term Domestic Terrorist Extremist (DTE) to identify such groups and their members. Like the OMGs, most DTEs are white, though a select few are Black or African American.

MILITARY-TRAINED GANG MEMBERS (MTGMs)

A military-trained gang member (MTGM) is defined as a street gang, prison gang, OMG, or DTE group member per the applicable jurisdiction's definition, with military training or experience, as perceived by a reasonable, typical, police officer. MTGMs display indicators that they received military training either directly or indirectly. Indicators of military training include the use of military tactics, weapons, explosives, or equipment to conduct gang activity, and the use of distinctive military skills, particularly if gang members are trained in weapons, tactics, and planning, and then pass the instruction on to other gang members.[139] Military tactics include the techniques and strategies taught in a variety of military occupational specialties, ranging from tactical assault to organizational leadership strategies. We will be discussing all the types of gangs with MTGMs in the coming chapters.

While examining gangs in the military was largely ignored in previous years, today the focus is not only on gangs in the military but how to respond to a gang member who has acquired military training.[140] Regardless of which category they fall into, the presence of an MTGM brings the training provided by the military to, at a minimum, engage an enemy with a small group and firearms. Due to the standard military enlistment requirements, MTGMs are most often adults. Additionally, the gang member with military training brings a degree of leadership and the skill set of his military specialty, many of which are beneficial to any organization.

GANG THEORY

There are several theories that attempt to explain why individuals commit crimes. Many of them address explanations for why youth commit crimes. As this book is about individual adults who operate in a group or gang, and because most members of the military are adults, we will limit analysis to those that strive to explain why individual, adult members of *groups* commit crimes.

Criminologist Edwin Sutherland proposed his social learning theory in contradiction to the widespread (then and now) notion that the commission of crime was limited to those in the lower social classes. Sutherland's Differential Association Theory explained how gang members acquired the knowledge and skills to be of use to the criminal organization.[141] The principles of differential association proposed by Sutherland included the premise that criminal behavior was learned in communication with others within intimate personal groups. The process of learning criminal behavior by association with criminal and anti-criminal patterns involves all the mechanisms involved in any other learning process.[142]

A modification to Sutherland's Differential Association Theory resulted in Glaser's observation that "individuals model their behavior on the basis of how others see them, rationalizing their behavior when role-conflicts exist."[143] Glaser identified the theory as differential identification, which meant "a person pursues criminal behavior to the extent that he identifies himself with real or imaginary persons from whose perspective his criminal behavior seems acceptable."[144] Prior identification and present circumstances play key roles in the selection of people with whom we identify and associate. The observation affects our ability to associate with one group (e.g., a criminal street gang), while maintaining employment by or membership in a second group whose institutional values and norms oppose those of the first group.

In his extensive 2006 study of Chicago-based street gangs, George Knox, director of the National Gang Crime Research Center, found that the gangs exhibited a patriarchal and hierarchal organizational structure.[145] The gangs exhibited a pseudo-warrior culture and embraced group identities that reflected a value for mental illness with words like insane added to the gang's name to make them seem fiercer to their rivals. Unlike Los Angeles-based gangs, Knox observed that the Chicago-based gangs were involved in local politics. The gangs used political corruption and misuse of social service funds for economic gain.[146] Although the current Chicago-based gangs began as youth gangs they evolved into adult gangs lasting over sixty years and expanding their operations all over the United States.

In his study of urban gangs, sociologist Martin Sanchez-Jankowski observed that in low income urban areas gangs were a natural response in the competition for scarce resources and comprised an alternate social order.[147] Sanchez-Jankowski found that gangs had adapted to their circumstances by adopting one or more of five entrepreneurial attitudes that included competitiveness, the desire and drive to accumulate money and material possessions, status seeking, the ability to plan, and the ability to undertake risks in pursuit of their goals.[148]

Economist Steven D. Levitt and Sociologist Sudhir A. Venkatesh observed that the rise of crack cocaine in the 1980's created a change in the mission, organizational structure, and operations of street gangs.[149] Due to the monetary benefits, many gangs began selling drugs. Levitt and Venkatesh found that earnings from drug sales were somewhat above the earnings for legitimate employment, but the risks inherent in engaging in drug selling more than offset the increased income. They suggested that economic factors alone did not adequately explain an individual's participation in a drug-selling gang.[150] We will look more closely at some of Levitt and Venkatesh's work on gangs later in this chapter.

Another Way to Tell if It's a Gang

Many citizens and police officers alike think they can tell whether someone is a gang member because of how they look or act. Some gang investigators initially default to their gut instincts when identifying gang members. A well-used saying by many a gang investigator depicts such a process. Let's call it the "Riley Method" for gang member identification. James Whitcomb Riley was among the most popular writers of the late nineteenth and early twentieth centuries. His poetry caused readers to recall a nostalgic and simpler time. He was a prolific writer, publishing millions of copies of more than fifty books.

James Riley, sometime around 1883–1885, said: "When I see a bird that walks like a duck and swims like a duck and quacks like a duck, I call that bird a duck."[151] The phrase was later used and paraphrased by many to describe the innate ability to identify a communist. At some point in the late twentieth century, gang investigators adopted the maxim to describe gang members.

More simply (and seriously), a gang is a group of individuals who: 1) agree to commit a crime, 2) commit crimes on a regular basis, and 3) one of them does something to further the commission of the crime. That definition contains the essential elements needed to prove the criminal charge of conspiracy in most jurisdictions.

GANGSTERS, BIKERS, AND DOMESTIC TERRORISTS IN THE COMMUNITY

Street gangs have been historically viewed as a sign of the failure of inner-city urban life. By the 1960s, a consensus among scholars formed regarding

Gangs in the Community. When gangs of any kind are present in the community, there are likely to be other troubles as well. Source: iStockPhoto

the idea that gang formation was a consequence of the conflicts that emerged in the socially disorganized lower-class, and that the social stresses commonly experienced in lower-class slum neighborhoods were at the heart of gang formation.[152] The academic analysis of OMGs and DTEs has often been either ignored or lumped in with the street gangs.

Much of what was considered gang activity has evolved in sophistication from random street crimes to criminal organizations engaged in drug trafficking, burglary, and theft.[153] Members of society express a wide range of views, from seeing gangs as a normal part of adolescence to viewing them as social parasites that must be routed from the neighborhoods.[154] Some citizens even consider the street gang, OMG, and DTE lifestyle as an acceptable (if not admirable) way of life.

In addition to criminal activity, street gang, OMG, and DTE groups often serve their members as a social network.[155] The social networks are closed, however, limiting the members' access to other, perhaps positive, influences. Group leaders control the behavior of the members, cutting them off from traditional relationships. That often produces members with serious social challenges in school, relationships, and employment.[156]

Street gang, OMG, and DTE groups provide their members with a feeling of belonging, as a surrogate family, a social group, and as a source for role models.[157] The groups sometimes protect their members and unaffiliated neighbors by inflicting violence on those who enter the community with bad intentions.[158] For example, some communities have asked, or allowed, the groups to act as law enforcers.[159] By providing basic products and services, the groups have assisted in defining the role their organizations play in the community—creating a symbiotic relationship in which the community becomes dependent on the group and the group becomes dependent on the community.

Challenges with Gangsters, Bikers, and Domestic Terrorists in the Community

Street and motorcycle gang culture has grown in acceptance (or perhaps tolerance) in the past few years. Many point to the societal adaptation of media-portrayed gang clothing and lifestyle as evidence of this growth. In any case, what concerns criminal justice scholars are the challenges experienced on the streets—perhaps because of the acceptance. Police use intelligence—the active collection of verifiable information—to classify gang members, and they use that intelligence to solve a variety of criminal investigations. It becomes difficult to use intelligence when it changes (or appears to change) as soon as it is obtained.

The Internet and the ability to access current information have brought many challenges for criminal investigators and analysts. Individual street gangs, OMG, and DTE group members often identify themselves with unique names and identify their gang with unique hand signs, the wearing of certain colors, and by displaying gang-specific insignia in their tattoos and graffiti.[160] Group members can easily learn about the intelligence indicators that police use to identify their group affiliation. Such things as gang colors, symbols, tattoos, graffiti, and hand signs have long been used by police to identify gang members, and those indicators are clearly identified in court and other venues. So what happens if those indicators are no longer used?

Tattoos have been an indicator of gang membership for many years. Gang-specific tattoos, bearing the logo or brand, some other symbol, or words related to the gang have been used to show allegiance to gangs. Each of the groups we are examining—street gangs, OMGs, and DTEs, have used tattoos to document their affiliation, though not all members get those tattoos. In research published in 2004, Knox found that only 38.2 percent of males and 7.4 percent of females who came into prison as gang members had permanent gang tattoos.[161] That may indicate either a limited dedication to the gang (evidenced by an unwillingness to mark one's body permanently) or an attempt to avoid detection.

Graffiti, too, has been used by many in law enforcement and corrections to identify gang (typically street gang or DTE) members. Graffiti is used by gangs to mark boundaries of the geographical portion of the city where they live by painting their symbols on the buildings, fences, and other property of non-gang members of the community.[162] Graffiti writers incorporate information regarding their neighborhood, nickname, group name, area of residence, and often telephone area code into their graffiti.[163] Gang members use a variety of signals and codes to identify themselves, their location, activities, relationships with others, and events.[164] Police officers (and members of other street gangs) learn to translate the messages contained in gang graffiti and respond as needed.

Perhaps the most basic and easily identified way for gang members to identify with their gang is to wear clothing and accessories that are the same color or style or display the same symbol(s). The wearing of gang colors may be a preliminary indicator of a community gang presence (in conjunction with the public display of graffiti).[165] The display of clothing representing the colors of a specific gang has been cited as a reason for implementing a school uniform policy and for obtaining a civil gang injunction.[166]

But those obvious indicators of gang activity may only be indicators of First Generation gang activity. The more advanced gangs, those in the Second and Third Generation, are more difficult to identify and investigate. Those are the gangs for whom the military does not provide an alternative, but a catalyst.

Gang migration has become a challenge, as well. Whether for expansion or because of social changes, gang members migrate from the larger cities to the smaller cities, and police who only recently had little need to understand gang activity are now finding themselves overwhelmed. In Tennessee, for example, the state gang investigators' association was founded with those expectations in 1998. The founders were from some of the larger cities in Tennessee, such as Memphis, Nashville, Chattanooga, Knoxville, Clarksville, and Jackson, and we (I was a founding member) realized that there were similar problems in each of the larger cities. We also realized that once those problems were addressed, it would not be long before the smaller cities, often suburbs of the larger cities, would experience the negative effects of gang activity in those jurisdictions. Criminal justice scholars call such activity crime displacement.

Gang migration patterns have indicated that gang members move into suburban areas adjacent to their original urban locations, and migrate to elsewhere in the country—often for social reasons (like job changes or transfers of the gang member or his or her parents). Among agencies experiencing a high percentage of gang-member migration, 45 percent reported that social reasons often affected local migration patterns.[167] In 1999, the Federal Bureau of Investigation attributed most gang migration to job transfers in both white-collar and blue-collar jobs, as well as military assignments.

Migration may also occur when the family moves to escape pressure from law enforcement, or to avoid gang activity or threats. Neighborhoods where migratory gang members relocate may find themselves somewhat controlled by a gang after the transplanted member begins recruiting new members and establishes a supplier and distribution base. Local law enforcement, in those cases, may have limited experience with street gangs and may not be able to counter the initial growth of the gang.

GANGSTERS, BIKERS, AND DOMESTIC TERRORISTS IN THE WORKFORCE

I realize it is a stretch for many readers to think about the possibility that active street gang, OMG, and DTE group members are in military service. I don't expect to convince anyone without significant evidence, which will be presented in the following chapters. In the meantime, let's take a step back. Earlier, we looked at gangs aligned with certain trades and professions. We just recently looked at the existence of gang members in the community, and I suspect none of that provoked a response of disbelief. The next step, then, is to look at the existence of street gangs, OMG, and DTE group members in the workforce.

Group members who choose to work may face difficulties. The Canadian Training Institute (CTI), for example, has identified specific barriers to employment of gang-involved youth, including:

- Lack of basic life skills;
- Low educational attainment;
- Poor work force preparation;
- Poor social skills;
- Absence of appropriate peer and adult role models;
- Disjointed service delivery plans and processes;
- Low expectations by self and others;
- Negative peer influences;
- Negative perceptions by the community and employers;
- Daily involvement with drugs;
- Previous history with courts and correctional systems;
- Inadequate self-regulation skills and a history of violence;
- School failures and problems with reading.

Those in the CTI study most often displayed a general lack of employability skills.[168]

Some would suggest, based perhaps on those barriers, that group members were completely unsuitable for traditional employment. There are indications, though, that at least the group leaders might have the skills necessary to succeed in the business world. Some gangs have become quite productive entrepreneurial organizations. Some gangs, such as the Chicago-based Gangster Disciples, have evolved into formal adult criminal organizations.[169] That gang is reputed to manage an extensive drug operation (hundreds of millions of dollars annually), involving tens of thousands of members in several states.[170] Many OMGs have a similar structure and operation.

Many street gang members have indicated they were often torn between working on the street and holding a conventional job.[171] That type of gang member tends to be unskilled in a specific field or profession, is usually insufficiently educated, and often has met with limited success in the traditional labor market.[172] So what kind of jobs can gang members hold? Depending on the degree to which they participated in the educational opportunities offered them, they may be relegated to the low-wage jobs, which can often be perceived as (and be) dead-end jobs. Less than 50 percent of gang member "foot soldiers" studied by Levitt and Venkatesh had legitimate jobs, though up to 80 percent held jobs at some point, and most were those deemed "entry-level" (in fast-food restaurants, dry cleaners, or performing manual labor on a construction site).[173] That is not so surprising, as CTI's basic life skills are critical to gaining and maintaining employment, and the gang lifestyle does not support those life skills. Gang researchers Scott Decker and Barrik Van Winkle found that less than 20 percent of the gang members they spoke with had legal employment, though many of them reported job hunting was a routine part of their average day.[174] Former gang members with whom I have discussed this matter have suggested that the typical gang member would choose the more profitable venture over a minimum-wage job.

Because of low-paying jobs, if they hold them, gang members may seek more meaningful activity outside their regular employment.[175] Those gang members will likely participate in the underground economy, where drug-selling and street-tax collection would provide additional, though more dangerous, income opportunities. Levitt and Venkatesh reported that few of the gang members they studied made more than minimum wage selling illegal drugs, which was even less appealing when considering the danger and increase of potential death in that "profession."[176] In this criminal economy, they see what they do as work and have been found to have the same motivation as those engaged in traditional (legal) employment.[177]

Challenges with Gangsters, Bikers, and Domestic Terrorists in the Workforce

Is there a real challenge with employing or working with street gang, OMG, and DTE group members? That would likely depend on the job and the individual holding the job. Group members have a sworn allegiance first to their gang. Any expected loyalty to anything else (family, job, even life) necessarily comes after membership. That does not mean that they cannot be good workers, though. It simply means that caution must be exercised when there is a conflict between the needs of the gang and the needs of the employer. Many gang members come from respectable, hard-working, and honest families. In many jobs, employers are not concerned with what employees do when not at work. That thought process may lead to a liability for the employer if gang membership impacts the workplace.

CONCLUSION

We have examined many important areas that provide a foundation for understanding the gangs that are represented by the military. Critical to understanding the threat of gangs in the military and military-trained gang members in the community, is understanding the existence of similar intersections in the past. In the early gangs, there were connections to specific areas in the cities, as well as connections to certain trades and government services. Following the early wars, veterans committed crimes against citizens or representatives of the government. Gangs have evolved over time, and the more advanced gangs have continued to engage in similarly advanced criminal activity.

I am sure you may find some sections of this book with which you disagree. You may also find sections that are a little, shall we say, dry. I have done my best to keep the legalese and number crunching to an interesting minimum without sacrificing the foundation you will need to be able to reach a logical conclusion. If you have insight or opinion regarding any of the following content, please take the time to let me know! I'm best contacted on social media sites like LinkedIn, Facebook, or Twitter (@carterfsmith). You should be able to find updates and ongoing conversation on the book webpage—http://www.gangsandthemilitary.com. You can also check out (and share, please!) the Facebook page at http://www.facebook.com/GBTITM.

Chapter Two

The Emergence of
Gangs in the Military

In April 2005, Army SGT First Class (SFC) Domingo Ruiz watched with his team as three cars stopped across the road from them. A man carrying a machine gun got out of one of them. SFC Ruiz told his sniper, "Take him out," and the man's head exploded. In an interview with a reporter afterward, SFC Ruiz said the activity reminded him of his days as a Brooklyn street gang member. He was a member of the Coney Island Cobras and explained he applied many of the principles he learned in the neighborhoods where he grew up as a leader in the U.S. Army.[1]

While this news coverage was of military actions in a war zone, I found the article troubling on many fronts. Primarily, it was a raw and apparently uncensored view of the realities of war. It was not that reporters had not covered such activity before—I think what troubled me was it contained a twisted before-and-after view of what can be a positive effect on a person's life. Many are the success stories I have seen and heard documenting a young person's transition from miscreant, or juvenile delinquent (or worse), to a successful and contributing member of the community. Although I didn't have an overwhelming amount of delinquent activity in my youth, my story was along those same lines.

But the above story didn't seem to depict a transformation—it seemed more like a transference. Here was an adult leader in the military who drew on the experiences in his violent past on the streets of Brooklyn to order violence in the present in a war zone. Something just didn't feel right about that and I was sure the public affairs folks were cringing as they read the article. But what disturbed me more than that was this non-commissioned officer felt it was appropriate to have that conversation with a reporter in the first place. Imagine how he initially felt when told by his chain-of-command he had been selected to do the interview. I suspect they gave him a briefing on what to say and what not to say, but trusted his judgment. And then this!

It was not that I could not imagine such a person being in the military. I could even imagine a scenario where it was clear, but unstated, that the perfect candidate for recruiting would be someone who had faced death before. In fact, many drug teams do just that – looking for people who can walk the walk and talk the talk while undercover, but who also have clean records. I just could not imagine how he could have considered it appropriate to be so bold (if that's the right word) as to say those things to a reporter. Imagine this—Hey, you want to see us take out the enemy? Watch this! Sniper dude— those guys over there—now! Yeah, that's how we used to do it back home. Wrong, just wrong! There are some things you must have enough sense not to say, and that was a fine example of one of them. But I digress.

The U.S. military has been in its share of battles and military service members have represented the country in internal, regional, and worldwide combat. Military service members have served the community following tornadoes, hurricanes, earthquakes, and other natural disasters. Most service members join the military to be a part of something bigger than they are. They rarely engage in activity that would harm or embarrass the military, and many of them see military service as a patriotic duty or a way to, as President John F. Kennedy suggested, find "what you can do for your country."

Some, though, enter the military with a pre-established and prioritized allegiance to another organization. While that organization may not be in an ongoing conflict with the military, the requirements of membership conflict with the requirements of military service. Those organizations include street gangs, OMG, and DTE groups.

The existence of gang members in the military ranks has been affected by a variety of factors, including the relaxation of standards. The process of increasing the number of enlistees often requires a relaxing, or lowering, of standards for incoming recruits. That relaxation of standards for enlistment allows more previously unqualified individuals to enlist. That has happened whenever a "surge" in troops deployed to the battlefield is needed and the enlistment numbers need to be increased.

Some leaders have intentionally recruited gang members and other delinquents with criminal records into the military. They appeared to believe the gang members would give up all connections to the gang for the more important connection to the military. The former gang members with whom I have spoken over the years typically supported the notion that a gang member would be enticed to join the military if they were dissatisfied with their lot in life at the time. None of them ever suggested that all ties to a gang would be severed if the move was made.

There are surely many success stories from such actions, and I have no doubt that many a young man has found a better way to live his life when he chose to leave the gang and join a more reputable and legitimate organization. My concern is that there is rarely a measurement and never a treatment for those who do not choose to leave the gang when they join the military, or those who do not stay out of them while serving. Unfortunately, both those that did and those that did not change their mindset about the gang life are released without notification of authorities to go back to the community when their enlistment period ends. To do otherwise would violate the individual's civil rights.

Once the need for increased numbers in the military passes, the higher standards are usually reinstated, making enlistment less available for individuals with criminal records and causing a similar restriction of the rules for retention, as those standards were simply overlooked, not erased. They may not be kicked out right away, but they are prohibited from reenlisting when their contract ends. Many would think that once they are in they can stay, but oftentimes when the military tightens the standards for recruitment they also tighten the standards for retention. Consequently, following such a restriction, civilian communities are more likely to experience an influx of military-trained gang members, veterans no longer deemed fit for service. Many times, a soldier with three, six, eight, and even more years has been let go by not being allowed to reenlist (the military version of downsizing).

In the previous chapter, we looked at the history of gangs in Western culture, identified the first known military-trained gang members, examined some definitions for gangs, considered some of the types of gangs, and evaluated the effect of a gang presence in the community and in the workplace. In this chapter, we will focus almost exclusively on gang members serving in the military. I'll continue to present the information by connecting them to historical periods of wartime. That is not to imply the occurrence of war influences the growth of gangs, although in the last chapter many of the gang members came from the Revolutionary War, the Mexican-American War, and the Civil War. Periods in which there was conflict have generally reflected notable growth, or transformation, of the existing gangs, or the way they have been addressed by the military. For readers seeking an academic application, this chapter contains a continuation of what would be considered the literature review on the topic(s). Let's look at the continued evolution of street gangs, OMGs, and DTEs, specifically those with a military connection, starting in the twentieth century.

THE POST–CIVIL WAR AND WORLD WAR I ERA (1865–1940)

One of the more well-known and intriguing gang members with a military connection was the gangster known as Eastman. Although it has been claimed that he was born Edward Osterman, biographer Neil Hanson reported that Edward Eastman was born in Brooklyn in December 1873 to Samuel and Mary Ellen Eastman.[2] While running his self-named gang, contemporaries and rivals of the Five Pointers, he used many aliases, but was best known to the police as William Delaney and to the gangsters and citizens of the streets as "Monk" Eastman. In addition to the pet store that had been established for him at the age of seventeen, either by his father, or as Hanson reported, a wealthy relative named Timothy Eastman, he made a living as a sheriff, a boxer, and a bouncer at various times during his life.[3] He ultimately used the pet store as a front for his growing pigeon collection and illicit trade.[4] Eastman was the example of a gangster's gangster for many years and was very well connected politically. His gang and the Five Pointers engaged in many street battles and were surely the first to conduct drive-by shootings. I suggest that because the automobile was invented in Germany in the 1880s and only started being produced in the United States in the mid-1890s.

Mugshot of Edward "Monk" Eastman, held as a witness to a shooting he was said to have committed, as no witnesses would identify him. Source: The Evening World, *September 16, 1903, Night Edition, Library of Congress*

Eastman met his downfall after the robbery of a young man from a wealthy family, after which his political supporters turned their backs on him.[5] He was convicted and served the better part of a ten-year sentence. Following his release, he attempted to regain control in the underworld but settled on work as a burglar and pickpocket. He was caught and convicted for manufacturing opium for consumption on the street, arrested for burglary and robbery, and served a short jail sentence. By 1917, Eastman decided to try another career, enlisting in the 106th Infantry of the New York National Guard under the alias William Delaney.[6] Although forty-three years old at the time, he told the recruiter he was thirty-nine and was shipped to South Carolina to begin training for war. He served during what was then known as *the* World War (WWI), and when his service ended received an order from the governor of New York restoring his citizenship in full. Sadly, he did not change his ways and was found to have been selling bootleg alcohol and drugs when he was murdered in 1921. He was buried, nonetheless, with full military honors.[7]

The gangs of the early 1900s in both New York and Chicago were often comprised of the children of recent immigrants. One New York gangster and military veteran who may have perpetrated immigrant status capitalized on the mystery associated with giving vague, suggestive responses to inquiries. Depending on to whom you spoke, the man known as either Spanish Louie or Indian Louie was either from Spanish and Portuguese nobility or Indian (Native American) chief lineage.[8] His given name was apparently John Lewis and he was nicknamed Spanish Louie to distinguish him from the many other gangsters who shared his given name.[9] He was said to have been in either the army or the navy, carried a huge Colt revolver, dressed in all black, and had black eyes. He always had money, had no police record, and his murderer was never identified. When he died, he was given a Jewish burial.[10] To add to the mystery surrounding that gangster, he was either killed for ripping off fellow gang members or he was the first victim of a drive-by shooting. Herbert Asbury's version claimed he was killed in 1900 by a fellow gang member after Lewis withheld his share from the proceeds of a political fundraiser. Another version, documented by Mike Dash, detailed his demise in a drive-by shooting by the Lenox Avenue Gang, on April 29, 1910. One evening, several men in a passing Pierce-Arrow called out to him as he stood on the doorstep of his East Eleventh Street apartment. The men opened fire and Lewis was killed as he tried to escape.[11]

Gang researcher James Davis observed that the Mexican Revolution of 1910–1920 was one of the causes for the increase of immigrants in Southern California. The revolution began in protest to the dictatorship of Porfirio Diaz. The dictator was ousted, and civil unrest followed. As the immigrants settled, usually near other expatriates, rivalries developed. Gangs such as

Bunker Hill, Boyle Heights, and San Fernando formed in the Los Angeles area in response to those rivalries.[12] Gang researcher and historian Howell noted that the Hispanic gangs in Los Angeles had stronger cultural, family-like bonds. Their gang associations were much stronger than their bonds at home, school, or church.[13] The solidarity Hispanic gang members exhibited appeared to come partly from the tradition of established, age-graded, non-territorial friendships in Mexico. Their strength may also have been in response to the inherent bias of the majority white population they encountered in Southern California. Howell observed Hispanics in the area were both physically and culturally marginalized.[14] The depression of the 1930s in the United States brought an influx of people from Texas, New Mexico, and Arizona to California, and Hispanic gangs like the White Fence, the Avenues, and Happy Valley started claiming turf there in the 1920s.[15]

Thrasher's study of 1920s-era Chicago gangs showed that delinquent gangs were most likely to arise in relatively poor, unstable neighborhoods.[16] Thrasher's oft-cited research documented the hundreds of gangs in Chicago in the 1920s. As with both past and current organizations, most of the gangs Thrasher identified were made up of adults, with a 60–40 percent majority. The gangs in Chicago at that time were representative of their communities in a very similar proportion to those in New York. Approximately 40 percent of the gangs had members of mixed nationalities. Polish immigrants, or individuals of Polish descent, made up approximately 17 percent of the gangs, while Italians represented 11 percent, and Irish represented just over 8 percent. Less than 10 percent of the gangs were made up of African-Americans. The second-generation youth of the immigrant groups seemed to be the most susceptible to gang involvement.[17] By the 1930s, gang researcher Joan W. Moore found gangs had been well-established in Chicago's African-American communities.[18] The members of gangs had a different make-up, she observed. They were primarily comprised of racial minorities—both African-American and Hispanic—but still represented those at the bottom of the economic scale.[19]

THE WORLD WAR II AND KOREAN WAR ERA (1941–1960)

The Outlaws motorcycle club was formed in 1935 in McCook, Illinois, so members could enjoy long-distance motorcycle rides together. Although World War II slowed the practice significantly, such motorcycle clubs grew after the war, as some veterans found their civilian lives relatively boring. They found camaraderie in the outlaw motorcycle lifestyle and embraced that subculture. Many veterans returning from World War II formed motorcycle clubs in much the same way the Ku Klux Klan formed after the Civil War.

While most were nothing more than social groups, some members began to engage in criminal activities and the clubs evolved to become Outlaw Motorcycle Gangs (OMGs).[20]

Retired Los Angeles Sheriff's Department Detective Richard Valdemar reported veterans also founded the Pissed Off Bastards of Bloomington (POBOBs) in San Bernardino, California, after World War II. The POBOBs later became the Hells Angels Motorcycle Club.[21] As the Hell's Angels grew in power and influence, rival OMGs such as the Pagans and Bandidos formed.

Valdemar also recalled that Army veteran Don Jordan, a famous boxer, founded the "Purple Hearts" street gang. Jordan was known in the boxing ring as the Geronimo Kid.[22] Jordan was the undisputed welterweight champion of the world from 1958 to 1960. He was in boxing at a time when the sport was controlled by organized crime. Jordan, however, was not. Very little about the Purple Hearts was documented, other than that they were a typical 1940s gang.[23]

Though not a classic gang-military connection, the Zoot Suit Riots provided an example of conflict between those with the gang mindset and those serving in the military. In 1943, World War II was underway and many military members were stationed in southern California. Several of the military men were dating and socializing with the local women. Al Valdez wrote that many of the local men disliked the competition from outsiders for the attention of local women.[24] Many in the Anglo community, especially military personnel, felt that Mexican-Americans were not contributing to the war effort, especially the young Mexican-Americans (including gang members) who wore the Zoot suits.[25] The perception was that people who wore the large, oversized suits did not support the war effort because the suit appeared to waste valuable fabric that could be used in the war effort. The thought was they had to be anti-American if they didn't support the war.[26] The Zoot Suit Riots started when some Navy personnel claimed that Mexican gang members attacked them.[27] The gang members claimed, in turn, that the Navy personnel were planning to attack them. The sailors returned to their base and reported one of them had received a broken jaw in the fight and about 200 sailors returned to the area to attack any Mexican wearing a Zoot suit.[28]

THE VIETNAM WAR ERA (1961–1975)

The development of gangs in Los Angeles followed a similar pattern to those in Chicago and New York. Alferdteen Harrison noticed that the development seemed to be predicated on the pattern of south-to-north African-American migration in the 1950s, 1960s, and 1970s.[29] Gang historian Steven R. Cureton suggested that also fueled the growth of African-American gangs in Los Angeles.[30]

Before and during the Vietnam conflict, gang members who joined the military usually severed their ties with the gang. At the time, the rigors of basic training, or boot camp, were much more demanding a recruit's demeanor was deemed incompatible with the gang after their discharge. After the Vietnam conflict ended, gang members who joined the military did not always sever their ties with the gang.

Valdemar recalled that several of the best fighting units in the Vietnam War had a significant representation of former gang members from New York, Chicago, and Los Angeles.[31] He was especially impressed with a platoon that called themselves the "Head Hunters," feared by the Viet Cong, who opposed the United States in Vietnam and Cambodia. The Viet Cong were so concerned by the Head Hunters that they placed a special bounty on their heads.[32]

Vietnam veterans returned from the war about the time the street gangs in Los Angeles were gaining a foothold in their communities. The Bloods and Crips were organized in or just before the 1970s, and like members of the Klan after the Civil War and OMGs after World War II, returning African-American veterans found they could get a sense of comradery in the street gangs that was comparable to what they felt in the military.

Profiting from the War

A criminal associate of the more typical organized crime figures, Frank Lucas also had a connection to the U.S. military during this period. After seeing a cousin killed by the Ku Klux Klan during the Great Depression, Lucas moved from North Carolina to Harlem, New York, in 1946 and immersed himself in street crime.[33] Lucas saw how real money was made and decided crime was his vocation. He robbed a local bar, stole diamonds from a jewelry store, and robbed the players in a high-stakes crap game at a local club. By the 1960s, Lucas had built a successful international drug ring. Then, in 1966, Lucas shot a man who reneged on a drug deal.

Ellsworth "Bumpy" Johnson, a long-time Harlem gangster who controlled gambling and extortion operations, took Lucas under his wing, according to Lucas.[34] Johnson's widow disputed those claims, claiming that Johnson distrusted Lucas. In her memoirs, she especially contradicted the claim that Lucas inherited Johnson's heroin business, claiming Johnson only dealt cocaine.[35] In any event, Frank Lucas learned the criminal mindset well from Johnson, developing one of the most lucrative crime organizations of the twentieth century. By the time it was finished being built, his vast drug empire was used to arrange and fund killings, extortion, and bribery.

Lucas realized that he needed to break the monopoly of the Italian Mafia on the drug trade. He decided to bypass the Mafia's heroin distribution

A wooden coffin. Frank Lucas was known for smuggling heroin into the United States from Vietnam using false-bottom coffins. Source: *iStockPhoto*

network and go directly to the source of the drug. He travelled to Bangkok, Thailand, in 1968, and met Leslie "Ike" Atkinson, a fellow North Carolinian who married one of Lucas' cousins.[36] Atkinson ran a bar and was well connected with many U.S. Army soldiers in Southeast Asia, often supplying them with drugs. Lucas and Atkinson created a network to send shipments of heroin on military planes to military installations on the East Coast. From there, the packages were sent to business partners who unpacked the heroin and prepared it for sale.[37]

Although some alleged that Lucas stuffed heroin into the bodies of dead servicemen, Lucas refuted those allegations, but admitted to using false-bottom coffins. He said he felt conflicted, but was using the means available to do business. With the slowing of transportation options toward the end of the war, the original means he had arranged to transport the drugs (as excess property on government planes) was getting harder to come by.[38] Lucas recruited a North Carolina carpenter and flew him to Bangkok to build over two dozen government-issued coffins with false bottoms, big enough to load in 6 to 8 kilos (about 15 pounds) of heroin. Lucas' "Blue Magic" heroin was far more potent than most heroin and caused many deaths due to overdose. After a jury trial, which resulted in a finding of guilty, Lucas became an informant, turning in his Mafia accomplices and several corrupt members of the New York police department. He also turned on Atkinson and thirty members of his family.[39]

The story of Frank Lucas didn't stop there, however. After Hollywood produced the film *American Gangster*, starring Denzel Washington, several former Drug Enforcement Administration Agents who investigated Lucas filed a class-action lawsuit.[40] Among the allegations were that the film, depicting Lucas' criminal enterprise, defamed them and grossly misrepresented the truth. Atkinson, one of Lucas' suppliers, said he shipped the heroin in furniture, not caskets. "I never had anything to do with transporting heroin in coffins or cadavers," Atkinson said.[41] Lucas claimed he only smuggled heroin through coffins once. A former DEA Agent reported that Lucas never mentioned any crooked DEA agents or cops.[42]

POST–VIETNAM WAR ERA (1976–1989)

In the 1970s and 1980s, there was a different paradigm in America with respect to gangs in the military. Following the Vietnam conflict, there were still many military members who had initially been drafted and had just returned home from war. There were several reports that gangs had formed on military installations, though many of those who had been gang members had successfully left that lifestyle after joining the military. There just wasn't much in the way of armed conflict during those years. Yes, I am aware that the United States invaded Grenada and Panama in the 1980s, but having served in the military during that time, I can tell you there was relatively little action in the way of combat for most of the U.S. military. Additionally, most of the gangs hadn't found their way into the military yet and the gang lifestyle hadn't gained acceptance in, or begun permeating, society. There were reports of groups of individuals hanging out together, often committing crimes as a group. Those groups were primarily members of the same unit, not criminals, and the primary purpose of their organization was not to commit crime.

In 1986, active duty military personnel were caught providing guerilla training and stolen military weapons to the White Patriot Party. The group was an offshoot of the Ku Klux Klan. Frazier Glenn Miller, a Green Beret, and Stephen Samuel Miller were instrumental in establishing the group in 1980. Military researcher and former Army CID Commander George Reed observed that Miller was an Army veteran of twenty years serving as a member of the elite Special Forces. Reed noted that in Miller's trial, an ex-marine admitted receiving $50,000 in exchange for arms, ammunition, and explosives stolen from military installations.[43] A government investigation identified 32,000 rounds of ammunition, 1,500 grenades, and 3,600 pounds of explosives missing.[44] You'll see more from Reed regarding MTGM DTEs in the afterword of the book.

The California Department of Justice (CDJ) reported that gang members have joined the military ranks since at least the 1980s.[45] However, their activity became more pronounced in the 1990s, as a rising number of street gang-affiliated soldiers began to get the attention of military law enforcement.[46] A CDJ bulletin in 2005 reiterated many of the things military investigators have typically recited when talking about gang members in the military. Some enlisted to try to start their lives over by escaping from the gang to get skills and knowledge that could be used to benefit them again.[47] Gang members who intend to stay with their gang enter the military for three primary reasons.

First, some gang members enlist to learn combat tactics. They can then take those combat tactics back to the gang and use the train-the-trainer method to assist fellow gang members with learning combat skills. The second reason gang members join is to learn medical skills. Obviously, especially with the First Generation Gangs, there is a lot of violence going on in their lives. Medical skills can be as critical on the street as they are on the battlefield. Finally, gang members join the military to gain access to weapons and supplies. As you will see in the following chapters, many civilians, gang members included, covet the semi-automatic weapons so prevalent in the military. Additionally, the ability to perform combat tactics increases the dangerousness of gang members in attacks against law enforcement and on members of rival gangs.[48]

THE PERSIAN GULF WAR AND SOMALIA ERA (1990–1994)

The presence of gang members in the military community became especially noticeable in the early 1990s. At Fort Campbell, we noticed different people had committed different crimes that were similar enough in method to indicate the perpetrators had planned the crimes together.[49] Until the 1990s, we generally had little experience dealing with gangs. Much of the gang activity that intersected with military service was happening in the civilian community adjacent to the military installation, and Military Police and investigators typically had enough to do without trying to solve the civilian community's problems.

We began noticing indicators that groups of people were committing crimes, burglaries, break-ins to cars, and thefts, around 1991–1992.[50] We found there were young people in the Fort Campbell community who travelled in groups and called themselves gang members. They were mostly juveniles—often the family members of active duty service members. At first, an increasing number of military-affiliated high school students, both those living on-post and off-post, were claiming to be gang members. They committed parking lot break-ins to automobiles and some burglaries, along with some other types of lower-level, non-violent crimes. By the mid-1990s, more soldiers were claiming gang membership and they were committing crimes both on- and off-post. We found the local police were seeing some of the same indicators.

We didn't have a clue about how to investigate gangs, as we knew no more than most civilians about gangs at the time. They were bad for the community, they were mostly made up of minority group teenagers and young men (or so we thought), and both young people and the producers in Hollywood acted like they were cool. The more that we got out and talked to people in the community and shared the indicators that we were looking for, the more those members of the community saw those indicators of gang activity and reported them to us.

As we will see in the following chapters, there has been gang activity in and around many of the larger military installations, such as Fort Bliss, Texas (located in El Paso, a city with a population of over 50,000 on the U.S.-Mexican border); Fort Lewis, Washington, now referred to as Joint Base Lewis–McChord, as it merged with the Air Force's McChord Air Force Base in 2010 as a result of Base Realignment and Closure Commission recommendations (located 9 miles from Tacoma, population close to 200,000); and Fort Stewart, Georgia (located adjacent to Hinesville, population in excess of 33,000). Those installations were frequently reported as the location of gang activity prior to the FY 2010 Assessment.[51] Since then, the assessments have not contained locations or descriptions of the gang-related activity, presumably to limit the amount of unsolicited oversight and critique coming from outside the CID Command.

It probably comes as no surprise that there is gang activity in some of those areas because of the proximity to a large installation. It may also be as unremarkable that there are often more gangs in larger cities (as compared to smaller cities, especially). In fact, when I was researching that topic for my dissertation from 2008–2010, I found it strange that the survey I was preparing needed to examine the effects of proximity to a large military installation and to a large city on the percentage of military-trained gang members in the community. That seemed like a no-brainer! But the scientific approach (used to an extent by both academics and criminal investigators) required us to assume nothing until it was proven.

The 1990s was the decade in which we started seeing gang and extremist indicators at Fort Campbell. Neither military leadership nor Military Police in the 1990s were prepared to learn there were soldiers doing their military jobs well, who had simultaneously sworn allegiance to leaders in another (competing) organization. At best, some in military law enforcement might have admitted a suspicion that there were some "really good" soldiers who were former gang members, but the majority was loathe to admit any of them were capable of some of the violent and serious criminal activity we will address later in the book. I don't know if they were in denial about the problem or if they were afraid of what could happen if what we were saying was true. To quote Erwin (played by Rob Schneider) in the movie *Demolition Man*, "We're police officers! We're not trained to handle this kind of violence!"[52]

For many, both in law enforcement and the general community, upon seeing gang-like indicators the initial thought was that the individuals who acted like gang members in the military communities were not appropriately qualified or were *wannabe* gang members. No one in the 1990s wanted to believe gangs existed outside of the large, typical-gang cities like Los Angeles, Chicago, and New York. But the more we examined the actions of the groups we were seeing, the more we realized they were groups of people who called themselves by a certain name, had similarities in manner and attire, had some semblance of leadership, and had formed the group to commit crime. Those indicators, even today, meet the criteria for gang membership.

Also in 1990, a Military Policeman at Carswell Air Force Base was identified as the KKK's chief recruiter in Texas. SGT Timothy Hall was also a Tarrant County, Texas, deputy sheriff. He, along with two fellow deputies he had recruited, were terminated from the department.[53] In 1991, an Army Green Beret demolitions expert was arrested on charges that he and another soldier stole military weapons and explosives for SGT Michael Tubbs' Knights of the New Order. Tubbs, who fought in the first Gulf War, had a list of African American and Jewish targets. He pled guilty to theft and conspiracy charges and served four years in prison. Tubbs was previously active in the Sons of Confederate Veterans and the League of the South.[54] Also in 1991, SGT Steven Barry formed the Special Forces Underground (SFU), a white supremacist organization for active duty and veteran Special Forces soldiers. Barry also published a magazine, *The Resister*, at Ft. Bragg, North Carolina. Barry served in the military for more than twenty years and received no more than a reprimand.[55] He briefly joined the neo-Nazi National Alliance as its military coordinator in the late 1990s.

Army soldiers in the Persian Gulf War were photographed flashing gang signs, and there were reports that gangs had claimed areas of aircraft carriers at sea as their "turf."[56] We often used the common-sense explanation that the U.S. military is inevitably affected by all the problems of society at large—including the spread of gang-related crime and violence, or as we said, "the military is a microcosm of society." Still, as gang experts like former marine SGT Wes McBride of the Los Angeles Sheriff's Department observed, military leadership was slow to react to the rise of gangs in uniform because the presence of gangs in the military destroyed the image of a disciplined organization.[57] Navy leaders along the West Coast were warned about rising gangs in the early 1990s. Meanwhile, the Army and Air Force compiled training manuals to help Military Police and investigators identify indicators of gang activity.

In 1992, Dr. George Knox conducted an exploratory study of ninety-one members of an Illinois National Guard unit. An incident involving the death of a child had occurred in a large public housing complex in Chicago that was known for gang violence. The shooter, a gang member, had served in the military, and public officials had suggested the possibility that the National Guard could have been called to assist in suppressing the gang problem.[58] Survey respondents, Army National Guard members from Chicago, estimated military service members with gang affiliations could be as high as 75 percent in some units. Only 2.8 percent of the respondents to the survey indicated there were no gang members in the U.S. military.[59] About one-tenth of the survey respondents reported being a victim of gang crime in the previous year.[60]

In December 1992, two Fort Lewis, Washington, soldiers assisted members of the Cedar Block Piru Bloods of Los Angeles in the murder of a father and his three children, all military dependents. In what may have been the first such murder in the military, street gang members killed Mr. Allen King Sr. and his three children. All four were hacked to death. SGT Lisa A. King, Mr. King's wife, was on duty in South Korea at the time.[61] The actions of the soldiers indicated a level of gang loyalty beyond that described, or understood, by military leadership. The soldiers drove the gang members to King's home and then waited in the car for about forty minutes, until the gang members returned. The soldiers then disposed of the bloody knives and scissors, burned bloody clothing, and drove the gang members to a motel.[62] The gang members killed Mr. King and his children because they believed King had reported them for operating a crack house in Tacoma. "We have a terrible problem with gangs in the military," said Tacoma police detective John Ringer.[63] Later in this chapter you will see another perspective on that crime.

Researcher Karen McMaster examined attitudes toward gangs on a military base in Arizona and found there was no significant difference regarding perceptions of the severity of the gang problem. In the 1993 study, 63.5 percent of the respondents did not believe that gangs were a serious problem in their on-base or off-base neighborhoods.[64] Few of the respondents reported direct contact with gangs, and 83.59 percent reported they had never been a target of gang violence. Few significant differences were identified in how military personnel living on and off base responded to questions regarding the gang problem.[65]

Street gang activity in 1994 included the stabbing of a U.S. Marine at an air base in western Japan. Lance Corporals Mark D. Jimenez, Kenneth E. Ruiz, and Michael R. Stelling were charged with killing SGT Michael A. Allen of Pittsburg, California, who was found floating in a ditch. The three killed Allen because they thought he was giving investigators information about La Familia, a California-based Hispanic gang to which all four Marines belonged.[66] DTE activity in 1994 involved five soldiers at Fort Benning, Georgia, who stole machine guns, hand grenades, military explosives, and booby trap components to give to the Aryan National Front, a white supremacist group based in Alabama, and the Confederate Hammerskins, the Georgia-based chapter of a national neo-Nazi skinhead organization.[67]

THE MID-1990s: EXTREMIST ACTIVITY ENHANCES GANG INVESTIGATION

The year 1995 promised to be an uneventful year for the military. The first Gulf War was over and Operation Uphold Democracy was underway (September 19, 1994–March 31, 1995) in the island country of Haiti. Other than some humanitarian issues in Rwanda and the fighting in Bosnia, the U.S. military had few major challenges other than continued budget decreases and personnel downsizing as they transitioned from a Cold War (and Desert Storm) fighting posture.[68] News reports advised us that street gangs existed in all four branches of the armed services and at more than fifty major military bases around the United States.[69] Little was being done to conceal the problem, if there was a problem. The crimes gang members committed included drugs, robbery, assault, and homicide. Most took place off duty and off base.[70]

Oklahoma City Bombing

On April 19, 1995, a vehicle bomb set off in front of the Alfred P. Murrah Federal Building in Oklahoma City, Oklahoma, killed 168 people and injured 674 more.[71] Although most citizens were shocked and appalled by the act, it did not seem to have a lasting impact on American perceptions of safety or on the political landscape, because it was viewed as an anomaly or common crime committed by Americans. Timothy McVeigh was captured shortly after the attack, and his accomplice, Terry Nichols, was arrested shortly thereafter.[72] Much was said about McVeigh's military service in the aftermath of the bombing, though there was little in the way of suggestion that the military had radicalized him. He served from 1989 to 1992, at Fort Riley, Kansas, and

The Murrah Federal Building. In 1995, Timothy McVeigh blew up the Federal Building in Oklahoma City, Oklahoma, killing 168 people and injuring 674 more. Source: FBI Image Repository

in the Gulf War, where he was a gunner on the tank-like Bradley fighting vehicle and rose to the rank of SGT.[73]

Enraged by the way the U.S. Government handled the Waco standoff between agents of the Bureau of Alcohol, Tobacco, and Firearms (ATF) and the Branch Davidians led by David Koresh on April 19, 1993, McVeigh and Nichols began experimenting with explosives.[74] They met with members of the Michigan Militia and tried to convince the group to launch violent attacks on judges, lawyers, and police officers. Inspired by the novel *The Turner Diaries*, McVeigh and Nichols formed their own group called the "Patriots." They met with at least one member of the Aryan Republican Army in eastern Oklahoma and frequented a white supremacist compound.[75]

The Oklahoma City bombing was a turning point for military investigators, as it brought a lot of national attention to the fact that military-trained folks ultimately leave the military, and some take their radical DTE beliefs and dangerous practices with them. Though it's not likely McVeigh received military training which specifically led to his ability to rig a truck bomb to blow up a large building, many in the press tried to insinuate just that. What it did show was that there was no filter for folks with extremist views while they were in the military, and there were no measures in place to protect the civilian community once those folks leave the military.

Extremists at Fort Bragg, North Carolina

A homicide that was apparently motivated by DTE views slightly different than McVeigh's occurred at the end of 1995. While it did not get the attention from the national media that the Oklahoma City bombing did, it marked an even more significant turning point in gang and extremist investigations in the military. On December 7, 1995, three white soldiers from the Army's 82nd Airborne Division at Fort Bragg, North Carolina, got into a car and drove around Fayetteville, North Carolina, in search of Black people to kill. They happened upon a couple out on a stroll, and two of them got out of the car and confronted the couple. Holding a 9mm pistol, one forced both to kneel and then fired several shots into their heads.[76] The next morning the principal shooter, PFC James Burmeister, was arrested. When police searched his room, they found Nazi flags, white supremacist pamphlets, and bomb-making equipment.[77] They also learned that Burmeister's chain-of-command was aware that he had an interest in Nazi regalia, had been in a fight with a Black soldier, and had used racial slurs.[78] Burmeister and Malcolm Wright were both charged with two counts of first degree murder in the December 7 deaths of Michael James and Jackie Burden.[79] Randy Meadows was charged as an accessory to murder for driving the car.

The homicides seemed to happen out of the blue. No one in the Army or community leadership seemed to have any warning or indication that such a problem existed at Fort Bragg, or anywhere else in the military. At the 82d Airborne Division, there was no significant history of reported extremist activity. In fact, there had only been three complaints filed with the Equal Opportunity Office in the previous year. That did not mean no problems existed—it just meant no one was reporting them. In that same year, skinheads reportedly committed eight assaults on the University of North Carolina, Chapel Hill campus, about seventy miles north of Fort Bragg. In all the assaults, the local police suspected some of the skinheads were soldiers.[80] In April 1995, there was an off-post fight between rival skinhead gangs. The neo-Nazi Skinheads and the local Skinheads Against Racial Prejudice (SHARPs) fought, and a neo-Nazi shot a SHARP in the chest. Fayetteville police investigated the incident, but the investigation was slowed by a lack of evidence.[81] Nothing linked Burmeister to any of the earlier shooting or assaults.[82]

As strange as it may seem, the Army's response to the racially-motivated homicides was the catalyst for empowering military investigators to conduct both military gang *and* extremist investigations. Secretary of the Army Togo West formed a task force to investigate extremist group activity in the Army's ranks. The task force members visited twenty-eight major Army installations in the United States, Germany, and Korea during January and February 1996. After conducting over 7,000 interviews and 17,080 written surveys, the task force concluded there was minimal evidence of extremist group activity in the Army. The survey found only 3.5 percent of the respondents had been approached by extremist groups members and asked to take part in their activities. About 7 percent said they knew another soldier they believed was a member of an extremist group. The task force also noted there was more of a "security concern" with street gangs than there was with extremists. Specifically, they reported "gang-related activities appear to be more pervasive than extremist activities as defined in Army Regulation 600-20. Gang activity both off-post and on-post (i.e., billets, military housing areas, schools, and Morale, Welfare, and Recreation facilities), sometimes involve family members and young soldiers."[83] Based on that information, Secretary West reinforced guidance, which was already in existence, that active participation in an extremist group was contrary to the good order and discipline of the military and would not be tolerated. Nothing was done officially about the task force observations regarding the pervasive gang problem. Make sure to read the *afterword* of this book, written by Dr. George Reed, then Commander of the Army CID at Fort Bragg during the Burmeister trial. His perspective was quite different than mine.

The key to the broad policy application was the use of the word *extremist*. Secretary West had a press conference and reporters asked him questions trying to narrow down or define the term. He said he would not further define the term, as that responsibility was delegated to the unit commanders. He explained that the term *extremist* broadly meant people who, for a variety of reasons, acted in such a way that was contrary to the good order and discipline of the military. He gave the commanders a lot of leeway, and a lot of discretion.[84] To prevent extremists from joining the military, West said the

Army would explore implementing screening procedures. We needed to "better inform ourselves as to whether we're bringing in an extremist—whether there is something we should know that we should be screening out," he said.[85] Thus, the word *extremist* became a catch-all, self-defining term that, as we will see elsewhere in the book, was originally intended to describe a far more different activity than that conducted by gangs.

In support to the Secretary of the Army, Department of Defense Secretary William Perry made it clear there was no place for racial hatred or extremism in all of the United States military. He said every service member took an oath to support and defend the United States Constitution against all enemies, foreign and domestic. "The men and women in the military understand the gravity of this oath," he said. "Department of Defense policies state that military personnel may not actively participate in organizations that espouse supremacist causes."[86] Perry said the policies of the Department of Defense clearly prohibited racial intolerance and discrimination in any form. "Equal treatment, respect and trust are values that the men and women in the military take very seriously," said Perry. "These values are fundamental to a just society, and they are fundamental to military effectiveness. Military training stresses these principles, military conduct requires their observance."[87]

You may be wondering how this event was such a turning point in the abilities of gang investigators. Relatively speaking, there were fewer identified DTEs in the ranks than either street gang or OMG members. The investigation commissioned by the Secretary of the Army had turned up only a few examples of extremist activity. But the presence of even a few of them in the Army was disturbing, given that the Army began integrating over fifty years prior, in the early 1940s, when civil rights leaders demanded an end to segregated Army units.[88]

The reason that was such a turning point was not only that Secretary West had refused to limit the definition of the term *extremist*. It was also that his Task Force had reported: "*Gang-related activities appear to be more pervasive than extremist activities*."[89] Other than a few indicators of gang members here and there, we had very little to work with in the mid-1990s. We found a few soldiers and a few family members who were engaging in gang activity at Fort Campbell, but the folks on the task force had determined that the presence of gangs was more pervasive in all the army, around the world, than extremists. And they had looked everywhere!

Just so the importance of this observation is not missed, let me explain it another way. An African American Secretary of the Army dispatched hundreds of investigators to conduct thousands of interviews to see if there was a looming problem elsewhere in the Army which might cause soldiers to behave as those at Fort Bragg had. The incident which provoked this tasking was the racially motivated homicide of two African American civilians by three white soldiers. The investigators were clearly told that their primary mission was to root out and identify the existence of extremists in the Army. And yet they reported back that yes, there was a relatively minimal extremist problem in the Army that should be addressed, but there was a much larger gang problem that needed to be addressed immediately! I hope I am satisfactorily explaining the significance of this bit of information in context. To me, it seemed to make it clear that there was, in fact, a huge problem with gang activity in the military. And yet, the military did relatively little to address that problem at that point, or at any point in the future, as we will see in the coming chapters.

Elsewhere in the Country . . .

Also in the mid-1990s, Rapid City, South Dakota, was experiencing the effects of military-trained street gang members in their community. *Newsweek* magazine reported in July 1995 that the Nation-Wide Posse (NWP) planned a drive-by shooting targeting the Original Gangster Posse (OGP). An NWP member had been beaten up by one of the OGPs. Seven of the suspects were active duty airmen at Ellsworth Air Force Base, South Dakota. [90]

In 1996, a suspected Sureños gang member shot and killed his Executive Officer and wounded the squadron Commanding Officer to protest the incarceration of his fellow gang members.[91] Marine SGT Jessie Quintanilla entered his squadron's command suite and confronted his Executive Officer, Lieutenant Colonel (LTC) Daniel Kidd in his office, pointed a .45-caliber pistol at him and, as LTC Kidd attempted to run to an adjacent room, shot Kidd in the back. As Quintanilla followed Kidd into the adjacent room, he encountered his Commander, LTC Thomas A. Heffner, who he shot in the chest. Quintanilla then shot Kidd a second time in the back, killing him. Shortly thereafter, Quintanilla fired two shots at Gunnery SGT W. E. Tiller, missing with both. Quintanilla was then disarmed and apprehended.[92]

Also in 1996, Army veteran Eric Rudolph set off a bomb at the Atlanta Summer Olympics, killing one person and wounding 111. Rudolph later bombed a lesbian nightclub and two abortion clinics, killing a police officer, before leading authorities on a five-year manhunt ending in 2003. Rudolph went to basic training at Fort Benning, Georgia, and briefly trained at the Air Assault School at Fort Campbell, Kentucky.[93]

In 1997, Jacqueline Billings, a Fort Hood, Texas, soldier ordered three gang members to kill Basel Maaz, the manager of a nightclub in Killeen, Texas. Billings was the "governor" of a 40-member faction of the Gangster Disciples—many of whom were soldiers at Fort Hood. Billings had the distinction of being perhaps the first, and surely the most violent, female military-trained gang member (MTGM). Instead of killing Maaz, the gang members shot Dorian Ellsworth Castillo and Robert Jharel Davidson, who were driving Maaz' car from the nightclub to his home.[94] Also in the summer of 1997, Billings' gang committed an armed robbery at the management office of the Monaghan Apartments, stealing approximately $2,500 in cash and a gold watch, valued at $18,500.[95]

MTGMs IN NEIGHBORING COUNTRIES

When considering the potential dangers of military-trained gang members, we would do well to consider the Zetas. The Zetas were created by a group of deserters from the Mexican Special Military Forces who became an unparalleled security force for the Gulf Cartel, a multi-national drug trafficking organization. The origins of the Zetas date back to the late 1990s when at least thirty-one Mexican Army commandos left military service to join the Zetas. Many of them had been part of the Grupos Aeromoviles de Fuerzas Especiales (Group of Special Forces of the High Command, or GAFE).[96] Military training was the key to the Zetas success, and the increase in discipline, professionalism, and violence they brought to the criminal world has caused rival groups to improve their recruiting and training. Not only did the group have members with elite military training, but the number two in command, Miguel Trevino, was a former policeman.[97] Trevino was listed as captured by the U.S. State Department as of December 2016.[98]

Mexican Soldiers. The Zetas started with a group of deserters from the Mexican Special Military Forces who became a security force for the Gulf Cartel. Source: *iStockPhoto*

The Zetas quickly became Mexico's largest drug cartel in terms of geographic presence. The group engaged not only in drug trafficking but also in sex trafficking and gun running. In February 2010, the Zetas broke away from the Gulf Cartel and formed their own criminal organization.[99`] The Zetas have lost some control of territory in recent years because of a turf war with the Jalisco New Generation Cartel (CJNG). Most of the original Zetas have either been killed or captured by Mexican law enforcement and military forces. As of December 2016, some of the Zetas have an alliance with the Gulf Cartel, as they were fighting against the Cartel Del Noroeste (Cartel of the Northeast). In a 2010 report, it was noted that street gangs like the Sureños, MS-13, Mexican Mafia, and Latin Kings maintained ties with the Zetas.[100] In a 2015 FBI report, the Sureños, Mexican Mafia, Norteños, Tango Blast, Bloods, Aryan Brotherhood, Gangster Disciples, Crips, and other less well-known gangs reportedly had ties to the Sinaloa Cartel.[101] The Sinaloa and Juárez Cartels, both rivals of the Zetas and the Gulf Cartel, were most frequently referenced for their ties to gangs. Within the United States, the Zetas have used social media as a method of communication and recruiting.[102] We will examine more about the connection between the Juárez Cartel and military members in the next chapter.

AN OFFICIAL RESPONSE TO GANGS IN THE MILITARY

At the Fort Campbell CID in 1997, our new Special Agent-in-Charge, Steve Chancellor, had implemented a very atypical strategy. Many military (and civilian) leaders tend to avoid acknowledgment of problems unless there was an effective solution in place. Many leaders wait until someone else has fixed the problem and then try to find a way to claim some of the credit. Few leaders respond to a problem by devoting sufficient resources to determine the extent of the problem. I had worked with Steve previously, and was not too surprised that he chose the direct confrontation method of addressing the gang problem we were experiencing. When he arrived, he asked the agents and investigators in the office what trends and crimes we were seeing, and we reported what we had seen. He decided to form a gang and extremist investigations team, and appointed the Assistant Special Agent in Charge, Tim Zimmerman, and a new (and experienced) Military Policeman in the community, Chuck Clapper, to launch it. Here's what Chuck recalled about those times:

> When I joined the Military Police in 1986 I never intended to be involved with criminal street gangs, radical militias or hate groups like the neo-Nazis or white supremacist movements. Following a three-year tour guarding nuclear weapons I moved to Fort Lewis, Washington, when the Crips and Bloods were getting

started scooping up turf across the greater Tacoma area. Many who investigate street gangs will remember the night in September 1989 where several Army Rangers shot up a crack house run by the Hilltop Crips street gang. My first two years I was assigned to an office in the Pierce County courthouse as a Military Police Civil Liaison to Local Law Enforcement. Over the next two years I noted a huge increase in military members becoming involved with street gangs on the periphery and documented this whenever possible. During my last two years at Fort Lewis I was assigned to the Military Police Investigations Section in charge of the Juvenile team. This was where I got my feet wet with street gangs as I began noticing many of the kids who lived on base started to "sag and rag," openly displaying gang colors. In fact, one group of Samoan kids who claimed "Blood" ties lived across the street from the Military Police station and openly flaunted their colors. There were no on-post schools for Middle School and High School so the dependent children were bussed to local off-post schools where they met up with local kids who were forming gangs. Many of these military dependents were jumped in and became members of either the Crips or Bloods.

As a result of the increase in Juvenile crimes involving kids who were potential gang members I began to work closely with the Pierce County Sheriff's Office (PCSO) to conduct on and off-post patrols of the areas known to be frequented by those youth and conduct joint Field Interviews in an attempt to identify military dependents and determine if there was a growing potential for gang violence on base. Gang violence spilled over onto the installation in 1992 when two known Blood gang members killed a dependent husband and his three children with a machete in on base housing. The husband had lived in the same off base apartment complex as the two blood gang members. The two gang members were arrested for distribution of narcotics from their apartment and the dependent husband had been called in to speak with the police to determine if he knew anything. An associate of the two gang members saw the husband leaving the Police department and informed the two gang members. By the time they were told, the husband had moved into on-post housing. The Blood gang members contacted two soldiers with ties to the Bloods and used them to gain access to the installation. One soldier drove the getaway car and the other helped destroy the bloody clothing and weapons used in the crime. That awakened members of the community to how gangs can invade a military installation.

Following this I coordinated with the Tacoma Police Department and Pierce County Sheriff's Department to provide a Gang information briefing to the major commanders on Fort Lewis. Even after the briefing the consensus among leadership was the problem was minimal. On the day of the briefing as everyone was leaving the post theater, which was located next to the Military Police Station, the two kids I mentioned earlier were walking in their front yard "sagging and raggin." The Tacoma Police pointed that out to many of the leadership and they seemed less than worried about the problem.

Following my time at Fort Lewis I was stationed in Korea and saw numerous soldiers openly flashing gang signs while in civilian clothes at the Post Exchange and other areas. Upon my return to the U.S. I was stationed at Fort

Campbell, KY and in 1997 was asked by Army CID to help establish a gang-extremist team to root out gang members on the installation. We decided to tackle this problem in a different manner and look at gang members from the perspective that many of them had fraudulently enlisted in the military. Since many criminal records would preclude them from service once we identified a potential gang member we conducted background investigations on them and determined if they had withheld information on their enlistment contracts. If it was determined they had the Army could separate them from the service. The other major initiative we started was an educational program which would educate the local command and give them insight into those individuals in the ranks who could become a threat to the order and discipline within the military. During the two years I was on the gang-extremist team we briefed several thousand soldiers, their unit commanders, and civilian Law Enforcement officers on the problems of gang members in the military.

Chuck Clapper, M.A., M.L.S.
CID Special Agent (Retired)

I was thankful to have Chuck's expertise and experience as we ventured in to the uncharted territory of gangs and extremists in the military. He could simultaneously identify relevant intelligence and share it with community leaders and other members in such a way that they could apply it. His assignment to Fort Campbell was a "win" for the Army CID. We also brought in a soldier named Tony Valdes who had some experience working on anti-gang initiatives in Los Angeles. Between Clapper and Valdes, I think we had more experience with gangs and the military than all the rest of the CID offices combined!

I took over the leadership of the Fort Campbell gang and extremist investigations team some time in 1998, and became the full-time team chief. We gave presentations to groups with just a handful of people, groups with a dozen people, and groups of a thousand people in a theater. We were simply identifying gang indicators, asking the attendees to tell us if they saw those indicators, and providing information with questions and answers. We were sharing what we learned with a lot of Fort Campbell's leadership, while giving what we called Gang Awareness Briefings. We gave hundreds of them. Inevitably, within days or weeks of giving a presentation, we'd get a call from someone who attended saying, *"Hey I went to your presentation and you know that tattoo you were telling us about, or you know that symbol you were telling us about? I saw a soldier with that on his car, on his locker, on his arm, ..."* That's where we got a lot of our information—from the folks who attended our training.

We also found the briefings served us well for two reasons. First, they allowed us to educate members of the community on what gang activity was and how it impacted the military. Second, the briefings served to let those that were active gang members know that we knew what was going on. We were just looking for the indicators. At first, there was not so much criminal activity going on. We noted the tattoos displayed by soldiers and the graffiti that was being sprayed in and around the base. We found paraphernalia, like pictures of soldiers throwing up gang hand signs; written correspondence, drawings, or clothing items with gang symbols, generally found during health and welfare inspections. Those were the main things we were looking for and often found.

Perhaps the best indicators of gang involvement were the tattoos. That worked well because the Installation Commander implemented a policy of tattoo checks for all soldiers who were assigned to Fort Campbell. We kept the leadership of the in-processing unit abreast of the signs and symbols to look for, and they called us if they found a soldier who had something with those signs or symbols. We then interviewed the soldier, and often examined their military records to check things like where they had previously lived and whether they reported a criminal arrest record to their recruiter.

We saw some changes because of the emphasis on tattoo checks. There was a slight decrease in tattooing of gang signs and symbols, and there was a decrease in soldiers admitting the gang connection of a certain tattoo. Sadly, that seemed to appease many commanders, as they took it to mean that soldiers were no longer allied with gangs. The problem was that simply hiding, or even removing a gang or other controversial tattoo, did not adequately change an individual's views or behavior. I am not suggesting that gang members should be allowed to keep their tattoos, but at least when we saw a tattoo or symbol, we knew what group the soldier was representing. Instead, the policy encouraged them to conceal their views with no real plan to monitor or track them. I think the message that sent was: "OK you, SPC Gangmember, and you PFC Extremist, you are being counseled to get your controversial tattoo removed. We, the Army, do not support those beliefs, BUT we will keep you, if you get your controversial ink removed, regardless of whether your views and affiliations change after the procedure." I always wondered why there was no follow-up plan after the counseling and tattoo removal.

After enough of the self-reported incidents and community-member contacts, we decided to call the "gang experts" to get some advice: Here's how the phone call to the Los Angeles Police Department gang unit went:

LA GangCop1: Hello.

Me: Good afternoon! This is Special Agent Carter Smith with the Army CID at Fort Campbell, KY. May I speak with someone on the gang investigations team?

LA GangCop1: Speaking!

Me: Great! It has come to our attention that some of the criminals in our jurisdiction are affiliated with the gangs in your area—namely the Bloods and the Crips.

LA GangCop1: Is that so? Where'd you say you are calling from?

Me: Fort Campbell, KY.

LA GangCop1: What's that near?

Me: It's just north of Nashville, TN.

LA GangCop1: Oh, OK, hang on, let me connect you with the migratory gang specialist.

LA GangCop1: (shouting across the room so I can clearly be part of the "hand-off") Hey Jim, there's a guy on the phone from Kentucky that says he's got some *bona fide* California gang members in his jurisdiction. Do you have time to talk with him?

(there was a long pause and silence before I heard)

LA GangCop2: Hello? (having noticeable difficulty controlling his laughing)

The conversation went downhill from there.

Many of the civilian gang officers we were contacting were senior investigators with their departments and often they were Vietnam veterans. Although there were a few gang members in the military during Vietnam, the general opinion or impression was that basic training had changed their minds regarding that lifestyle. Basic training in the 1990s, and the following decades, did no such thing. Once the "real" gang cops started realizing how dangerous their "real" gang members could be with military training, though, the friendly joking ceased, and we started to address the gang problem together.

There was quite a learning curve and we learned by simply being inquisitive. We found many gang members, like members of many other organizations, were very willing to explain things if you respected them and showed them you were sincerely interested in learning more about them and their gang. Not surprisingly, as we learned more, we were more effective in our identification and investigation of gang-related crimes.

THE FOLLOW-UP

In 1998, right after we started up the gang-extremist team, DoD leaders published a comprehensive follow-up study to the task force report following the Fort Bragg murders. Mr. Marc Flacks and Dr. Marty Wiskoff conducted the study and reported, among other findings, that gang members adversely affected the military in a variety of distinct ways. They noted that while there was no official accounting of the scope and nature of the problem, it was enough of a problem to inspire each of the branches to publish gang identification manuals.[103] The researchers also observed recruiters, and other relevant personnel, were in need of better guidance on gang identifiers and the policies that guided decisions to allow gang members to enlist, as the goal should be to eliminate the possibility that gang members can enlist in the military.[104] In addition, due to a decline in optimal quality and quantity of enlistees, recruiters in the military had more of a propensity to recruit from the less-desired population, of which gang members were a part.

The three primary areas found to need attention were policies used by recruiters and those processing enlistees, connectivity and coordination with local law enforcement, and access to the juvenile records of potential enlistees.[105] The recruiter policies in need of work included identifying gang membership indicators beyond tattoo inspection. Personality factors, biographical data, and additional screening measures should also be added, they suggested. Coordination and liaising with local law enforcement should focus on identifying ways to determine the criminal history of potential enlistees.[106]

The researchers found access to the juvenile records of potential enlistees had been blocked by Congress.[107] They suggested continued efforts and coordination with legislators should be attempted to prove the need for access to juvenile records for potential enlistees. They noted the alternative to legislation was a continuance of the creative practice of some recruiters who persuade enlistees to unseal the records.[108] Flacks and Wiskoff also recommended a coordinated effort by all military branches to determine the scope and nature of the gang and extremist group problem. The follow-up report was not a turning point to me because I didn't see it until many years later, while researching this topic in graduate school. It might have been a turning point for others, though, had something in the list of recommendations been tried or implemented by anyone in military leadership. It was as if no one knew about it. If nothing else, the report seemed to reinforce that the military should focus not only on gangs and extremists, but also on finding a solution.

During that time, we learned that what was needed to address the gang problem was a variety of approaches to training. We targeted training primarily at military leadership, but also included some soldiers, depending on the requests of unit leadership for an expanded briefing, and we were seeing results. It was time to expand to the local community, so we organized the first Military Gang and Extremist Training Conference in February 1998.[109]

Also, at about that time, we arrested an Infantry soldier who was associated with a group who called themselves the Clarksville (TN) Area Skinheads (CASH). The CASH-affiliated soldier assaulted individuals off-post, vandalized a church in Oak Grove, Kentucky, attempted to build a pipe bomb in his barracks room, and distributed CASH literature on- and off-post. He was convicted of attempted manufacture of an explosive device and distribution of extremist literature and received a Bad Conduct Discharge (BCD), reduction to E-1, forfeiture of all pay and allowances, and two years' confinement.

A CHANGE IN TERMINOLOGY: SECURITY THREAT GROUP

Although we had the unit briefings down to a science, after we had been doing them a while, we started having difficulty scheduling them. We were learning new things so often that our briefings never became stale or repetitive—in fact, many of the leaders saw value in second and third briefings within just a few months. But there were some units that seemed to have no interest in having the battalion or brigade leadership sit through one of our briefings. Sometimes it felt like we hit a brick wall when we tried to arrange a briefing. Battalion Commander LTC X was one of those brick walls.

Here's how the phone call often went:

LTC X: 123d Infantry Battalion, LTC X, sir!

Me: Good day, sir! I am Special Agent Carter Smith with the Army CID here at Ft. Campbell. I'm the team chief of the Gang and Extremist Investigations Team, and I would like to schedule a briefing for your unit leadership.

LTC X: A briefing on what, Agent Smith?

Me: On Gangs and Extremists, Sir!

Lt. Col X: Thankfully, we don't have those problems in our unit, Agent, but thank you for your time! Goodbye!

Now, I know you may be criticizing me for calling on the battalion commander to schedule training, but that was a strategic decision made to avoid getting the run around. Our thought was that if we called a training sergeant or even the Executive Officer, they would still have to sell the idea to the commander. All the Battalion Commanders had surely heard of our successes through either formal or informal channels, so we figured that was the way to go. Many times, I had to bite my tongue when I heard "we don't have those problems." What I wanted to say was, "Oh, I know that, Sir, but the unit next door to yours is ate up with that stuff and we are afraid some of your guys will get caught up in their problems," or, "That's excellent news, Sir, because the rest of the Division has those problems and they were hoping I could do a case study of your unit to collect some lessons learned." The reality in most instances, in my opinion, was that either the Battalion Commander was uninformed, or his leadership was actively concealing problems—neither of which were likely to turn out well. While training with the British Police at Scotland Yard a couple years earlier I learned they had a saying which was quite appropriate for this sort of issue, "You don't look, you don't find."

Instead of shifting into Smart Alek mode, I decided to shift into problem-solving mode. I contacted as many gang investigators as I could and explained the dilemma to them, asking for their advice and insight. It wasn't so much that I thought they may have encountered the problem before—the military is a unique institution where recidivism is a relatively unused word. My thought was that the gang investigators were experienced at fixing a variety of perception problems, of which this was one.

After many such phone calls and visits, I happened across a fellow who was the prison gang expert for the state of Michigan. He seemed, initially, to promote a corrections solution to a military problem. He suggested that we stop referring to our gang and extremist group members as such, and start referring to them as Security Threat Group members. He advised me to stop giving Gang and Extremist briefings as the Team Chief of the Gang and Extremist Investigations Team and start giving Security Threat Group briefings as the team chief of the Security Threat Group Investigations Team. The use of the term Security Threat Group to refer to the groups like street gangs, prison gangs, white supremacy groups, Outlaw Motorcycle Gangs, subversive groups, and cult groups is patterned after various states' departments of corrections.

So, I figured, what the heck? Let's change the terminology! And who better to start with than my old friend LTC X?

Here's how that phone call went:

LTC X: 123d Infantry Battalion, LTC X, sir!

Me: Good day, sir! This is Special Agent Carter Smith with the Army CID here at Ft. Campbell. I'm the team chief of the Security Threat Group Investigations Team, and I would like to schedule a Security Threat Group briefing for your unit leadership.

LTC X: Hello, Agent Smith! Would you hang on a second?

Me: Yes, Sir!

LTC X: (yelling to someone in another office) SGT T, could you bring the training schedule down here?

Give me just a minute, Agent Smith. When are you available?

Me: (thinking we were on to something and should spend the next week making sure of that) I have an opening about 3 PM on Thursday of next week, Sir. We can schedule next month if that doesn't work.

LTC X: (as SGT T arrived out of breath and told Lt. Col X that they have mandatory training scheduled out for two months) SGT T, cancel whatever we have for 3 PM on Thursday of next week. Agent Smith, can I get my leadership (all Commanders and First Sergeants) in that briefing?

Me: Yes, Sir!

LTC X: Excellent, and the Sergeant Major, Executive Officer, and I will be there too, Is that OK?

Me: Yes, Sir!

LTC X: Great! Goodbye!

I talked with LTC X after the briefing and asked him about what appeared to me to be a change of heart. I had looked through all the recent military police reports, checked with informants, and done everything I could to find out why he would have become so receptive to our briefings in just a matter of weeks. He explained that the term Security Threat Group seemed to limit the need for an explanation—it was defined in the words. In any event, we called that a win, and our team name and focus was changed forever (well, at least until I retired in 1999). In our briefings, we explained that we called them Security Threat Groups to eliminate any recognition the members may draw from publicity about their group or its activities. Also, we felt the term accurately described how those groups can impact the security of military operations and law and order.

That change in terminology was a turning point to me because I felt like we had happened across a term that was not as "offensive" to commanders (it felt like we had called them out for a problem they should have fixed), and the term was well and rapidly accepted. The added benefit was that when we called them gangs, extremists, and so on, many in leadership expressed only a passing interest. When we used the term "Security Threat" Group, it was like the light bulb instantly turned on regarding why those groups should be important to them.

I realize that these efforts seem to be quite passive in application, so let me remind you that the issues we were trying to address were occurring at a time when the country was focused on "more important things" such as the political and military adjustments that happened after the Persian Gulf War, the first attack on the World Trade Center in New York, and the bombing of the Federal Building in Oklahoma City. Additionally, those of us that saw a gang problem in the military were pushing back against the organizational leadership (both in my organization and the military community) that traditionally adopted a status quo posture. There was resistance and reluctance to accept our observations that the issues existed, and there was resistance when we tried to engage, train leaders, or explore the problem. That sort of inaction went against every-thing I had learned as a military law enforcement professional, and I was of the belief that leaving the issue alone would ensure it would get much worse. Inaction would have been a foolish response. Our only potentially successful option was to subtly identify indicators of the problem and hope we were in the room when they asked for ideas. As was recently pointed out to me about a similar issue, the logical approach had we been in the civilian community would have been to contact the media and go forward as an "official who was familiar with the matter and could not be identified." That option was not something we could or would do in the military.

IT'S NOT JUST US!

In the fall of 1998, I attended a Countering Violence conference put on by the Department of Justice in Gatlinburg, Tennessee. While there, I met several detectives, agents, and investigators from across the state of Tennessee. One night we were sitting outside after a hard day of parking our butts in the seats and we were talking about how what the conference presenters were address-ing applied to the communities we represented. There were guys from Mem-phis, guys and gals from Jackson, some folks from Nashville, Murfreesboro, Chattanooga, and Knoxville, and we all realized that we had the makings of a "gang problem." That night's conversation was the spark that lit the organiza-tion now known as the Tennessee Gang Investigators Association, or TNGIA. I'll talk more about the organization later in the book.

During the coming months, we recommended many local and Army-wide policy changes and some were implemented. For example, as Clapper noted, we realized soldiers who had been gang members prior to joining the military were likely to have committed a crime to get that membership or once they had joined. It was learned that many of the recruits with a criminal record had not reported their record to their recruiter or their recruiter had not identified a record prior to allowing the recruit to enlist. That happened sometimes because the background checks which were conducted were local and were only implemented in the county where the enlistment occurred. Oftentimes, recruiters, or friends of the recruit, would suggest they enlist in a county where they did not have a record. As a result, no record was found unless a national fingerprint check was conducted. Many such instances were found, although most commanders took no action again the soldier for fraudulent enlistment—often claiming the individual was one of their best.

From January 1, 1999, to August 20, 1999, Major Rafael Davila, retired Washington Army National Guard intelligence officer and his ex-wife conspired to illegally transfer documents classified as "top secret" outlining plans for U.S. troop deployments during a domestic crisis to the Aryan Nations.[110] The documents had titles like "Strategic, Korea, Russia, chemical warfare, chemical mixtures, nuclear, biological." Davila was a Vietnam veteran who won the Bronze Star.

In October 2000, the Army began requiring national fingerprint checks of all recruits. That requirement was added after we brought to light the faults of the policy of coordinating local background checks for recruiters. Partly due to that requirement, more recruiters sought waivers to accompany the records of criminal activity that were discovered. For example, from 2003 to 2006, the number of criminal background waivers grew about 65 percent.[111] The majority of the Army's moral waivers are for serious misdemeanors, including aggravated assault, burglary, robbery and vehicular homicide. Felony waivers increased from 8 to 11 percent of the moral waivers granted from 2003 to 2006.

SEPTEMBER 11, 2001: NO MORE GANG INVESTIGATIONS, THE FOCUS IS ON TERRORISM

Citizens of the United States of America had just finished celebrating 125 years of freedom and were looking forward to a bright future. The dangers expected from the Y2K technology disaster at the turn of the millennium were behind us and the first Gulf War seemed like an old memory. On the 11th day of September, 2001, much of that changed. A group of men from a handful of far-away countries demonstrated their hatred for the United States in a way never before seen and hardly ever imagined.

Four planes, flown by well-coordinated members of a previously little-known terrorist group engaged in suicide attacks in New York City and the Washington, D.C., area. The men intentionally flew commercial passenger jets into the North and South towers of the World Trade Center in New York City and the Pentagon, headquarters for the Department of Defense in Arlington, Virginia. A fourth jet, intended to be flown into the U.S. Capitol Building in Washington, D.C., crashed into a field near Shanksville, Pennsylvania, after its passengers physically confronted the hijackers. Nearly 3,000 people died in the attacks, including all 227 civilians and nineteen hijackers aboard the four jets and many of the occupants in the buildings which were targeted.

Most people will acknowledge the September 11, 2001, attacks altered the political and financial landscapes of the United States. Prior to 9/11, there had been only a few terrorist attacks within the United States and only one perpetrated by terrorists from outside the country. But what most

Destruction of the World Trade Center Towers. After 9/11, many ongoing gang investigations ceased, and many gang investigations teams were reassigned to investigate the terrorist threat. Source: iStockPhoto

people don't realize is that many ongoing gang investigations ceased almost instantly, and many gang investigations teams were not open for business for quite a while. I've told many people it seemed like many gang cops got instant job reassignments on September 11th, and they became terrorism task force officers or homeland security specialists almost overnight. I saw first-hand how the attacks on 9/11 changed the operations strategies for several organizations. Although I was unable to attend while in law school, the 2001 TNGIA conference was scheduled for Memphis, Tennessee, less than two weeks after 9/11. To say that attendance was down would be an understatement. Thankfully, the hotel was understanding and didn't hold us to our room block commitment.

New Legislation

Following the 9/11 attacks, on October 26, 2001, President George W. Bush signed the Uniting and Strengthening America by Providing Appropriate Tools Required to Intercept and Obstruct Terrorism (USA PATRIOT) Act (commonly known as the Patriot Act) into law. The act significantly reduced restrictions on law enforcement agencies gathering intelligence within the United States, expanded the Secretary of the Treasury's authority to regulate financial transactions, particularly those involving foreign individuals and entities, and broadened the discretion of law enforcement and immigration authorities in detaining and deporting immigrants suspected of terrorism-related acts. We will address the USA PATRIOT Act more in chapter 4.

The events of 9/11 led to a rapid and significant decrease in the focus in all law enforcement agencies, local, state, and federal on gang-related activity. Terrorism task forces sprang up or immediately received multiple commitments of manpower, and law enforcement everywhere was focused on preventing attacks like the ones experienced in New York City and Washington. The gang problems didn't go away, though. It's not like a bunch of gang member leaders from across the United States gathered at an emergency session and one of them said, "Hey, bro, that terrorist activity was pretty nasty. They got terrorists in DC and New York, they probably got 'em up in Chicago and out in Los Angeles. Let's go ahead and take a break and just not do any gang-banging while the cops go chase terrorists." That conversation never happened! But to hear most government leaders talk they stopped having a gang problem for at least a little while.[112]

The aftermath of 9/11 was a turning point because it not only gave the gangs in the military a head start (think of the game of hide-and-seek and the military counted to about 200), it also expanded the laws that would ultimately apply to the investigation of gang members (including those with military training) by the civilian police. The USA PATRIOT Act and anything that comes after it, while "focused" on terrorists, are likely to continue to expand the abilities of law enforcement to investigate gangs and other organized crime groups.

The Grassroots Investigation Model

In September 2002, we scheduled another TNGIA conference, in Nashville. It was at the 2002 conference that I met Dr. Ronal Serpas, then the Chief of Police for the Metro Nashville Police Department. He was invited to the conference for the opening ceremonies. At the time we met, he was out in the parking lot, just outside the conference area, and a crowd had formed as he appeared to be answering questions. At the time, the Nashville Police Department was in one stage or another of what some referred to as their "recognize the gang problem" or "don't recognize the gang problem" plan, and many of the cops in the city were more than a bit frustrated. An officer from a neighboring jurisdiction, clearly sympathetic to the cause, asked Chief Serpas a not-so-subtle question about it, something along the lines of, "What should detectives do if darn near every case that comes across their desk has a clear gang connection but the politicians in their jurisdiction won't acknowledge that there is a gang problem?"

What Chief Serpas said in response was simple: If as a law enforcement professional you see a problem, do what you can to address the problem. Look for others who also see it as a problem, and as much as you can, address the problem in the most efficient way possible. If you think additional resources, whether they are dedicated officers, funds, vehicles, or equipment, would help you address the problem, find out who can provide the added resources. Then, approach them, or get as close to them as you can (referring to the impenetrable hierarchy in some organizations, I suspect) and make sure they get (understand) three things: 1) What the problem is and how you have been successful at addressing it. 2) How big a problem it is, in context, and what it would take in the way of resources to address it if there were unlimited resources available, and 3) What you think will happen to the problem if it is not addressed in the way that either of the first two provide. I saw a lot of folks acknowledging the applicability of that response, but I am not sure how many folks it impacted long term. I have used this model in many situations since then, and as often as possible I have shared it with others. I encourage you to do the same!

Many professionals are in the habit of doing a great job at whatever they are asked, ordered, or paid to do. They study hard, achieve mastery, and become the best widget-salesman or flying carpet-cleaner in the company.

Cops are different, and military cops are especially different. Cops have to learn to master things quickly, often on the fly, as a lot of what they are asked, ordered, or paid to do involves dangerous activities—someone's life is often in danger. Cops tend, though, to wait for the organization to tell them about their need for specialization. They may notice trends happening, such as an increase in burglaries or a high number of fatal accidents at a certain intersection, but they aren't likely to choose to specialize in something unless it's part of their assigned duties.

The thing about cops who know a lot about gangs, especially when they are one of few in the area, is that they were usually just being inquisitive in the beginning. Perhaps they noticed that a group of folks had the same method for thefts, or maybe they realized that victims had similar reports regarding the subject descriptions. On further inquiry, they found that a group calling itself the ABC Thugs or 789th Street Hustlers was responsible. It they were anything like us in the early years, they would send a report containing the discovery up the chain of command, expecting an "Atta boy" from above. Again, if they were like us, they would be shocked when the message came down that the word gang should not be used anywhere in any official report put out by the organization. But that didn't make the gangs disappear.

Despite the pause for military gang and extremist investigations following the events of September 11, 2001, in October 2002, U.S. Army veteran John Allen Muhammad (born John Allen Williams) launched the Beltway sniper attacks as part of a scheme to extort $10 million to establish a Black separatist nation in Canada. For three weeks, he and Lee Boyd Malvo, then seventeen, killed ten people at random in the Washington, D.C., area.[113] Their victims were in the middle of otherwise normal activities when they were shot—pumping gas, shopping, walking to school, mowing lawns, going to a restaurant. Investigators learned Muhammad had joined the Nation of Islam (a Black separatist group) in 1999, and later connected with Jamaat Al-Fuqra, a Pakistan- and U.S.-based DTE group.[114] Muhammad had previously served in the Louisiana National Guard and the regular Army during the 1980s, in jobs such as combat engineer, mechanic, truck driver, and metalworker.

In 2003, the Fort Hood area Gangster Disciples' new leader SGT Jerome Smith was charged with robbery at an off-post residence and an armed robbery of a convenience store. Smith reportedly motivated his gang members with fear, and once placed a plastic bag over the head of someone who owed him money and ordered him to explain how he was going to get money before the air ran out.[115] Smith joined the Army in 1993 and was involved in several incidents during his enlistment. He had been arrested in Virginia for malicious wounding and had faced charges for unlawful carrying of a weapon, drunk and disorderly conduct, failure to obey a lawful order from a noncommissioned officer, and indecent assault.

James Ross Jr. served in Iraq during 2004 as a military intelligence officer. Ross was caught shipping disassembled confiscated AK-47s to the United States. When Military Police searched his house, they found not only a stockpile of weapons and ammunition, but also neo-Nazi and white supremacist literature.[116] He was allowed to keep the weapons and moved to Washington State, to serve as a leader in the Eastern Washington Skins, a neo-Nazi gang. His job was to recruit active duty soldiers to the gang.[117]

GANG AND EXTREMIST INVESTIGATIONS ARE BACK IN FOCUS!

The year 2005 became known as the year that military-related gangs and extremists returned to the national spotlight. On January 8, 2005, Lance Cpl. Andres Raya shot and killed Ceres, California, police Sergeant Howard Stevenson and wounded Officer Sam Ryno with a semiautomatic SKS rifle outside a Ceres liquor store before police returned fire and killed him. Raya, a U.S. Marine, was a Norteño gang member and was high on cocaine at the time. During the investigation, it was learned that he had just returned from Iraq, but had not faced combat. Raya had made odd statements when he entered the liquor store, left and fired off a couple of rounds from his rifle, and then returned to the store and told the clerk to call police because he had been shot. Officer Ryno and Sergeant Stevenson then arrived. The investigation also uncovered ties to the Norteño gang, including a book by a member of the related prison gang, Nuestra Familia, and numerous pictures of Raya wearing the gang's signature color red and making gang signs with his hands. A video showing Raya and his friends smoking marijuana, making gang signs, and showing off gang graffiti was also found.[118] The video of the shooting is readily available on YouTube, Keywords: Ceres Gang Police.

Later in 2005, two deaths occurred in Germany and Alaska which were clearly gang-related. On July 3, 2005, in Kaiserslautern, Germany, gang leader Rico Williams knocked out Juwan Johnson with one punch. Williams, thirty-four, a former airman, ran the Gangster Disciples in the area. After two gang members helped Johnson to his feet, Williams punched him again. Johnson fell to the ground a second time. Johnson then stood up under his own power, at which time nine of the Gangster Disciples descended on him in a beating typical of those experienced for initiation and discipline.[119] The punishment lasted six minutes. Soon, Johnson could no longer stand, and he curled on the ground in the fetal position, to block Williams' kicks. After six minutes and more than 200 blows, Johnson lost bowel control.[120]

The other gang members helped him into his car, and drove him to their barracks on Kleber Kaserne. Three of them carried him to his room.[121] Johnson took a shower and returned to his room. Later, Johnson turned blue and stopped breathing. Someone called an ambulance and he was taken to the local hospital, where he died from his injuries. That afternoon, Williams concocted a cover story for all to tell: a bunch of Turks beat up Johnson in downtown Kaiserslautern the night before.[122]

All the news reports quoted the Army investigators who were saying that the homicide was a gang initiation (beat-in) gone awry. That seemed strange and illogical to me, as Johnson was set to leave the Army and return to the United States a mere three weeks later, had a new child, and was going to be in Baltimore, Maryland, not the most popular location for Gangster Disciples. I suspected he was being beat-out, not beat-in. I had seen past instances of military-affiliated and hybridized gangs offering a beat-out exit option. It would have made sense that, given the circumstances, the local set was giving him their version of a military "Hail and Farewell." His mother found it strange, too, and said, "I just don't picture my son joining a gang. Does it make any sense that he would join a gang in Germany just weeks before he's going to leave?"[123]

There was a trial going on, so I didn't offer (and wasn't asked) my opinion, but I was well acquainted with the relatively few other gang experts whose area of expertise included gangs and military personnel. After the trials, I spoke with a gang expert who investigated the murder, and he advised that Johnson's beating was discipline for being too much of an individual. Johnson had apparently become full of himself and was provided some gang-sanctioned discipline. The History Channel's *Gangland* series covered the Johnson murder. You can purchase the video of that episode or find it readily available on YouTube, Keywords: Gangland Basic Training.

In Alaska, as reported by CID in August 2005, three soldiers became involved in a dispute with civilian gang members off-post, and after an exchange of gunfire, one civilian was killed. The three soldiers, suspected gang members stationed at Fort Wainwright Army Installation, Alaska, were indicted on second-degree murder charges for their involvement in the gang-related shooting death of a Crip member at a local nightclub off-post near Fairbanks. They were later acquitted.[124]

While at an off-post club an argument ensued, and someone took one of the soldier's red bandannas and burned it in the street. Red is the color of the Bloods, Crip gang rivals. The soldiers encountered the civilians they suspected of burning the bandanna at a nearby Community Center, and each of the soldiers fired a weapon at the vehicle in which the civilians were traveling. One of the civilians leaned out of the passenger door with a shotgun and was shot in the chest and groin area. He died shortly thereafter. The incident occurred just days prior to the soldiers' deployment to Iraq.[125]

Also during the summer of 2005, Petty Officer 2nd Class Sheila Daniels, a sailor stationed in Okinawa, Japan, solicited a gang member to kill her husband's girlfriend. The gang member, Marine SGT Michael Avinger, claimed to be the godson of Crips gang founder Stanley "Tookie" Williams, and was himself a high-ranking Crips "lord." Daniels asked Avinger to kill then Staff SGT Christina Miller who was pregnant by Daniels' husband.[126]

The year 2005 was a turning point because not only did we see a military-trained gang member actively engaging in the ambush of police officers, we also saw a return to at least a passive monitoring of the gang and extremist posture in the military. The homicides in Ceres, California, further demonstrated the level of dangerousness that military-trained gang members can bring to the civilian community. Prior to that event, we had few ways to convince civilian law enforcement that they should pay attention to gang-affiliated military veterans who returned to their communities.

The two military homicides, one in Germany and the other in Alaska, showed that despite ignoring the problem, gangs continued to form in the military, and they conducted their activities on military installations overseas much the same as gangs conducted their affairs in the United States. Relatively little is known about the homicide in Alaska, but the Johnson killing catalyzed a returned focus on gangs in the military. As a result, on August 23, 2005, the Chief of Staff of the Army tasked the CID to do an assessment of gang activity in the U.S. Army.[127]

The response by the Army was initially reminiscent of the task force assigned after the murders in Fayetteville, North Carolina, in 1995. While there was ample intelligence that such activities were occurring, no investigative assets were devoted to following up on the intelligence until something big happened. I thought it strange that the person tasked with conducting the initial gang and extremist assessment for the Fort Campbell CID office area of responsibility (southern Illinois, western Kentucky, and all of Tennessee) was a computer crimes specialist, self-identified as someone who "wouldn't know a gang member if one walked up and smacked him." I suspected the assignment of a computer crimes specialist to tally gang reports was an indicator of the level of interest the CID Command had in identifying gang members in the military.

I had recently (in 2004) returned to the CID as a civilian in the battalion headquarters for the CID office, and was also located at Fort Campbell. I was puzzled that I was never asked about any of the gang indicators to look for or asked for assistance in any way, and neither was the fellow who followed me as the gang and extremist team chief, who was a senior special agent at the time. The U.S. Army Chief of Staff began requiring an annual report from CID on the current gang and extremist threat because of the events of 2005. We will see the results of these annual reports in the following chapters. I left the CID in 2006 to pursue a career in higher education.

In December 2005, a National Guard soldier sold several machine guns to a gun dealer in Georgia. The soldier had smuggled the foreign-made machine guns (that usually means AK-47) back to the United States and attempted to trade them to a gun dealer near Atlanta for an all-terrain vehicle and a pistol.[128] From March 2005 until October 2006, William Ivery, a U.S. Army Gulf War veteran with two purple hearts, bought two Jennings .380-caliber handguns and sold them illegally. One of the purchasers was a New Jersey gang member. Ivery also mailed a Smith & Wesson .40-caliber handgun to two others, who retrieved it from an address in Burlington County, New Jersey.[129]

In 2006, the House of Representatives Subcommittee on National Security and Foreign Affairs asked the U.S. Government Accountability Office (GAO) to investigate the unauthorized sale of military equipment on the Internet.[130] That was problematic, as it demonstrated the lack of accountability of surplus and stolen military equipment, much of which could be stolen by gang members in the military or acquired by gang members in the civilian communities. Also in 2006, Michael Smith, a Marine reservist and Maniac Latin Disciple gang member was charged in Aurora, Illinois, with attempted murder in the shooting of three teenagers.[131] With an accomplice, he shot the three teens and then led police on a daring high speed chase before being captured.

In the fall of 2006, four Marines in Columbia, South Carolina, were found to be recruiting local teenagers into the Crips street gang per the direction of a gang leader in Florida.[132] The Marines were contacted by the gang leader and asked to follow up on an online inquiry by the teenagers, who had used computers at schools and public libraries to make the connection. The teenagers met with the gang member-Marines outside a high school, near a fun park, and at a home in the community. Many Crip gang members, including the Marines, were arrested for planning an attack at a high school football event in Columbia, South Carolina.[133]

CONCLUSION

We have examined the emergence of street gangs and OMG and DTE group members in the military from before World War I until the revisiting of the problem not long after 9/11. I paused the summary at the end of 2006, and will continue to identify the chronological events in the next chapter. I wanted this section to catch us up from the historical beginnings to the start of the current period and, in the interest of time and space found an easy-to-identify stopping point. As you can see, at different times, different groups of street gangs, OMGs, and DTEs have been in the spotlight, and you may see some similarities in their behavior and criminal activities. I did my best to point out the turning points and include the context so you could evaluate the importance of each of these events yourself. The listed events do not represent all the street gang, OMG, and DTE activity in the military, only the activity with which I was familiar and felt typified the activity that occurred with some regularity. As with criminal activity in the civilian community, no one can know about crime that is not reported, and gangs and extremists have a lot of motivation to keep things quiet.

While some will choose to dismiss these claims as alarmist in nature, the existence of gang members in the military and MTGMs in the community is very real, and it represents a very dangerous threat to both. Without fail, as I have talked to military members who know gang indicators and have been in the military both in the Continental United States and overseas, I hear stories of wide-open gang representation from all the street gangs, OMGs, and DTEs. This is especially troublesome when I hear it from a police or corrections officer returning from an overseas deployment with the Reserves or National Guard. They often report that no one in the military, not even military law enforcement, acts like they know that these gang members are openly representing their criminal affiliation. As you can see from the breadth of resources cited throughout this book, there is much support for the information presented to you. My hope is that you will see the seriousness of the issue, but even if you don't it is still there. I've been investigating gangs and the military from several perspectives for over a quarter century, and I assure you that this book is no work of fiction. I have heard from many along the years that there is no way that someone could be a member of a group that formed to commit crimes *and* be a member of the military. I have also heard that some folks will deny things even when you show them the video!

Chapter Three

Contemporary Issues with Military Gangs

On May 15, 2009, Michael Apodaca, a soldier stationed at Fort Bliss, Texas, shot Jose Daniel Gonzalez outside of Gonzalez's home in El Paso.[1] Apodaca agreed to kill Gonzalez for the Juárez drug cartel for $5,000. The Mexican drug cartel believed Gonzalez, one of their lieutenants, had become a government informant and he owed the cartel money.[2] Apodaca and an accomplice followed Gonzalez to his neighborhood, where Apodaca shot Gonzalez eight times as he walked toward his home.[3] The murder brought to light the extent to which drug trafficking organizations, which collaborate and do business with gangs on both sides of the border, will seek the expertise of military service members to protect their criminal activities from detection by the authorities.

In the last chapter, we covered gangs and extremists in the military from the World War I era to the military's revisiting of the problem not long after 9/11. I paused at the end of 2006 for a variety of reasons, perhaps mostly because it represented the historical period of analysis that culminated about a decade prior to writing this book. The year 2007 was the year our efforts (identifying gang members in the military) received repeated nationwide attention—first with a follow-up gang threat assessment by the FBI's National Gang Intelligence Center, and threat assessments conducted not only by the Army, but also the Air Force and the Navy. The media learned of the problem, too, with coverage by the *Army*, *Navy*, *Air Force*, and *Military Times* newspaper conglomerate, and then by the History Channel.

In this chapter, we will continue to examine the events which shaped military gang and extremist investigations. As the Army CID has provided some written summaries of their gang and extremist-related investigations, I will include a sampling and summary of those findings among the otherwise compiled news articles and FBI reports. The incident summaries were available as far back as 2004, with data to 2002, but the street gangs, OMGs, and DTE groups involved, the crimes reported, and the general locations of events were very similar and I am trying hard to restrict the focus of the book. If you would like to see additional summaries, check out the website for the book: http://www.gangsandthemilitary.com.

MORE ON MILITARY GANG AND EXTREMIST ACTIVITY

In January 2007, a Staff SGT and a Captain from the Illinois National Guard stole military-grade body armor, night-vision equipment, tasers, and other military gear and sold it for $37,000.[4] They sold the military equipment on the South Side of Chicago, a part of the city well known for the presence of street gangs. During the transaction, one of the soldiers agreed that street gang members would benefit from the use of the equipment.[5] And gangs have been increasingly able to access such military equipment. Government Accountability Office (GAO) investigators later seized body armor plates manufactured in June 2007 that were stolen from the U.S. military or the manufacturer.[6] The GAO investigators also identified storeowners who purchased military Kevlar vests, flak jackets, and gas masks from military service members and sold the equipment through the eBay online auction site to the public.[7] Also in 2007, the American public started learning about the presence of gangs in the military.

The FBI on Gang Activity in the Military

The FBI established the National Gang Intelligence Center (NGIC) in 2005, to integrate gang intelligence across federal, state, and local law enforcement. In January 2007, the NGIC released a report titled *Gang-Related Activity in the US Armed Forces Increasing*. Data for the report was obtained from FBI information, open-source documents, and a variety of (about twenty) law enforcement sources. Many of the findings have been cited elsewhere in the book, and NGIC reports since then have updated or validated the general findings. Among the information in the report, not covered elsewhere, were these tidbits:

- From 2004–2007, the FBI and El Paso Police Department identified over forty military-affiliated Folk Nation gang members stationed at Fort Bliss who were involved in drug distribution, robberies, assaults, weapons offenses, and homicide, both on and off the installation.

- Fort Hood officials identified nearly forty gang members on base from 2003–2007. Military-affiliated Gangster Disciple members at Fort Hood were responsible for robberies, assaults, theft, and burglaries on- and-off-base.
- Nearly 130 gang and extremist group members were identified on the Fort Lewis Army Installation from 2005 to 2007. Those gang members were believed to be responsible for many of the criminal misconduct incidents reported on base.
- Army CID documented many gang-related incidents at Fort Bragg and Fort Campbell during that time.
- The Defense Criminal Investigative Service reported in 2006 that gang members, particularly MS-13 members, were increasing their presence on or near U.S. military installations.
- Criminal courts in the United States have allowed gang members to enter military service as an alternative to incarceration. Several incidences wherein gang members have been recruited while facing criminal charges or on probation or parole have been documented. In many instances, a gang member facing criminal charges was provided the option to join the military or serve a jail sentence. Furthermore, some Army recruiters have been known to conceal recruits' gang affiliation to help boost their enlistment numbers.
- A Latin Kings gang member from Milwaukee, Wisconsin, joined the Marines while under federal indictment for racketeering. The recruiter reported that despite the gang member's indictment, he was still eligible for military service because he had not yet been convicted. He was, however, ultimately denied enlistment before reporting for duty.
- An MS-13 member stationed at Fort Lewis reported that he and several other MS-13 members joined the military after their leader was incarcerated. The soldier claimed he was candid about his gang membership when recruited.
- Black Disciple, Gangster Disciple, Hells Angels, Latin Kings, Mexican Mafia, Norteños, and Sureños graffiti was reported in Iraq.
- Crips graffiti was reported near U.S. military bases in Germany, Italy, and Japan. Gangster Disciple and Latin King graffiti was reported in Germany.
- Many current and former OMG members have military experience. For example, the Hells Angels have recruited soldiers for their explosives and firearms expertise.
- Both U.S. and Canadian law enforcement officials suggested that many Hells Angels and Bandidos OMG members were former members of the military.

- Several Hells Angels members, including an Army lieutenant colonel from Illinois, served in Iraq.
- A Nomad OMG prospect was recruited by Hells Angels members upon returning from Iraq in 2006 due to his military expertise.
- Gang members in the military were commonly assigned to military support units where they had access to weapons and explosives. Military personnel may steal items by improperly documenting supply orders or by falsifying paperwork. Law enforcement officials throughout the U.S. recovered military-issued weapons and explosives—such as machine guns and grenades—from criminals and gang members.
- A 2006 GAO probe revealed that undercover government investigators purchased sensitive surplus military equipment, such as launcher mounts, signal converters, and body armor, from a DoD contractor. A 1993 GAO report similarly concluded there was widespread theft of military small arms due to lax inventory control. Army CID maintained the military implemented stricter inventory controls over weapons.
- In June 2006, an incarcerated soldier and active gang member identified sixty to seventy gang-affiliated military personnel in his unit involved in the theft and sale of military equipment and weapons. The soldier reported many of the military personnel in charge of ammunition and grenade distribution were sergeants and active gang members. The soldier also reported military commanders were aware of the actions of the gang-affiliated personnel.
- A May 2006 interview with a former Marine and Gangster Disciple member incarcerated in Colorado detailed how easily soldiers—many of whom were gang members—stole military weapons and equipment and used them on the streets of U.S. cities or sold them to civilian gang members.
- In December 2005, a National Guard soldier smuggled several machine guns back from Iraq and sold them to a gun dealer in Georgia.
- In 2004, an Army sergeant and suspected National Alliance white supremacist group member from Fort Bragg was caught mailing an AK-47 home to his father in the state of Washington. The soldier had numerous weapons, ammunition, and racist propaganda in his possession. Local police in Washington state later reported several incidents involving the discharged soldier's weapons.
- Military weapons and supplies were stolen by both gang-affiliated and by non-gang-affiliated military personnel who sold the weapons to gang members, or criminals, on city streets in the U.S. Law enforcement officials nationwide encountered active service members selling, or attempting to sell, stolen military weapons, supplies, and drugs to civilian gang members and criminals. Senate testimony dating back to 1993 revealed that military

weaponry has been sold at public gun shows, some in their original government packaging.

- In August 2006, a parolee in San Bernardino, California, was arrested in possession of an armed military shoulder-mounted rocket launcher.
- In January 2006, a Navy veteran in Ingleside, Texas, was arrested for stealing military equipment from the Ingleside Naval Station and selling it on the Internet.
- In November 2005, two senior airmen at an Air Force base in Montana were charged with drug distribution after selling drugs to an undercover police officer. A firearm purchased by one of the airmen had been reported stolen and was subsequently recovered in Calgary, Canada, in the possession of Asian gang members. The airman further admitted to trafficking guns across the U.S.-Canadian border and selling them to a friend in Canada.
- In November 2005, a gang member and active duty Navy service member in California was discovered in the possession of firearms and bullet-proof vests and was suspected of distributing stolen firearms and hand grenades.
- In August 2005, a soldier in San Antonio, Texas, was suspected of supplying hand grenades and bullet-proof vests to the Texas Mexican Mafia (Mexikanemi).
- Gang members in the military have joined forces with rival gang members, even crossing racial and ethnic boundaries to commit crimes and use each other to recruit members. Those unusual alliances made it difficult to prosecute gang-related activity, since judges were often not convinced the defendants were gang members based on their understanding of the stereotype that a member of one gang would not associate with a member of another gang.
- FBI and military authorities report incidents of rival gangs, such as the Bloods, Crips, and Gangster Disciples joining forces while in the service and engaging in gang-related criminal activity. Rival gang members stationed at Fort Bliss, for instance, joined forces to commit assaults on civilian gang members.
- In a May 2006 interview with the Colorado Department of Corrections, an incarcerated Gangster Disciple member and former Marine discussed the advantages of military training and how it assisted gang members in bank robberies, home invasions, and confrontations with police.
- A 2006 news interview revealed that a Marine, who was a King Cobra gang member stationed at Camp Pendleton, taught members of his gang to engage in military-style ambushes and how to position themselves for tactical advantage. He further admitted that he joined the Marines "to learn how to shoot guns."

- In August 2005, a naval chaplain's assistant, and United Blood Nation (UBN) member from Bremerton Naval Station, attempted to kill a state prison corrections officer in a contract killing in Lakewood, Washington.[8]

Army, Navy, Air Force, and *Military Times*

In September 2007, *Army Times* reporter Michelle Tan wrote a long article (covering seven pages, as I recall) on gangs in the military. I won't recite everything she reported, but among the interesting bits were:

- In fiscal 2006, 1,002 of the 8,330 moral waivers granted to incoming soldiers were for a felony on that individual's record.
- In 2003, the total was 459 waivers for felonies out of 4,644 moral waivers. Waivers for felony criminal charges were reviewed by a general officer.
- Waivers were not granted for offenses such as convictions for sexually violent offenses, alcoholism, drug dependency, and the trafficking, sale, or distribution of drugs.

As I told her, I thought offering a waiver to otherwise qualified recruits was the right thing to do for most citizens who wanted to enlist, but there were potential pitfalls. Sure, let former gang members go off and serve their country and fight a war! I'm concerned about when they come home, though. When they return, they would likely be instant gang leader material, because of their exposure to a unique form of violence and inherent leadership skills. Former gang members may deserve a shot at military service, but not if they intend to continue their criminal gang affiliation! If the Army is going to recruit and accept former or current gang members into the service, it should also make sure those people successfully get out and stay out of the gangs.[9]

My friend, Hunter Glass, was also interviewed for that article. He said the gang problem in the military was a growing problem and if left alone could be a true powder keg.[10] "Everybody always assumes the most dangerous things a gangster can learn in the military is moving and shooting," he said. "The most dangerous thing a gangster can learn in the military is leadership." His concern was what soldiers affiliated with gangs took back to the streets when they were released from the service.[11] Lt. Steve Lucero, an intelligence officer who specialized in Security Threat Groups for the Colorado Department of Corrections, was also interviewed. He said that members with military training typically rise to the top of the gang structure. "They learn their military styles and they use them to embellish the gang productivity, their networking, all that stuff," he said.[12] There is more insight on incarcerated MTGMs from Lucero in chapter 6.

Detective Hunter Glass, Fayetteville, North Carolina, Police Department wearing a Military Police Ballistic Vest recovered by the Fayetteville Police Department's Narcotics Unit in a drug raid conducted on a known gang members residence. Source: *Hunter Glass*

I had only met Hunter about a year before those interviews, when a mutual acquaintance told me that our focus on military gang members was very similar although we had never met. Hunter was gracious enough to provide some of his memories and experiences here.

I first became aware of gangs in the military while assigned as a School Resource Officer (SRO) in Fayetteville, North Carolina. Fayetteville is the largest city connected to Ft. Bragg and Pope Field (formerly Air Force Base). Fayetteville has a population of around 204,000 with the majority being current, former, or retired military.

I started as a patrol officer in Fayetteville not long after leaving the Army. When the city was tasked with the schools within the city limits the chief decided he would take the cops that worked the crappiest zones and make them SROs. His belief was that all kids should feel safe at school except the ones who tended to be trouble. When first assigned to the SRO position in 1992, I was assigned to work in a middle school known for problems. I figured as much as I disliked the position I was going to make the most of it. I set about locating as many problem children as I could. After the first day of school, I realized that due to the large number of them, locating them was not going to be a problem. Most of the kids in my school were military dependents or children of veterans.

Because of the nature of Fayetteville these kids do not stand out. To be honest they are the norm. Their lives revolve around the military and world affairs.

One child who caught my attention early on was a tiny female with a huge chip on her shoulder. I nicknamed her Peanut although I would learn later her gangster name was Queenie. Peanut was a firecracker and my interactions with her were frequent. Rather than continually dragging her before some form of disciplinary board, I decided it was much easier for me to just let her sit in my office and discuss her issues. No one is born that angry. Once during the warmer months, I noticed what appeared to be a scar on her upper right arm slightly covered by her shirt sleeve. When I asked her about it she nonchalantly raised her sleeve to expose not a scar but a brand of a six-pointed star. I was immediately taken aback and went into Cop mode. I asked her if she was being abused and she laughed and said no. When I asked her how she got a brand of a six-pointed star on her arm she replied that it was the symbol of her gang the Folk Nation.

Having grown up in New Orleans in the sixties and seventies I was very familiar with mobsters and street level narcotics but I had never heard of such gangs as Folk, Crips, Bloods and Latin Kings. Even the KKK kept a low profile due to the number of Catholics in that part of Louisiana but I was about to have my eyes opened to a point where they never shut.

As time progressed I would learn that this child was no regular kid. Her name Queenie came from her status inside the gang. She had the ability to command even adult members of her set (gang). She demonstrated this to me on several occasions. Queenie became very attached to me over the year and began giving me an insight on gangs and gang life that you just can't find in books or movies. I decided to exploit this avenue into gang life to better understand something that was so much bigger than I could have ever imagined. I asked her when did she become a gang member. She stated when she was a little older than ten she was beat in by other military dependents while her stepfather was stationed in Italy with the US Air Force. This would have been sometime around 1990. Being a Veteran I was fairly surprised. I say fairly because I was aware of Outlaw Motorcycle Gang members, Nazis, Black Panthers, and basic Thugs over the eight years that I had served in the military. I'm sure there were probably more than I knew about but I was busy being a soldier and unless it conflicted with my duties it did not matter. I asked her if there were many gang members in the military and she stated that yes there were plenty and that some were in her set. Queenie, under her given name Christina Walters, became the fifth woman on North Carolina's death row in 2008. A jury sentenced her to death for leading a gang that kidnapped and shot three women in 1998, killing two of them, in a gang-initiation rite. Her sentence was later commuted to life without parole under the provisions of the 2009 Racial Justice Act.

After several years, I was assigned to the Gang Intel Unit in Fayetteville where I would work with numerous Law Enforcement agencies including Federal, State, Local and Military. For many years, I worked closely with Military Police Investigators (MPI), and occasionally with the US Army Criminal Investigation Division (CID) and Air Force Office of Special Information (OSI).

Shortly after being assigned to the Gang Unit I received an Information Exchange report from one of our SWAT team members. It stated that while visiting a local gun shop and range he observed a soldier loading several Kalashnikov (AK-47) rifles into his vehicle along with a large amount of ammunition. Being very familiar with the Russian rifle and knowing it was not commonly found in a military arsenal outside of Special Forces he approached the soldier and inquired as to why he had so many. The officer was in civilian apparel and did state that he was a law enforcement officer. He stated that the soldier was very candid and explained that he was a Gangster Disciple from Chicago and that he was in charge of all the rifles in his set. There was no civilian law being broken so the officer noted the conversation, the vehicle tag number, and a basic description and name. That information was then forwarded first to my office and then to Ft. Bragg.

I found working with the military to be highly influenced by current politics and world affairs. During peacetime, the Army and Navy seemed concerned as to the background and current affiliations of their service men and women whereas during war those concerns were reversed. Many times during the early years of the Iraqi and Afghanistan wars I was told that if those kinds of individuals liked killing then what's wrong with them killing for Uncle Sam to which I always replied I guess they could rape, steal and sell dope for Uncle Sam as well.

As the wars progressed we observed a definite change in the military attitude towards soldiers with ties to known criminal organizations. This created a definite split in the military law enforcement community. Many soldiers would be chastised for continuing to go after gang members in uniform. I was not immune to the harassment either as I was verbally attacked on many occasions by Army CID as everything from hysterical to anti-American. Although I could back all my data with photographs, video and statements they continued their assault which in the end gave them a black eye.

For many years, I became a recognized expert on the phenomenon of gangs in the military and received many requests for information on the topic. The FBI and the High Intensity Drug Trafficking Areas (HIDTA) were very concerned and police in cities such as Los Angeles, California, considered the issue to be of great concern. Understanding that thousands of potential gang members returning home with combat skills and experience was something they needed to prepare for. LA had already dealt with this type of activity after the Vietnam war in which members of The Avenues street gang openly bragged about using the skills obtained during the war to increase their drug territory. From 1998 to 2006 I found myself dealing with gang members associated with the military on a monthly and sometimes weekly basis. Much of the time military gang members were associated with our local gangs except in the case of Gangster Disciples (GD). Usually the GDs we dealt with had come into the military with criminal intentions and in some cases their civilian counterparts had followed them to Fayetteville and surrounding areas. GDs were usually the most organized gang outside of Latin Kings that we dealt with.

The idea of criminal gangs in the military should not be a shock to anyone with a law enforcement or business background. It would only make common sense if you want secure a future for your criminal enterprise that you would have your personnel trained. What better place than the military can you think of where someone can obtain the skills and training without a license or registry. Many people immediately assume that armed tactical training would be the draw for criminal organizations but they would be wrong. The infantry leaves little time to be devoted to the gang and it is a skill that can be taught to others with some success and without much effort. During my time in the Gang Unit I found most of my military gang members to be assigned to support units. Military Occupation Specialties (MOS) such as Finance, Quartermaster (Supply), Transportation, Communication, Riggers and Intelligence were more desirable to a criminal organization than someone who can kill.

I think the saddest thing I found about the upper echelon of the military was their unwillingness and to some degree arrogance to accept that criminal gangs were both smart and organized and that they had little fear of criminal charges placed upon them under the UCMJ.

Hunter Glass
Private Consultant and Investigator
Criminal Entities and Security Threat Groups

FROM GANGS IN THE MILITARY TO MILITARY-TRAINED GANG MEMBERS

Shortly after the *Army Times* article, in October 2007, I was at a conference in Missoula, Montana, with the Northwest Gang Investigators Association. A few of the speakers had gone out to a great dinner with the association board. As we were talking, I told some in the group that it was the last time I was going to be talking about *gangs in the military* and would start talking about *military-trained gang members* in the civilian community. I realized that we had a lot of service members who were trained to go to war and had already left the military, or were soon getting out, and that was the main thing that needed our attention. Coincidentally, it was at that conference that my first appearance on the History Channel's *Gangland* series was filmed, but I'll talk about that later. That conference was also the only time (to date) that I did a joint presentation with my friend Dr. Al Valdez, who wrote the forward for this book. The full video of the Gangs in the Military presentation we did is available on my YouTube Channel at https://youtu.be/_8ZF_MLDPPs. The History Channel folks used it as B-roll, but it's worth checking out because Al and I did a pretty coordinated, albeit unrehearsed, job of handing the mic back and forth during the presentation, if I do say so myself.

I had previously (and have since) traveled around the country talking to hundreds of gang investigators and other police officers, and I found them much more receptive to the idea of military-trained gang members than the average military (including law enforcement) professional. That was true while I was in the Army, and has not changed much, if at all, since I retired. Do you remember the conversation with LTC X? His problem was that I was insinuating he had allowed gang and extremist group members to infiltrate his fighting unit. Imagine if it was LTC Y, the head of all things security (think Public Safety Commissioner), and my call was interpreted as informing him of his responsibility in a security breach of the military installation by dozens of organized criminals. Or, worse yet, imagine if I was calling Colonel Z, who thought I said he was personally responsible for the systemic weakness of the background and security clearance system which had failed to identify hundreds of criminal gang and extremist group members! No, none of those military officers in the latter parts of the alphabet leadership would want to hear anything I had to say about those issues. I know I've tried to talk to each of them several times!

But the civilian investigators? They listen and some even take notes! Sure, there are the nay-sayers, thinking they are being appropriately patriotic by denying any possible existence of gang and extremist group members in the military. I've even had a few of them try to sabotage the validity of the surveys I started handing out (more on those later). They responded to questions asking what percentage of the jurisdiction's gang members had military training with astronomically high (like over 50 percent) numbers for jurisdictions where few of the population have ever been in the military. They weren't hard to cull out, thankfully, as they aimed for overkill on almost all their responses to my questions.

Most of the investigators I have spoken to are engaged and I have received a lot of good feedback wherever I have gone. They realize, as do I, that this is both a strange and very sensitive topic. It's not unpatriotic to point out flaws in one of the systems which is tasked with screening folks to fight in wars and represent the country around the globe.

I have received some instant validation in my travels, too, with folks who served in the military, sharing stories about the gang and extremist group members they had to deal with, and I have received some delayed feedback weeks, and months, after they heard my presentation. The civilian investigators who have served or are serving in the military all verify what I am saying and many share their own anecdotes.

As with my classes at the university, I try to make sure my presentations are interesting, informative, and interactive. I often ask the attendees how many of them had received SWAT tactics training. In other words, how many knew how to enter a building with a rifle pointed at whatever they're looking at, and know how to tell people to get down on the ground and make sure the area's safe and all that? Somewhere between a quarter and a half of the room will typically raise their hands.

And then I ask how many of them were trained to *respond* to attackers that use SWAT-like tactics? In other words, how many were trained to be the recipient of those same commands, given by someone on the opposite end of the gun? My thought is that if you don't know how to be on the receiving end of a handgun, shotgun, or rifle you don't know what it's like to be the victim of a home invasion. That's what it's called when gang members do the activity we train service members to do when they raid a building in Iraq, or Afghanistan, or wherever the war is. We're teaching those combat troops how to do a proper home invasion if they are a gang member and neither our police officers, nor our citizens, are trained to respond to that.

The realization I needed to change my focus for training was a turning point for me because it required not just a paradigm shift, but a change in perspective. Before, I was explaining to fellow gang cops and corrections officers what we had learned about gang members in the military. Now I am explaining to cops and other criminal justice professionals the skill sets those gang members were likely to bring to the streets, jails, and prisons and suggesting they consider some of the options available for dealing with them.

The Air Force Survey

In 2007, agents of the Air Force Office of Special Investigations (AFOSI) prepared an unclassified report to document their efforts at intelligence collection to determine if Air Force personnel or resources were adversely affected by gang activity. The agents reported that gang members joining the military were a problem over the previous decade.[13] Gang members were becoming increasingly more sophisticated in their recruitment of young people, including military dependents, using popular hip hop culture, websites, and chat rooms, the report said. That was problematic because gang members may seek to "join the military for weapons training and use of combat tactics, such as evasive skill and cover and concealment."[14]

Among the gang-related incidents included in that report (not elsewhere in the book) were:

- In August 2005, an airman from the F.E. Warren AFB, Wyoming, was arrested for armed robbery of two local gas stations. The airman purchased two hand guns and gave them to friends who had local Bloods gang connections. He had never been formally jumped in to a gang, but had been around gang members since high school. The airman was also under investigation for selling stolen military body armor to civilians.

- In September 2005, an airman assigned to Davis Monthan AFB, Arizona, was shot near a party with three friends (all civilians). Prior to arriving at the party, one of the individuals accompanying the airman provided him and the others with blue bandanas to wear. The airman declined to wear the bandana but his friends agreed and put them on. Upon arriving at the house, they were informed the party was full. As they were leaving, another group of individuals pulled up next to them and one of the occupants started shooting, killing one of the civilians and badly injuring the airman. All denied being gang members, but admitted to being associates.

- In July 2006, an airman assigned to Misawa AB, Japan, was the victim of a drive-by shooting incident while on leave in Denver, Colorado. The airman was riding in a car with a known gang member who had informed her that he was no longer involved in gang activity. While they were stopped at a traffic light, two unidentified individuals approached their car and fired several rounds into the car, striking the airman twice—in the arm and the ribs.

- In October 2006, an airman was arrested for possessing a concealed weapon and suspicion of committing multiple homicides. The airman was observed parked outside the residence of a person who was in the Pittsburgh Police Department's Witness Protection Program. The airman had a fully loaded 9mm pistol, a balaclava-type face mask, a blue bandana, and leather gloves with him when he was stopped. Several of the 9mm bullets matched casings found in two separate homicides in the local area, and the airman was observed by police surveillance with several gang associates who were under investigation on separate homicide charges.[15]

Gangland: Basic Training

In January 2008, the History Channel's *Gangland* series featured gangs in the military in a documentary, part of a multi-year, multi-episode series. *Gangland: Basic Training* was about the infiltration of gangs, primarily street gangs, into the United States military. The writers noted that gang members in uniform were participating in serious criminal activity on, or near, military installations around the world, and national security was at risk as they stole advanced weaponry, learned military tactics, distributed drugs, and committed murder.[16] If you are interested, the episode is available for purchase in many locations and you can find it online by searching for *Gangland: Basic Training*.

The production of that episode was a turning point for me for a couple of reasons. First, I realized it had been quite a few years since we had started investigating gangs in the military. I realized that's not why the *Gangland* series was made, but it *was* on the History Channel, and wouldn't they be the best ones to decide whether it was a historical activity? Regardless, the episode also served to acknowledge the presence of gangs in the military and military-trained gang members in the community. There had been many other related documentaries and news reports, but that one seemed to be the most well-organized. It brought together (in the episode, if not physically) a variety of investigators and researchers, and laid the foundation for continued communication and collaboration among the folks who had a personal and professional interest in the topic. I don't know if any of the reporting activities by the military were influenced by the *Army Times* article or the *Gangland* series, but I did find the timing remarkable.

STREET GANGS AND THE MILITARY

The FBI has long stated that street gangs have been documented on military installations, although recruiting gang members violates military regulations.[17] Both the CID and FBI have reported a variety of gangs affecting the military, though the Gangster Disciples were considered more sophisticated and widespread. Street gangs have posed a serious domestic threat to many communities, and the Department of Justice has reported they were expected to increase their role in trafficking drugs and increase their relationships with international criminal organizations and drug-trafficking organizations as a means of obtaining access to the global illicit drug market.[18]

The Army CID provided paragraph-length summaries of the gang-related investigations in their annual assessments from FY 2005–2009. The summary of the gang-related investigations from FY 2007 included:

- Fort Bliss, Texas, had an aggravated assault that culminated in a drive-by shooting on-post. One of the individuals involved was a prior member of the street gang known as Hated by Many which supported Crips and Folk nation gangs. One of the soldiers involved had previously admitted gang membership to his commander.
- Fort Campbell, Kentucky, had an investigation into the attempted murder of two civilians, one with ties to the Gangster Disciples, by a soldier affiliated with the Latin Kings. A gang of civilians (some military family members) identifying themselves as the Birchwood Bloods assisted the soldier with evading arrest.

Several members of a local Blood set in front of a Fayetteville, North Carolina, department store. Upon refusing to surrender identification, the tallest subject was later identified as a Staff SGT from Ft. Bragg, North Carolina. The Staff SGT was later discharged from the Army on drug-related charges according to Detective Hunter Glass. Source: *Hunter Glass*

- Fort Campbell had an investigation of assault on a military family member, formerly a Latin Kings gang member, by a soldier, who was a member of the Sureños.
- Fort Stewart, Georgia, CID investigated the robbery of a soldier. The subjects were both soldiers, and robbed the victim of about $4000 in cash and $1400 in jewelry. One of them claimed to be a Crips gang member.
- Fort Stewart was the site of an aggravated assault when a soldier was shot in the arm after leaving an on-post club. The soldier, a former Crips gang member, reported that several patrons were displaying Blood gang hand signs while dancing at the club. The soldier/victim was found to be in possession of a blue bandanna and a loaded, unregistered Springfield .40 caliber pistol.
- Fort Stewart authorities investigated a murder in which a soldier, an affiliate of the Dog Pound Posse gang, drove the civilian murder suspect from the crime scene. The Dog Pound Posse was apparently in an altercation with a rival gang, the Headhunters.

- Fort Wainwright, Alaska, was the site of an accidental shooting and stolen property investigation. A soldier was accidentally shot while mishandling a handgun brought to the home by a relative, a member of the Gangster Disciples. The handgun was stolen.
- Fort Campbell reported the aggravated burglary (home invasion) of the off-post residence of a soldier and his girlfriend by two other soldiers. The subjects were suspected members of the Asian Pride gang.
- Fort Lewis, Washington, investigators documented information from the San Bernardino, California, Police Department regarding the theft and wrongful disposition of military property. A soldier was involved in selling protective military body armor to gangs in San Bernardino while on leave after a tour in Iraq.
- Fort Irwin, California, was involved in the investigation of the murder in Los Angeles of a civilian by four members of a local street gang, the Mental Boyz. One of the subjects was identified as a soldier, although the incident apparently occurred before he enlisted.

The summary of the gang-related investigations from FY 2008 included:

- Fort Belvoir, Virginia, had an investigation of arson and burglary of a soldier's residence by suspected Bloods gang members.
- Fort Bliss had a drug trafficking investigation by gang members from the Georgia Bois and Kommishun gangs.
- Fort Bliss had an investigation of armed robbery, on-post. Two armed, civilian Georgia Bois gang members robbed two out-of-state civilians of $23,000 after arranging a drug deal in an unoccupied on-post home with them.
- Fort Bragg was the site of an attempted murder when a soldier, a member of the Black P-Stone Nation, shot at two civilians outside a local store after an argument. One of the two civilians was killed.
- Fort Bragg was where two soldiers created fraudulent accounts at a local bank to steal over $5,000. The purpose of the crime was to start the non-traditional local gang "Young Stunnas Car Club," they said.
- Fort Hood CID investigated an off-post murder with the Killeen Police Department. Two active-duty soldiers were in an argument with the son of a former soldier and one of the soldiers, a Norteño gang member, fired several gunshots into the victim's vehicle and hit the victim, who died shortly thereafter.
- Fort Irwin was the site of an attempted kidnapping, rape, and aggravated assault, when a civilian woman was attacked by two soldiers. The soldiers

were members of the Florencia 13 and Latin Kings street gangs. The attack occurred on the installation.

- Fort Myer, Virginia, had an aggravated assault and illegal firearms possession when a soldier struck his civilian girlfriend with a pistol. The incident happened at his off-post residence. He and his roommate, another soldier, admitted to having past affiliation with the Vice Lords street gang, and there were various articles of gang paraphernalia in the house.
- Schofield Barracks, Hawaii, CID investigated a series of break-ins and larceny while soldiers were training at Fort Irwin, California. The subjects were soldiers affiliated with the Bloods and the Crips, as well as a former soldier affiliated with the Gangster Disciples. The proceeds, from the sale of a total of $85,000 in stolen personal property from 30 victims, were used by the Gangster Disciples.

In December 2008, a former soldier in Oklahoma City, Oklahoma, admitted to making multiple improvised explosive devices (IEDs) that he had tried to sell to gang members.[19] The former soldier made weapons like those used against soldiers in Iraq and offered them for sale to gang members and other criminals in Oklahoma City for as little as $100.

As mentioned previously, on May 15, 2009, Jose Daniel Gonzalez was shot outside of his home in El Paso, Texas. His death was the first documented cartel-related slaying in El Paso since the drug wars erupted in Juárez in 2008. Michael Jackson Apodaca, a soldier stationed at Fort Bliss had served in Afghanistan and admitted shooting Gonzalez.[20] He said he was told that a member of the Juárez drug cartel was looking to hire someone to kill Gonzalez and that he would pay $5,000. The cartel believed Gonzalez had become a government informant and he owed the cartel money.[21] Apodaca agreed to kill Gonzalez. Ironically, Gonzalez was a government informant who lived on the same street as the El Paso police chief, who told local reporters he heard shots being fired that day while standing in his backyard.[22]

After locating Gonzalez on the night of the murder, Apodaca and an accomplice followed him to his neighborhood. Apodaca got out of the vehicle, ran up to Gonzalez and shot him eight times as he walked toward his home.[23] Apodaca then met with another accomplice, who took the murder weapon apart, sprayed the weapons parts with WD-40, and burned Apodaca's shirt in a barbecue grill.[24] Apodaca was paid $7,500 for the murder.

Street Gangs in the Sandbox

In Taji, Iraq, in 2009, dozens of tanks were spray painted with gang symbols.[25] The graffiti was suspected to be from a Los Angeles gang since the number 323 was painted on the vehicle. 323 was an area code in Los Angeles. Inside a guard shack at a base near Nasiriyah, a star and "GDN" represented the Gangster Disciple Nation in Chicago.[26] On a concrete barrier, EL MOCO and LA EME (representing allegiance with the Mexican Mafia) was painted. On a wall, in Camp Scania, was written "Amor de Rey" ("King Love" in Spanish), the motto of the Chicago-based Latin Kings. Jeff Stoleson, an Army Reserve sergeant, said there were soldiers in Iraq with tattoos signifying their allegiance to the Vice Lords and the Simon City Royals, a street gang spawned in Chicago. "They don't try to hide it," Stoleson said.[27] He knew what the gang symbols were from his civilian career as a corrections officer with the Wisconsin Department of Corrections and his membership in the International Latino Gang Investigators Association. Elsewhere in the war zone, the word 1Norte4 (showing allegiance with the Norteños) spray-painted on a concrete barrier was lined out and "SUR 13" (depicting allegiance with the Sureños) was painted directly below it.

The summary of the gang-related investigations by the CID from FY 2009 included:

- Fort Bliss CID investigated a soldier and three civilians for the murder of a known drug cartel member in El Paso. The subjects were all members of the Crazy Mexican Killers gang, a recruiting source for the Barrio Azteca transnational criminal organization, allied with the Juárez Drug Cartel from Mexico.
- Fort Bliss CID along with the El Paso Police Department investigated an altercation at a club between a soldier and three associates and several other individuals, which escalated when individuals began throwing rocks at the soldier and his associates. After leaving the club, the soldier reinitiated the altercation when he began hitting one of the assailants, the driver, in another car at a stop light, through an open car window. The driver responded by exiting the vehicle and shooting the soldier multiple times in the chest. It was suspected that some of the individuals involved in the altercation were members of a group identified as "Militia."
- The Fort Hood CID investigated a murder for hire involving an active duty soldier and his mother. The soldier's mother was apparently in a dispute of some kind with her father over the soldier's younger siblings. As a former member of the Sureños, the soldier was authorized by the gang to conduct a drive-by killing of his step-grandfather.
- The Fort Lewis CID investigated several minor felonies, in which the subject was determined to have "various gang-related tattoos" which were not specifically identified. Those investigations included drug

possession and distribution, altering of military identification cards, and conspiracy.

- The Fort Meade, Maryland, CID investigated an armed robbery at the Burger King restaurant on the installation. The subjects were all family member dependents connected to a Bloods-affiliated gang, which was identified as All Bout Money.
- Fort Stewart CID investigated the shooting of a civilian Crips gang member by a military family member who was a member of the Bloods gang. The shooting happened on-post, in the housing area.
- Fort Wainwright, Alaska, CID investigated the stabbing of a soldier by another soldier who was affiliated with the Bloods gang. The victim apparently made the claim that there were no real gangs in Fairbanks, the city adjacent to Fort Wainwright.

A partial list in the FY 2010 Army CID assessment (transitioning from the narratives to a simple listing format of the reports) identified these street gangs:

- Barrio Azteca
- Bloods
- Cowboys from Hell
- Maras
- Norteños
- G Enterprise

THE NAVY SURVEY

In 2011, the U.S. Navy (USN) published their only gang threat assessment to date (so far as I know), in a review of NCIS criminal investigations and criminal intelligence reports produced during calendar year 2011. The review found that the number of reports identifying gang activity largely stayed the same from 2010 to 2011 and gang activity did not appear to pose a significant threat to the operational readiness of the Navy or U.S. Marine Corps (USMC).[28] The review addressed the threat to the civilian community post-service only by referencing media reports suggesting gang members purposely entered the military to gain skills they could teach fellow gang members.[29] In contrast to the U.S. Army, the Navy survey experienced a slight drop in all gang-related investigations but a slight increase in those, presumably felonies, with a Navy connection.

For 2011, there were twenty-one gang-related investigations and fifty-eight gang-related intelligence reports with a Navy connection, or nexus, resulting in seventy-nine total.[30] That represented barely over 1 percent of the total NCIS investigations and intelligence reports opened and written in 2011. As the authors of the report noted, of the 322,629 active duty U.S. Navy sailors and 200,255 active duty Marines in 2011, a statistically negligible percentage, 0.0086 percent and 0.0164 percent for the USN and USMC, respectively, were linked to gang activity with a Navy nexus.[31]

Between November 2009 and November 2010, Stanislav Sazonov, a graduate student at John Jay College of Criminal Justice, conducted interviews of self-identified military-trained gang members and other service members in New York City, Chicago, and San Diego to explore threats posed by active gang members on national security, and the safety of military personnel and law enforcement in the military. Respondents included current or former soldiers who served in those branches for at least one tour of duty within the previous eight years; were at least eighteen years of age or older and had been exposed to gang activities or were affiliated with a gang while serving in the military. African-Americans made up 50 percent of the participants, followed by whites at 39 percent, with Asians and Hispanic at 5.5 percent each. Most of the participants (67 percent), were not affiliated with any gang, while 33 percent claimed gang affiliation.[32]

The number of gang members Sazonov estimated to be serving on a military base varied significantly from one or two to hundreds, based on the size of the base. Large military installations, such as Fort Hood and Fort Bragg had the highest reported number of active gang members.[33] An Army corporal stationed at Fort Stewart who was also a Crips member, estimated the total number of gang-affiliated soldiers in the area was twelve. A Staff SGT from Fort Hood, who was a Gangster Disciple, estimated the total number of gang affiliated personnel there between 100 and 150. However, a non-gang affiliated Army SGT, also stationed at Fort Hood stated that he encountered between fifteen to twenty gang members on the base.[34]

A respondent from the Army installation at Fort Benning, Georgia, reported observing the presence of at least five gang members. A participant stationed at Lackland Air Force Base, Texas, stated that he encountered six gang members. Another respondent reported observing about thirty-five members of various gangs at the base in Iraq where she served.[35] A respondent stationed at Fort Bragg estimated the number of gang-affiliated personnel there to be about 170 to 200. A respondent stationed at Naval Station Great Lakes, Illinois, estimated there were forty-five gang affiliated service members at the base. Another Navy respondent said when deployed on a ship with about 5,000 on board, there were approximately 260 active gang members.[36]

An Army SGT from Fort Hood stated that he heard gang members talk about how they would train other gang members to use military tactics in civilian life.[37] A Crips affiliated Army private from Fort Lewis stated that he would teach his gang associates skills he learned at boot camp, including how to shoot and how to fight. Another respondent said he would be willing to teach a gang associate how to shoot, but he wasn't "gonna teach him to be no killer."[38] Sazonov didn't identify the population of the military installations represented in his research, but they were all large installations, with more than 10,000 troops.

As I noted earlier, after 2010, the Army threat assessment summaries were replaced by a simple listing of street gangs, OMGs, and DTE groups identified as having a military nexus. No listing of either type was found in the 2011 assessment I received. The simple listing of groups encountered occurred from FY 2012–2015 and are listed below. The street gangs investigated by Army CID from FY 2012 included:

- A Town
- Barrio Pobre
- Bloods
- C Boys
- Crips
- Dead Man Inc.
- East Terrace Crips
- El Hoyo
- Fresno Bulldogs
- Gangster Disciples
- Gulf Cartel
- Juggalos
- Kommishun
- Latin Kings
- Los Zetas
- Money over Bitches (MoB)
- MS-13
- Norteños
- One
- Skyview
- Sureños
- Tango Blast
- Tiny Rascals
- United Blood Nation
- 40 Boyz
- 107 Hoover Crips
- 410

The documented CID gang investigations and intelligence reports from FY 2013 included:

- Barrio Azteca
- Bloods
- Crips
- Disciple Lords
- El Hoyo Maravilla
- Gangster Disciples
- Get Back Squad
- Goons
- Los Carnales
- MS-13

- Norteños
- South Side Locos
- Sureños

- Vice Lords
- West Texas Syndicate
- Young Bosses and Gentlemen

On March 1, 2014, a video-clip was posted on the Internet by the Middle East Media Research Institute (MEMRI) showing two men representing themselves as members of the Westside Armenian Power gang and the Sureños gang from Los Angeles fighting in Syria.[39] One of them, Wino Ayee Peeyakan, posted a picture of himself on Facebook in Hezbollah garb. Neither appeared to be of Hispanic descent.[40] According to an unnamed source, the two gang members had been deported from the United States for criminal activity. The video and a transcript can be found on the MEMRI website, at http://www.memritv.org/clip/en/4170.htm.

From August 2014 to March 2015, Jaime Casillas and Andrew Reyes, worked at the National Guard Armory in El Cajon, California. While stationed there, Reyes travelled several times to Texas to obtain numerous weapons, which he then sold in San Diego.[41] Casillas also agreed to sell military property including firearms, body armor plates, and ammunition to an undercover agent, who told Casillas he was working to procure weaponry for drug traffickers in Mexico. Casillas sold the undercover agent 1,600 rounds of .223-caliber ammunition, identified as military inventory, for $700. Casillas later sold the agent a .40-caliber pistol for $800, and an AK-47 for $1,700. In all, Casillas and Reyes sold six rifles, one pistol, the body armor plates, ammunition, and magazines, for a total of $15,450. The last deal was for a $15,000 .50-caliber rifle, but that sale was never completed.[42]

The gangs investigated by CID in FY 2014 included:

- Armenian Power Gang
- Barrio Azteca
- Black Gangster Disciples
- Bloods
- Crips
- Juggalo/Insane Clown Posse
- Las Palomas Krew

- Latin Kings
- MS-13
- Straight Edge Crew
- Sureños
- West Side Longos
- Zae Street Gang

In 2015, Captain Leon Brown was convicted of sexual assault of a child younger than 16; use of psilocybin; willful dereliction of duty; conduct unbecoming an officer and a gentleman; pandering; unlawful entry; and communicating threats. He reportedly led a violent street gang that ran an underage prostitution ring, distributed drugs, and gave alcohol to teenagers, per the *Air Force Times*.[43]

The street gang investigations by CID from FY 2015 included:

- Bloods
- Crips
- Desert Blazers
- Folk Nation
- Gangster Disciples
- Get Money Clique
- Gorilla Stone
- Harlem Crips
- Hoover Crips
- Las Palomas Kings
- Latin Kings
- Money Mafia
- Money Over Bitches
- Organized Chaos
- Savage
- So Icey
- South West Cholos
- Squadd
- Stay Fly Get Hoes Crew
- Sureños
- United Blood Nation
- Young Mob
- Youth Gang

OUTLAW MOTORCYCLE GANGS (OMGs) AND THE MILITARY

The U.S. Department of Justice has defined Outlaw Motorcycle Gangs (OMGs) as organizations whose members use their motorcycle clubs as conduits for criminal enterprises.[44] There are more than 300 active OMGs within the United States, ranging in size from single chapters with five or six members to hundreds of chapters with thousands of members worldwide. OMG members engage in criminal activities such as violent crime, weapons trafficking, and drug trafficking.[45] Some OMGs have posed a serious national domestic threat, especially with their cross-border drug smuggling. In 2015, the NGIC reported OMG members or associates who had been employed or applied for employment with the military included: Bandidos, Devils Disciples, Hells Angels, Iron Horsemen, Mongols, Outlaws, Pagans, Sin City Deciples, Vagos, and Warlocks.[46] The crimes that OMG members committed were often economically motivated. Crimes such as drug trafficking, motorcycle theft, and prostitution funded the club and needs of the individual members. Unlike members of many street gangs, OMG members typically had legitimate employment.

The summary of the OMG-related investigations from FY 2007, as reported by Army CID, included:

- Fort Bragg CID investigated a drug trafficking incident in which the second subject was the sergeant-at-arms of the Rough Riders motorcycle club, a validated OMG.

ST. JOHN THE BAPTIST PARISH LIBRARY
2920 NEW HIGHWAY 51
LAPLACE, LOUISIANA 70068

Hells Angels. Members or associates of Outlaw Motorcycle Gangs like the Hells Angels have served in many branches of the military. The ATF has designated many of those gangs as "Highly Prioritized Organized Crime Groups." Source: *iStockPhoto*

- Fort Bragg, in conjunction with the Fayetteville Police Department, investigated a drive-by shooting in which a soldier was hit in the head with a bullet, resulting in non-life-threatening injuries. One of the subjects, a civilian, was a member of the Rough Riders motorcycle club.

There were no noteworthy OMG-related investigations from FY 2008 or FY 2009. As noted previously, the Army CID provided paragraph summaries of the OMG-related investigations from FY 2005–2009. After that, the summaries were replaced by a simple listing of gangs and extremist groups identified as having a military nexus. That occurred from FY 2012–2015, as represented below.

The OMG investigations from FY 2012 included:

- Bandidos
- Chosen Riders
- Cremators
- Cochise Riders
- Death Dealers
- Dem Boyz
- Dog Pound Crew (Bandidos)
- Grim Reapers
- Grings
- Hells Angels
- Imperial
- Infidels
- Kingsmen
- Legacy Vets

- Malvados
- Nomads (Hells Angels)
- Outlaws
- Renegades
- Ruff Riders
- Sin City Deciples (*sic*)
- Sons of Silence
- Strays
- Street Soldiers
- Unforgiven
- Vagos
- Veterans MC
- Wingmen
- 69ers OMG

The OMG investigations reported by Army CID from FY 2013 included:

- Assassin Street Rydaz
- Bandidos
- Battalion of Death Ryders
- Brother Speed
- Brothers in Chains
- Chaos Ridaz
- Cochise Riders
- Cremators
- Divine Jewells
- Dysfunctional Few
- Grand Assassins
- Hells Angels
- Illusions
- Infidels
- Iron Order
- Kingsmen
- Los Soldados
- Masonic Riders
- Mongols
- Organized Chaos
- Outcasts
- Regulators
- Ruff Riders
- Silent Warriors
- Slack Jaw
- Sons of Hell
- Sons of Silence
- Special Forces Brotherhood
- The Revolution
- Vagos
- Veterans
- Wheels of Soul
- Wingmen

The OMG investigations from FY 2014 reported by CID included:

- Black Hawk
- Black Devils
- Dysfunctional Few
- Dysfunctional Veterans
- Hells Angels
- Infidels
- Legacy Vet
- Los Soldados
- Outcast
- Outlaws
- Road Brothers
- Silent Brotherhood
- Sin City Deciples

In 2014, members of a Dutch motorcycle gang, armed with Kalashnikov rifles, reportedly fought alongside Kurdish forces battling the Islamic State in Iraq (ISIS). Three members of the OMG No Surrender traveled to Mosul in northern Iraq to take up the fight against ISIS, according to a group leader of the gang, which had dozens of chapters in the Netherlands and across Europe.[47] A Dutch public prosecutor said it was lawful for Dutch citizens to engage in combat in service to other entities, as long as they did not fight against The Netherlands.[48]

The ATF Reports on OMGs and the Military

The Department of Justice, represented by the Bureau of Alcohol, Tobacco, Firearms and Explosives (ATF), has generated annual reports titled "OMGs and the Military" since 2009. In September 2010, the Department of Justice Organized Crime Program designated the Hells Angels as a "Highly Prioritized Organized Crime Group." In March 2013, the Vagos, Bandidos, Mongols, and Pagans were added to the list. ATF reports from 2014 included the following information, which was not documented from other sources:

- OMGs in the northeast, south, and western portions of the United States recruited military personnel to further their expansion. OMGs and their support clubs have courted active-duty military personnel for their knowledge, reliable income, tactical skills, and dedication. Many support clubs have utilized active-duty military personnel and U.S. Department of Defense (DOD) contractors and employees to spread across the United States.
- OMG and/or support club members who were in the military or serving as government employees or contractors participated at numerous OMG events, including the Hells Angels U.S.A. Run, Rockford, Illinois; Sturgis Bike Rally; Swap Meets in Colorado and Maryland; Myrtle Beach, South Carolina, and Ocean City, Maryland, Bike Weeks; Yuma, Arizona, Prison Run.
- As traditional white OMGs have moved to the suburbs, African American OMGs such as the Outcasts, Wheels of Souls, Sin City Deciples, and Thunderguards have increased their presence in the inner cities. Many of the members were former military or street gang members.
- The Infidels MC was comprised of active-duty military, government contractors and employees. Many of its members were also in the Special Forces community, either as operators or in support roles. The Infidels MC has tended to side with the dominant OMG in their area.
- OMG members have displayed their gang colors while serving in Iraq, Afghanistan, and other destinations across the globe since at least 2010. The Hells Angels, Bandidos, Mongols, and Warlocks have created soft colors and t-shirts to support their members serving in theater.

- On March 3, 2012, gunfire erupted outside the Sin City Deciples clubhouse in Colorado Springs, Colorado. Virgil "Jason" Means was tossed out of the clubhouse after getting into a fight with a member. Means returned about an hour later to retrieve his wallet. Means was shot and killed. A U.S. Army soldier and Sin City Deciples sergeant-at-arms was convicted of manslaughter and sentenced to twenty-one years imprisonment.
- On October 20, 2013, an officer with the Richmond, Virginia, Police Department conducted a traffic stop on Eric Roman for speeding. Roman was a member of the Down and Dirty MC, a support club for the Wheels of Soul OMG. Roman was wearing his colors and carrying an 8-inch knife and a handgun, both concealed under his colors. He explained to the police officer that he was employed as a Federal police officer at Quantico Marine Corps Base. The officer determined that Roman was not authorized to possess a concealed firearm off-base, and arrested him.[49]

The OMG investigations by CID from FY 2015 included:

- Aka Manah Motorcycle Club (MC)
- Arbiters
- Bandidos
- Blackhawks
- Black Lyfe
- Cossacks
- Dirty Dawgs
- Dirty South Stunners
- Dominant Breed
- Dysfunctional Veterans
- East Coast Soldier
- Eastside
- Hells Angels
- Infidels
- Iron Order MC
- Kandid Clutch
- Kings
- K-9
- Liberty Ryders
- Los Cabelleros
- Los Solitarious
- Malvados
- Mongols
- Nam Knight
- Nasty Dogs
- No Surrender
- Nu Boyz Wit Attitude
- One Fist Ryders
- Outcast MC
- Outsiders
- Pistoleros
- Rebels OMG
- Red Devils MC
- Regulators
- Renegades
- Research
- Rezurrected Riderz
- Ruff Riders
- Scimitars MC
- Silent Brotherhood
- Silent Heroes
- Sin City Angels
- Sin City Deciples MC
- Sons of Hell
- Sons of Sinners
- Southern Riders
- Steel Horsemen
- Street Soldiers MC

- Swagg City
- War Mongers MC
- Thunderguards

- Twisters
- Wheels of Soul
- Wingmen

DOMESTIC TERRORIST EXTREMISTS (DTEs) AND THE MILITARY

The FBI has long stated that various DTE groups have been documented on military installations although recruiting gang members violated military regulations.[50] The CID summary of DTE-related investigations from FY 2007 included:

- Fort Bragg was the location of an undercover FBI investigation into white supremacist soldiers selling narcotics and military body armor. The soldiers stole body armor, medical supplies, and a military vehicle, all of which were recovered.

There were no noteworthy DTE-related CID investigations in FY 2008.

In 2008, the Southern Poverty Law Center (SPLC) reported that forty-six members of the white supremacist web forum New Saxon identified

Ku Klux Klan members. Domestic Terrorists and Extremists like the KKK have been found in every branch of the military. Source: iStockPhoto

themselves as active-duty military personnel.[51] It quoted a racist skinhead, who wrote on a neo-Nazi online forum, that he had joined the Army and specifically requested an assignment where he would learn how to make an explosive device.

In February 2009, Marine Lance Cpl. Kody Brittingham was arrested at Camp Lejeune and charged with threatening President Barack Obama. Investigators found white supremacist materials and a journal containing a plot to assassinate President Obama among his belongings.[52]

The summary of the investigations from FY 2009 which were DTE-related included:

- Fort Hood CID investigated the kidnapping and assault of a female by a soldier, his spouse, and others. The soldier was found to have neo-Nazi and lightning bolt tattoos indicative of white supremacist affiliations.
- Fort Carson, Colorado, CID documented the existence of a soldier on the FBI terrorist watchlist. The soldier was associated with the skinheads or another white extremist group. He was identified as a "Ghost Skin," a skinhead who has neither tattoos, nor a documented criminal history of participating in extremist activities.

In July 2011, members of the DTE group Forever Enduring Always Ready (FEAR) planned to destroy a dam and poison several apple orchards in Washington State, set off explosives in a park in Georgia, and assassinate President Obama.[53] The group leader, Isaac Aguigui, had purchased ninety acres of property in Washington State and had stockpiled nearly $90,000 worth of military-grade weapons. Members of the group, although in the military at the time, used cocaine, marijuana, and Ecstasy.[54] Aguigui killed his wife and purchased property and weapons with the insurance money he received after her death. He and members of the group also killed a member of his unit, Michael Roark, and Roark's girlfriend, Tiffany York, because they thought Roark knew about the organization and was going to tell the CID about their activities. The families of Roark and York sued the Army for wrongful death and negligence, claiming the investigation was flawed and many unit members knew of FEAR's existence and did nothing.

As with the street gangs and OMGs, the Army CID provided paragraph-length summaries of the DTE-related investigations from FY 2005–2009. After that, the summaries were replaced by a simple listing of DTE groups they identified as having a military nexus. That occurred from FY 2012–2015, as represented below.

The DTE group investigations reported by Army CID from FY 2012 included:

- Anonymous
- Aryan Brotherhood
- Black Hebrew Israelites
- Chatsworth Skinheads
- FEAR
- Hammerskins
- Ku Klux Klan

- Lone Wolf Militia
- Moorish Nation
- New Saxons
- Orange County Peckerwoods
- Texas Militia
- Volksfront
- Westboro Baptist Church

On August 5, 2012, Wade Michael Page shot six people and wounded four others at the Sikh temple in Oak Creek, Wisconsin. Page was shot in the stomach by a police officer who was trying to arrest him, and ultimately committed suicide by shooting himself in the head. Page was an Army veteran and leader of a white-power band called End Apathy, a white supremacist rock group.[55]

The DTE group investigations by CID from FY 2013 included:

- Aryan Brotherhood
- Church of Kaweah
- Hammerskins
- Heidnischer Sturm Pforzheim
- Kentucky Mountain Rangers

- NC Citizen Militia
- Oathkeepers
- Pan African Freedom
- Peckerwoods
- Texas Militia

In December 2013, Keith Michael Novak, the "commander" of an anti-government Minnesota militia was arrested for selling undercover FBI agents the roster of 400 members of his former military unit in the Army's 82nd Airborne Division for $2,000.[56] Novak was trained as an intelligence analyst, and was a member of the Minnesota Army National Guard at the time. He promised to provide the undercover agents with training on various military intelligence-related tasks, including the creation of "target packages" and the effective conduct of interrogations.[57]

The DTE group investigations from FY 2014 included:

- 44th Spatha Libertas
- Arizona State Militia
- Ku Klux Klan
- Moorish National Republic

- Northwest Front
- Skinheads
- XXX Minutemen

The DTE group investigations from the FY 2015 Army CID assessment included:

- Hammerskins
- Klu Klux Klan (*sic*)
- Moorish National Republic

- New Black Panthers
- Skinheads
- Sovereign Citizens

On July 7, 2016, Micah Johnson shot fourteen police officers in Dallas, Texas, killing five. The incident occurred at a Black Lives Matter protest against the police killings of Alton Sterling in Baton Rouge, Louisiana, and Philando Castile in Falcon Heights, Minnesota, which had recently occurred.[58] It was the deadliest day for U.S. law enforcement since the September 11, 2001, terrorist attacks. Johnson had been a member of the Houston chapter of the New Black Panther Party (NBPP), a group that advocated violence against whites a few years prior. A leader of the organization, Quanell X, reported that Johnson was only a member for about six months and had worked some security details.[59] Johnson didn't want to follow the chain of command and questioned why the group was not buying guns and ammunition to fight the government.

Detectives found bomb-making materials, ballistic vests, rifles, ammunition, and a personal journal of combat tactics. Johnson had stated he wanted to kill white people, especially white police officers. Johnson was in the Army Reserve from March 2009 to April 2015, and served in Afghanistan from November 2013 to July 2014. After the attack, Johnson tried to take refuge in a parking garage and exchanged gunfire with police. Police killed Johnson using a bomb disposal remote control robot armed with about 1 pound of C-4 explosive after negotiations for his surrender failed.[60]

The NBPP was a Black separatist group. They believed African Americans should have their own nation.[61] They claimed to be entitled to reparations for slavery from the United States. Its leaders have blamed Jews for the 9/11 terrorist attacks and for the slave trade. The original Black Panther Party (BPP) was founded in 1966 as a response to police brutality. Members of the original BPP, which had no connection to the NBPP, have heavily criticized the NBPP.[62] Bobby Seale, a famous founding member of the original Panthers, called the organization "a black racist hate group." Ironically, the BPP had been identified by many sources as a contributing force or influence to the foundation of both the Bloods and the Crips street gangs. Both gangs initially formed based on ideas of community power similar to those the Black Panthers had, but neither had the necessary leadership to replicate the success of the BPP with motivating members of the community.[63]

THE 2015 NATIONAL GANG INTELLIGENCE CENTER REPORT

While the National Gang Intelligence Center (NGIC) 2007 report was one of the first seen outside of government law enforcement channels, subsequent government reports have tended to contain less and less specific information and more and more generalities. Both with the CID and the FBI, the earlier reports highlighted specific incidents and activities. As the reports recurred, there was more of a general coverage, and the details found in the summaries of the initial reports occurred less and less. The most current assessment by the FBI's NGIC included the following anecdotes that aren't found elsewhere in the book:

- Approximately 26 percent of jurisdictions and 44 percent of prison facilities reported that gang members had joined DTE groups. A mutually beneficial arrangement, DTEs used gangs to spread their doctrine, while gangs turned to DTEs to increase membership and facilitated collaboration with other criminal organizations. Gangs also referred to DTE ideology to respond to perceived injustices and to enact social change.
- Over the past two years known or suspected gang members from over 100 jurisdictions had applied for positions or gained employment with the military, law enforcement agencies, corrections facilities, and the judiciary. Employment with the military ranked as the most common.
- Street gangs continued to engage in financial crimes, such as identity theft, credit card fraud, prescription drug fraud, counterfeiting, check fraud, fencing stolen goods, money laundering, mortgage fraud, social security fraud, and tax fraud. Over the last few years, street gangs became more involved in white-collar crimes due to weaker sentencing guidelines and the ease of making money in those endeavors.
- Approximately one-third of jurisdictions reported an increase in threats to law enforcement. The attacks carried out against law enforcement and judicial officials were violent and brazen. However, the actual number of attacks against law enforcement had remained relatively stable.
- OMGs recruited mainly from fellow motorcycle enthusiasts and from the U.S. biker community at large. Larger OMGs often had proxy gangs or support clubs, which accounted for the clear majority of OMG recruits. Some larger OMGs required smaller motorcycle gangs or sport bike clubs to wear support patches. Those OMGs demanded monthly payments from each motorcycle club or sport bike club member in exchange for their use of support patches. Refusal to wear a support patch has resulted in violence. Accordingly, membership in an OMG was an extremely violent existence marked by frequent assaults by rival gangs and intra-gang aggression.
- Street gangs, prison gangs, and DTE groups have served as significant recruiting pools for OMGs, with approximately equal recruitment from each category. African American OMGs were known to recruit members from street gangs.
- Gangs provided fertile grounds for recruitment by DTE groups, including Black separatist extremists, white supremacist extremists, and sovereign citizen extremists. Recruiting gang members enabled these groups to

expand and spread their doctrine. Gangs then used these groups and their teachings for several reasons, including the ability to exploit freedom of religion rights; to increase membership and collaboration with other criminal organizations; and to respond to perceived injustices by attempting to enact social change, often by engaging in criminal activity.

- Traditionally all-white OMGs and predominantly African American OMGs were both identified as associating with white supremacist groups and Black separatist groups, respectively. Some gang members may also adhere to anti-government ideologies, for example claiming sovereign citizen (DTE) status to escape criminal charges or indictment.
- Military members' access to weapons and their perceived ability to move easily across the border may render them ideal targets for recruitment. Members of all gang types have been reported to have military connections or training.
- According to a report by the Virginia Department of Corrections, in March 2015, an inmate with gang membership had been corresponding with other members of his gang to recruit an Army soldier. The active duty soldier knew the inmate through hometown contacts.
- OMGs such as the Hells Angels, Vagos, and Mongols, have successfully gained access to military installations; recruited and associated regularly with several active duty military personnel. OMG members have been employed as federal employees and contractors, active duty military, reservists, and National Guardsmen, which enabled expansion of the organization.
- A senior airman from Robins Air Force Base, Warner Robins, Georgia, was arrested for the 2013 death of his fiancée and their unborn child. The airman, who was linked to another death in 2011, was allegedly the national secretary for the Outcast Motorcycle Club.
- In January 2014, an Army CID investigation revealed a soldier was the vice president of the local chapter of the Silent Brotherhood Motorcycle Club, a support club of the Outcast Motorcycle Club. Law enforcement executed a search warrant of the soldier's vehicle and discovered his personal vest bore an Outcast support patch.
- Members of the Pagans assaulted several members of the Mongols in a Pennsylvania bar. In retaliation for this assault, members of a San Diego Mongols chapter traveled to Pennsylvania and actively "hunted" for Pagan members. One of the Mongols from San Diego was allegedly an active duty U.S. Marine Corps helicopter crew member, and two Pennsylvania Mongols also had military affiliation—one was an Army National Guard member and the other was a civilian employee at a Department of Defense facility.

• In 2014, an active duty member of the U.S. Army was found to be the president of the Colorado Springs Chapter of the Colorado Sin City Deciples Motorcycle Club. He shot a member of Hell's Lovers Motorcycle Club during an argument.

THE WORD FROM THE STREET

I have conducted over a dozen surveys of hundreds of gang cops since 2009. I'll share the results of many of the surveys in the following chapters, but I think some of the comments I have gathered are important to examine here. The survey questions have been modified and expanded over the years, but what has remained consistent is the LAST question, which asked the respondent to:

> "Please provide any feedback or comments that you feel are important regarding the presence of gang members in the military or gang members that were formerly in the military."

As you may imagine, most respondents either completely ignore the question or put something that every member of law enforcement or corrections can observe, like "I think that any person wanting to join any branch of the military should be screened and inspected for any signs of gang related tattoos" or "gangs have no place in the military." It's probably a good thing for the folks I draft into transcribing the survey responses that more people don't get too in-depth with their responses, but I put the question there for a reason. I may know a bit about this problem, but I don't know everything, for sure, and I don't know "your" perspective at all. The question was designed as a "what did I forget to ask that you cannot wait to share" question. Here are some of the more thought-provoking responses (edited slightly for brevity or readability). Remember that the survey is handed out and collected *before* I say anything from the podium. Do with them what you will:

• Recruiters need to work hand in hand with civilian gang detectives to lower the number of gang members in the military.
• I feel that if an active gang member in the military is discharged, his local home town or police/sheriff should be notified.
• When I was in basic training, a white male in my platoon continuously claimed he was a gang member. Because he was in the military, and based on lack of knowledge on my part and the part of my other platoon members, no one believed him. Based on my knowledge now, he probably was a gang member (his knowledge, hand signs, etc.).

- I believe all ex-military gang members who were discharged or disciplined for their gang activity in the military should be reported to local, state, and federal authorities. I believe they can present a huge problem because they can take the tactics they have learned and teach them to the other gang members out on the street. I believe recruiters and other military personnel should be aware of gang tattoos, paraphernalia, and so on, so they can make an informed decision when deciding to accept a military applicant.
- The presence of gang members in the military is evident. I believe that encounters with such gang members will become increasingly more prevalent as the military members return home from Iraq and Afghanistan. We will now potentially be dealing with gang members who have been trained and battle-tested their skills in an urban environment.
- We currently have a white supremacist in the Army. He said he signed up with the intent of going to Iraq or Afghanistan to fight in a war. I believe that he wants the training and experience provided in war to bring back to his group. He also wanted to work with weapons and/or explosives while he was in the military.
- Inmates we get in the state prison that have military backgrounds tend to be natural leaders and are less hesitant to set things off. A lot of times they are leaders behind the scenes and shot callers.
- My primary assignment is domestic terrorism and extremists (KKK, neo-Nazis, Militia, etc.). I have noted on several occasions military members self-identify within extremist websites with white power ideology and openly display their military photographs from the combat theaters. Additionally, during my tenure as an Oxnard, California, police officer we noted Asian gang members within the Navy ranks as early as 1992. Military members continue to be involved in criminal gang and violence cases that I have assisted Army CID with.
- I previously worked with probation and parole and was aware of several incidents of gang members in the military or military members affiliated with current street gang members. I know the numbers are growing which makes those members extremely dangerous given their military training and security clearances.
- When I first started my military career in the late 1970s former gang members in my unit wanted to leave the gang life and start a new life where they could raise their families peacefully. In 2001–2003, I deployed with my reserve unit and noticed apparent gang members on the base utilizing the fitness centers on a regular basis at Fort Bragg/Pope Air Force Base, North Carolina. The subjects were displaying colors associated with street gangs.

- We had one OG in the 5/2 Hoover Crips that was former Army. He tried to organize the gang after getting discharged from the Army. We prosecuted him federally on gun charges.
- The current generation of gang members is the first in a very long time to grow up during a time of high military activity. As a result, more gang members are now joining military service for a wide variety of reasons and are returning to the jurisdiction with basic military training at the very least. I have seen gang members in the military encourage others in their gang to enlist as well. The percentage of military trained gang members will continue to rise for the foreseeable future.
- Since I work primarily with teenagers and young adults (14–21), many of the gang members I see are not currently in the military, but talk about their big homies or OGs encouraging them to enlist to come back and teach tactics to those in the streets. Many of my kids feel this will help increase their street rep, because they will have info the gang needs. Others talk of their big homies or OGs teaching them what they learned when they were in the service.
- The greatest concern I have is gang members in the military recruiting new members and using military services (weapons, armor, training material, supplies, access to security levels, and personal access to soldiers' private data) to further their roles and purposes. Not only are they being deployed into combat, but they are also learning new tactics and weapons specializations that were unseen in the streets until the last couple of years. These tactics and training are showing up in home invasions and ambush style shootings. The weapon selections are also becoming a concern as military and ex-military know the firepower of an AK-47 or military-style assault rifle, as compared to a smaller handgun. This along with the massive amount of military equipment (such as tac-vests and armor) missing or unaccounted for should be of great concern.
- I believe background checks should be more thorough and more strict to be in the military. Home assessments by parents should be taken into consideration to younger men of twenty-six years old and below. If the individual has any gang identifiers he should not be allowed to join the military, and if he is, a special training unit should be established by the military for those that otherwise meet the standards. They should be housed and trained together. This would be a true test of the affiliation with their gang and to see if they would stay in good conduct during the boot camp period and give the military a chance to assess one-on-one to see whether they can pass boot camp or not.
- The military has many gang members and a wide base of gangs were represented, as I have seen both in Iraq and in the former Yugoslavia. Gang

members with military experience present a major threat to law enforcement as not all officers have a knowledge of military tactics.

- Military tactics and Army BDU uniforms were used in one aggravated robbery I investigated. When the offenders entered the residence, they announced themselves as local law enforcement. One of the offenders was trained by the U.S. Army Military Police School at Fort Leonard Wood, Missouri, but prior to the incident was discharged for unknown reasons. This offender was linked to the Vice Lords.
- Military combat training is far superior to police officer survival training. Military doctrine teaches soldiers how to advance and take fortified positions. Police training is centered on retreating to a position and waiting for backup to arrive, which does NOT work against a good soldier or marine.
- It seems to be a growing problem with gangs being military trained and having access to military weapons. It is my opinion that legislation should keep gang members from a military career. I personally work with juvenile offenders and have three years' previous law enforcement and I get juvenile offenders, both past and present gang members, that are very interested in the military. When I ask them "why the military?" they explain to me that they want "good training." This raises a serious red flag with me.
- One military-trained gang member we identified and verified by his own admission, was in the National Guard unit. He is no longer in the unit. The other person identified is still in the National Guard. The one that is out was charged with aggravated assault.
- In basic training in 2009, I had at least thirty gang members from around the country in my unit. We had a Crip, a Sureños 13, a member of the Juggalos, and a Mongol. While in Afghanistan, I witnessed gang graffiti on almost every base. I am in the Army Reserve.
- Military-trained gang members are an alarmingly increasing threat to the community and law enforcement personnel, particularly among the OMG 1 percent and support clubs. We have seen a tremendous increase in military style assault weapons/stolen law enforcement grade SWAT weapons in recent years.
- I debriefed a white supremacist gang leader, who described in detail, their efforts to recruit former military members. This info was used to plan and execute home invasions by gangs.

CONCLUSION

In this chapter, we examined the events which shaped contemporary military gang and extremist investigations following the shift in priorities caused by

9/11. I included some of the known street gang, OMG, and DTE events, summarized investigations on those events reported by Army CID from FY 2007–2009, and listed the gangs, OMGs, and DTEs in felony CID reports from FY 2012–2015. Assessments by the FBI, AFOSI, NCIS, and ATF were also reviewed and summarized. I suspect this chapter has given you a different perspective than the mostly historical and anecdotal information contained in the previous chapters. As we continue examining this phenomenon in the coming chapters, we will look at some of the laws and policies controlling the investigations of these groups, as well as some of the reports the Army CID has prepared. I will also include the results of my own research. It may be helpful to refer back to the previous chapters as we do this, as I think you will see not too much has changed.

Chapter Four

Prohibitions and Prevention Measures

In January 2008, legislative efforts restricting recruitment and enlistment of gang members were added to a defense-spending bill, H.R. 4986. The legislation included a directive to the Secretary of Defense to "prescribe regulations to prohibit the active participation by members of the Armed Forces in a criminal street gang."[1] The bill essentially ordered the Pentagon to put membership in a criminal street gang on the list of prohibited activities for service members. Previously, Defense Department regulations only prohibited membership in any organizations that espoused "supremacist causes; attempt to create illegal discrimination . . . advocate the use of force or violence; or otherwise engage in efforts to deprive individuals of their civil rights." But they didn't explicitly list street gangs among those groups. The legislation was the first official acknowledgment of a problem with street gangs in the military. Though it occurred over a decade after the task force investigating the Fort Bragg hate crime murders, I took it as a positive, albeit significantly delayed and underdeveloped step in the right direction. But there were issues.

In the last chapters, we looked at the history of gangs, the emergence of street gangs, OMGs, and DTEs in the military, and contemporary issues with gangs in the military and military-trained gang members. We also examined some of the turning points, or events affecting the existence of and ability to investigate gang members in the military. In this chapter, we are going to look at some of the laws and regulations used to limit the effect of gangs on the community. It's not often that reading through the law is very interesting, but I will try to make it so here by including some context, a few stories, and insight (opinionated, I'm sure), whenever possible.

We will start with a look at several anti-gang regulations and policies, as well as other attempts at prohibiting and preventing gang activity. We will then examine military law, specifically the process depended on to investigate

117

and prosecute street gangs, OMGs, and DTEs. Finally, we will consider a sampling of community-based counter-gang approaches which have been used with some success in the civilian communities and may be implemented in the military communities to limit the negative effects of gang activity, specifically activity by military-trained gang members.

As we will see in this and subsequent chapters, "what works" often depends upon what the problem is. Just like you wouldn't expect to rid your home of cockroaches with a mousetrap, it's not wise to use strategies to limit juvenile delinquency to remove entrenched adult gang members. Many people tend to think (or more often hope) that by saying something should not happen it will not happen. I am sure parents all over the world can relate to my frustration when trying to explain to a three-year-old that he or she shouldn't act a certain way. Those same parents likely learned from those mistakes and found ways to limit access to whatever it was their three-year-old (or maybe their teenager) was getting into. For managers, police officers, and a variety of other professionals, it's the same story. Physical limitation works better and faster than regulatory prohibition.

Sadly, it appeared some lawmakers (and some military leaders) have yet to learn simply saying something wasn't going to happen amounted to little more than wishful thinking without an agreeable second party or the means to physically ensure your wishes. They seem to spend a lot of time passing laws that are unenforced (often unenforceable) and rarely seem to apply what others would see as a "common sense" approach.

Let me give you an example of what works and what doesn't. Are you familiar with the Drug Abuse Resistance Education (D.A.R.E.) program? D.A.R.E. is a substance abuse prevention education program that seeks to prevent use of controlled drugs, membership in gangs, and violent behavior. It was all the rage in the late 1980s and early 1990s. Police departments everywhere wanted to implement D.A.R.E. and assign a D.A.R.E. officer and a D.A.R.E. vehicle that was decked out and very cool looking to every elementary, middle, and high school in the area. A few years into the trend, I was approached by a friend of mine, a local police chief, and he asked my opinion of the program. I told him the problem I had with D.A.R.E. was that there was no measurement plan. He asked what I meant by that, and I pointed out that there was no way to determine whether the perceptions or actions of children who went through the D.A.R.E. program had changed. They were not measuring to see if the program had an effect! That's what I mean by a commonsense approach. Have a reason for implementing a program and then check to see if it's working. Let's apply some of that commonsense approach to preventing (or at least limiting) gangs in the military.

As noted by David Curry, Scott Decker, and David Pyrooz, noted gang scholars, professors, and authors, while most anti-gang programs lack a direct measure of their effectiveness, what matters is whether the implementing agency (and, obviously, their community) see the program as effective.[2] For the most part, D.A.R.E. was a feel-good program, not one that was expected or required to work in any measurable way. With that said, if the community felt like it was working to keep drugs away from kids, it was probably a good idea to keep it around.

DEFINING GANGS

As a reminder, we previously defined the types of organizations we are dealing with, but it is important to also legally define those terms, or you will not be able to enforce the law.

- Street gangs are an association of three or more individuals; who collectively identify themselves to create an atmosphere of fear or intimidation, to engage in criminal activity, with the intent to enhance or preserve the association's power, reputation, or economic resources.[3]
- Outlaw Motorcycle Gangs (OMGs) are highly structured criminal gang organizations whose members engage in criminal activities such as violent crime, weapons trafficking, and drug trafficking.
- Domestic extremists (or DTEs) engage in domestic terrorism, such as crimes dangerous to human life; intended to intimidate or coerce a civilian population, influence or affect the conduct of a government, within the territorial jurisdiction of the United States.[4]

We will see from the next section that little has been done to identify gangs or gang activity in the military until recently, and the effectiveness of measures that *were* implemented was questionable.

Army Guidance

Army CID Policy, CID Regulation 195-1, made no mention of investigating gangs.[5] While that did not mean that CID agents would have no authority or responsibility when it comes to investigating gangs crimes, it did mean that the folks in charge of Command policy didn't think the issue was significant enough to highlight specific action that should be taken when investigating gangs or gang members.

There were two references to gangs in the 2013 version of Military Police (MP) Field Manual (FM) 3-39, which guided MP Operations. The FM covered topics such as the Army's Military Police School, the Criminal Investigation Command (CID), and Corrections Command, along with the Police Intelligence Operations, Investigative Mission, Use of Force, and Transporting of Dangerous Prisoners.[6]

- In section 7-14 of FM 3-39 it was noted that MPs may be attached or assigned to support CID elements to perform duties as Military Police Investigators and can be found conducting drug suppression operations, gang activity investigations, or other criminal investigative functions as designated by the CID special agent in charge.
- In section 7-17, which covered Criminal intelligence, a critical portion of installation police intelligence operations, guidance included the treatment of criminal intelligence such as gang violence is to be reported to commanders and shared with various intelligence and law enforcement agencies.

The old FM system was/is being replaced by Army Tactics, Techniques, and Procedures (ATTP) Manuals, and Military Police doctrinal manuals changed from 3-19 Series to 3-39 Series in 2010.

ATTP Manual 3-39.10 (formerly FM 19-10) Law and Order Operation, June 2011, addressed gangs in the following ways:

- In Section 2-12 (addressing policing models and strategies), the broken-window theory of policing (was) "based on the theory that allowing minor problems (broken windows, trash accumulation) encourages vagrants, gangs, drugs, and other more serious problems to take root."[7]
- In Section 2-52, as identified (other) duties and responsibilities of Military Police Investigators (MPIs).
- In Section 2-119, addressing crime categories such as Organized Crime and Terrorism. Organized crime (including criminal gangs) and terrorist activity are an asymmetric threat to the restoration of peace and stability of the AO.
- Identifying Crime Prevention Measures in Section 3-45. Many crime prevention programs (Drug Abuse Resistance Education [D.A.R.E.], Gang Resistance Education and Training [G.R.E.A.T], and McGruff the Crime Dog) are tightly controlled and require specific training for Military Police personnel conducting the programs.
- In Section 7-50, civilian police advisers are comprised of veteran police officers from across the U.S. who come with a wide range of experience and education. Their LE experiences can cover a large specialty range, including:

- Organized crime.
- Gang units.
- Patrol officers.
- Special weapons and tactics units.
- Hostage negotiations.
- Criminal investigations.

Army Techniques Publication (ATP) No. 3-39.12 (formerly FM 3-19.13/ FM 19-25) Law Enforcement Investigations included the word gangs in two areas:

In section 1-19, addressing the responsibilities of MP Investigators (MPIs) who handled minor crimes and routinely conduct juvenile crime investigations, gang-related investigations, and crime prevention activities.[8]

When explaining the functions of the U.S. Army CID Command in Section 1-33 the manual explained that investigations typically fell into the six primary categories, one of which was:

- Criminal intelligence, derived from the collection, analysis, and interpretation of all available information concerning known and potential criminal threats and vulnerabilities of supported organizations (ATTP 3-39.20). It noted that CID Special Agents collect, analyze, and process criminal intelligence from both the installation and external sources, and report, when required, based on threat and investigative impacts, specific criminal intelligence including gang violence and terrorism to commanders and supported installation activities, and share with various intelligence and LE agencies.[9]

Army Tactics, Techniques, and Procedures (ATTP) Manual No. 3-39.20, on Police Intelligence Operations, addresses the investigations of gang activities in these ways:

- In Section 5-34, covering Police intelligence resulting from trend analysis. The manual suggested that ideally, trend analyses should be depicted visually and in a report format, and that trend analyses are extremely useful for investigations such as sex crimes, drug offenses, homicides, and gang activities.
- In Section 5-46, addressing police intelligence collection folders, where guidance includes the thought that many ideological threat groups and gangs place great emphasis and importance on symbolism, and that symbols (among other things) related to those specific threat groups should be included in the working files.

- In Appendix C, Section 14, in an overview of the capabilities of the Regional Intelligence Sharing System (RISS) network, conduits for the exchange of criminal information and criminal intelligence among participating LE agencies. Typical targets of RISS activities are terrorism, drug-trafficking, violent crime, cybercrime, gang activity, identity theft, human trafficking, and organized crime.[10]

Many of the Army regulations had little guidance. Army Regulation 190-45 (Law Enforcement Reporting) defined a gang as: A group of individuals whose acts of crime are committed against the public at large as well as other groups. A gang usually has in common one or more of the following traits: geographic area of residence, race, or ethnic background. They have a defined hierarchy that controls the general activities of its members.[11]

Army policy on MP Investigations, Army Regulation 190-30 (2005) made one reference to gangs. In paragraph 4-2, it noted that MP Investigators were responsible for gang, or hate crime-related activity, when not within the investigative responsibilities of USACIDC.[12] Likewise, Army Regulation 195-2, containing policy on Criminal Investigation Activities, made no mention of gangs.[13]

Army Regulation (AR) 600-20, until recently, had nothing directly about gangs, and now it has only a little. As we saw in the previous chapter, at the time of the Fort Bragg homicides there was no prohibition against gang membership of any sort by military service members. Both AR 600-20 and DoD Directive 1325.6 (later changed to DoD Instruction (DoDI) 1325.6—Guidelines for Handling Dissident and Protest Activities Among Members of the Armed Forces) prohibited active membership in extremist groups, and many leaders and investigators considered street gangs to be extremist groups, although neither of the documents specifically mentioned street gangs.[14] When I say we considered them extremist groups, that was a consideration of necessity. It would have been nice to have a law that was current or workable, but in the absence of such a law, we got creative.

At the time the instruction was initially published as a Directive in 1969, the DoD was concerned with the infiltration of anti-war and anti-military organizations. The directive focused on dissident and protest activities within the military, and especially on activities such as underground newspapers, demonstrations involving military service members, and serviceman organizations. In 1986, the Secretary of Defense updated the directive with the first inclusion of anti-discriminatory language, trying to apply tools previously used to counter anti-war protest and unionization to now combat hate group membership. Dr. George Reed found that the timing of that change was right after the discovery of alleged participation of soldiers and marines from two military installations in North Carolina, Fort Bragg, and Camp Lejeune, in training activities of the White Patriot Party, the group headed by Frazier Glenn Miller, Jr.[15]

The directive's language prohibited "active" participation in "extremist organizations." That came from language in Executive Order (EO) 11,785 issued in 1953, during the height of the Cold War, when the government leaders feared Communist infiltration. It was later changed to forbid designating any groups as "totalitarian, fascist, Communist, or subversive" and forbade any circulation or publication of a list of such groups.

Department of the Army (DA) Pamphlet (PAM) 600-15 - Extremist Activities (2000) does not include the word *gang* anywhere in the document. The general guidelines included:

- Modern extremist groups run the gamut from the politically astute and subtle to the openly violent. Their involvement in fomenting conflict and unrest in the Armed Forces, their implication in the theft of military weapons, and their tendency to have former military members as leaders and trainers make it imperative that commanders be aware of their threat to discipline, cohesion, and good order.
- Extremists in the Army have an immediate impact on the unit. The mission continues and work is accomplished, but the overall command climate changes as it adjusts to this extremist element. In many instances, soldiers who oppose, or disagree, will not confront the extreme views of another. They either do not feel directly affected by these views or fear damaging the unit's working environment. The unit, however, will usually divide into opposing factions and the "team concept" is gone. Time and effort are now required to deal with the situation.
- Examples of how units are affected include:

  1. The command climate changes to adjust to the extremist views presented by individuals.
  2. Positions are taken (some in favor, some against, some in-between), polarizing the unit.
  3. Productivity is hampered as unit cohesion starts to break down.
  4. An enormous amount of time must be spent to retrain, counsel, investigate, or initiate administrative or disciplinary actions.[16]

PROHIBITING MILITARY STREET GANGS, OMGs, AND DTEs

Although policies and regulations differ in wording across the military branches of the Defense Department, most guidelines on participation in extremist organizations are the same. When there is no information, the other

branches default to the Army. Service members must generally reject participation in organizations that:

- Espouse supremacist causes;
- Attempt to create illegal discrimination based on race, creed, color, gender, religion, or national origin;
- Advocate the use of force or violence or otherwise engage in efforts to deprive individuals of their civil rights.

Additionally, DoD policy instructions have prohibited service members from:

- Participating in supremacist or extremist rallies or demonstrations;
- Knowingly attending meetings or activities while on active duty, when in uniform, when in a foreign country, or in violation of off-limits restrictions or orders;
- Conducting fund-raising activities;
- Recruiting or training members (including encouraging others to join);
- Organizing or leading a supremacist or extremist group;
- Distributing extremist or supremacist literature on or off military installations.

The regulation has prohibited involvement in any organization—extremist
or otherwise, which adversely affected the good order and discipline of the
military, observing that involvement in such organizations affects the ability
of the unit to work together regardless of background.[17] Membership in the
organizations alone was not forbidden. Active participation was what was prohibited—not to the extent of murder or shouting at a rally. It took things such
as handing out literature, recruiting others, going to meetings in uniform, and
a whole host of other things. It was clear, though, that superiors could consider
membership without active participation for consideration of promotion or assignments. The thought behind such policy appeared to be that commanders
could prohibit people from being active in these organizations.[18]

CONSTITUTIONAL PROTECTION

Many folks, confronted for the first time with a gang presence in their community, have suggested simply that the gangs be broken up, done away with,
or outlawed. Don't fall into this trap! It is not easy to rid a community of
gangs—even in the military. Gangs are protected—they are a legal organization that anyone can join. According to some, that's because of the United

The Constitution of the United States has been interpreted to mean that affiliation with or membership in a street gang, OMG, or DTE group does not automatically prevent service in the military. Source: *iStockPhoto*

States Constitution. Do you remember the last time you read the First Amendment? It says, in part, that Congress cannot:

1. establish or prohibit religion
2. restrict freedom of speech, or freedom of the press
3. or restrict people from peaceably assembling.

In fact, as strange as it may sound, each of these provisions may apply to the groups that we are looking at. Some gangs and many DTEs have a religious component, and could be protected under the freedom of religion clause. Street gangs, OMGs, and DTEs may also enjoy the Constitution's protection of much of their freedom of speech. The third part is often found to permit groups to meet in public areas. But it's a strange twist on the freedom of speech clause, tied to the Fourteenth Amendment, that empowers those organizations to form. The "right of association" was identified in the 1958 decision of *NAACP v. Alabama ex rel. Patterson*. The state of Alabama had sought to compel the NAACP to produce membership lists to determine whether the organization was operating in violation of the law. Justice Harlan identified the "right of association" inherent in the Constitution, explaining:

Effective advocacy of both public and private points of view, particularly controversial ones, is undeniably enhanced by group association. . . . It is beyond
debate that freedom to engage in association for the advancement of beliefs and
ideas is an inseparable aspect of the "liberty" assured by the Due Process Clause
of the Fourteenth Amendment, which embraces freedom of speech.[19]

Said another way, mere affiliation with or membership in a street gang,
OMG, or DTE group does not automatically prevent service in the military.
While there is a good argument that neither the Constitution nor the Bill
of Rights "gave" us the freedom to do anything, both are often cited as the
authority that allows gangs (and legally behaving groups) to gather, or "as-
semble" without interference by government representatives.

EXTREMISM OR TERRORISM

The more recent Army CID assessments (since 2010) have included the word
Extremist in the title of the report. There was no indication or explanation in
any of them as to why the term was added, though that's how the military has
identified what the rest of the government has called domestic terrorists for
as far back as I can remember. The report also started distinguishing clearly
between the groups, just as I have identified them here: Street gangs, OMGs,
and DTEs. None of the reports since 2010 have explained the shift, but I have
my suspicions. I suspect you will be able to see what they are as we examine
the annual reports in the coming chapters. That was important because only
the existence of DTE groups appeared to be specifically prohibited. Army
Regulation (AR) 600-20, paragraph 4-12 contains the Army's official definition of extremist organizations and activities:

(Those that) advocate racial, gender, or ethnic hatred or intolerance; advocate,
create, or engage in illegal discrimination based on race, color, sex, religion,
or national origin; advocate the use of force or violence or unlawful means to
deprive individuals of their rights under the U.S. Constitution or the laws of the
U.S., or any state, by unlawful means.

When identifying terrorist groups as extremists, the Department of Homeland Security, as well as the Department of Defense, officially incorporated
terminology previously used interchangeably. Extremism has been defined as
a radical expression of one's political values. According to Gus Martin, a terrorism researcher and textbook author, it is a precursor to terrorism, used by
terrorists to justify their violent behavior.[20] Violent extremism occurs when
individuals openly express their ideological beliefs through violence or a call

for violence.[21] The substance and form of one's beliefs are the elements for defining extremism. It is characterized not only by *what* one believes, but also by *how* an individual expresses those beliefs.[22]

The FBI's typical definition of extremism has suggested two inter-related components. First, extremism involves following a particular ideology. That ideology often serves as a guide for behavior and interaction with other individuals and the world around us. Second, extremism includes the use of criminal activity to advance the ideology.[23] Some do not advocate such a broad use of the term. According to government policy researcher Bjelopera, for example, using the term "extremist" allows prosecutors, policymakers, and investigators to discuss terrorist-like activity without having to officially label the activity as terrorism.[24]

Randy Borum, who has studied the psychology of terrorism, found that part of becoming an extremist means accepting four positions, especially for violent extremists, who were typically characterized as being:

- *Polarized:* Having an "us vs. them" mindset.
- *Absolutist:* Their beliefs are truth in the absolute sense.
- *Threat-Oriented:* External threat causes group members to grow closer.
- *Hateful:* Hate energizes violent action, and allows principled opposition to impel direct action.[25]

Issues with Extremism

Captain Walter Hudson, writing in the *Military Law Review*, criticized the Army's definition of extremism. He noted that the Army's definition did not focus on style or "taking political ideas to their limits."[26] He noted that the regulation (AR 600-20) paid attention to types of extremism which advocated intolerance toward gender and racial, religious, and ethnic minorities, thus providing a narrower category of extremism.

Hudson observed one of the regulation's definitions spoke generally about activities or organizations which may advocate the "use of force or violence or unlawful means to deprive individuals of their rights."[27] The regulation, he noted, did not cover anti-government right-wing extremism, or any solely political extremism, which often indicated white supremacist extremism. It simply declared a behavior (the type that expresses intolerance toward gender, racial, ethnic, and religious groups, and those who advocate violence or unlawful conduct) as extremist.[28] Hudson also observed that the Army avoided designating certain groups or causes (such as environmental activists) as extremist. That, he suggested, allowed the policy to avoid the debate of which political side is favored.[29] Hudson also pointed out that the policy's focus on race and ethnicity highlighted the serious extremist problem that existed in the military.

The regulation distinguishes so-called "passive" participation, such as "mere membership, receiving literature in the mail, or presence at an event" from "active" participation, which includes recruiting others to join and participating in public rallies or demonstrations. The policy does not prohibit passive participation in extremist organizations, though it does not condone it. It prohibits active participation only.[30] At the time of the Fort Bragg shootings, the Army policy on extremism was in the March 30, 1988, version of AR 600-20, paragraph 4-12.[31]

DOMESTIC TERRORISTS

The Army's definition for *Domestic Extremist* is one who is "involved in domestic terrorist activities as defined" in Title 18 of the U.S. Code, Section 233(5), so we will turn our attention to the term *Domestic Terrorism*.[32] Domestic Terrorism, according to the Department of Homeland Security (DHS), is any act of violence that is dangerous to human life or potentially destructive of critical infrastructure or key resources committed by a group or individual based and operating entirely within the U.S. or its territories without direction or inspiration from a foreign terrorist group.[33]

Domestic Terrorist Groups, as identified by the DHS, include the following:

- Animal rights extremists, who are against people, businesses, or government entities perceived to be exploiting or abusing animals.
- Environmental rights extremists, who are against people, businesses, or government entities destroying, degrading, or exploiting the natural environment.
- Anti-abortion extremists, who are against the providers of abortion-related services, their employees, and their facilities.
- Lone offenders are individuals who appear to be motivated by one or more extremist ideologies and, operating alone, support or engage in acts of violence in furtherance of that ideology or ideologies.
- Anarchist extremists, who say they believe that all forms of capitalism and corporate globalization should be opposed and that governing institutions are unnecessary and harmful to society.
- Militia extremists, who profess belief that the government deliberately is stripping Americans of their freedoms and is attempting to establish a totalitarian regime.

- Sovereign citizen extremists, who claim belief that the legitimacy of U.S. citizenship should be rejected; almost all forms of established government, authority, and institutions are illegitimate; and that they are immune from federal, state, and local laws.
- Black supremacist extremists, who claim they oppose racial integration and/or support efforts to eliminate non-Black people and Jewish people.
- Racist skinhead extremists and white supremacist extremists, who both claim belief that Caucasians are intellectually and morally superior to other races and that the government is controlled by Jews.[34]

EXTREMIST GANGS

So, while Hudson suggested that the Army's definition of extremists was not inclusive of many types, it appeared that by referencing the federal law, the intent (or at least the result) was that the term would be inclusive. That appeared closer to Secretary West's understanding, as he made it clear to his commanders over twenty years ago that they were empowered by the intentional absence of a narrowly and rigidly defined term.

Though the intent of AR 600-20 was to thwart typical DTE activities, in the mid-1990s, we at the Fort Campbell gang-extremist investigations team received a tentative (not tested in court) SJA opinion that the prohibitions of distributing extremist literature covered in AR 600-20 would apply to a gang member who "distributes" his literature using a can of spray paint for a writing instrument and a wall or other flat object for his media. We saw that there wasn't likely to be a change to the regulation soon, and we needed something to work with, so we approached a military attorney with the Office of the Staff Judge Advocate (SJA) and pitched the scenario as a solution, and he agreed. The SJA officer in question will remain nameless, partly because I am not sure which of my two favorite prosecutors it was and partly because his name is not relevant to the story. He knows who he is, though! We did not realize that it would be at least fifteen more years before legislation that could be used against gangs would be implemented.

In 2008, legislative efforts to prohibit street gang members from joining the military were added to a defense-spending bill (Public Law 110-181, 2008).[35] It started in 2007, when Rep. Mike Thompson (D-CA) added an amendment to the 2008 Defense Authorization bill that required the military to prohibit service members from associating with criminal street gangs, whether on duty or at home. Thompson found that a growing number of gang members in the military were returning to the streets with combat training, and that put local law enforcement at a disadvantage. Thompson explained that he knew that some gang members joined the military to change for the better, but some were not there to change. He observed that those who intended to change would not be hurt by the amendment.[36]

The legislation included the provision to add active membership in a street gang to the standing prohibition against active group membership by military members in extremist groups. The legislation was intended to extend the prohibitions of Department of Defense (DoD) Instruction (DoDI) 1325.6. H.R. 4986, the National Defense Authorization Act (NDAA) for 2008, SEC. 544, was titled: Prohibition against members of the armed forces participating in criminal street gangs. All that was included in the add-on to the NDAA was: The Secretary of Defense shall prescribe regulations to prohibit the active participation by members of the Armed Forces in a criminal street gang.[37]

Military gang investigators have had problems linking the DoD instruction to gangs because of the history of the original legislation.[38] It was clear what actions the original legislation was designed to prohibit—there was no mention of gangs or anything like those groups. One need only look to the introductory statement *whether the employment or retention in employment in the Federal service of the person being investigated is clearly consistent with the interests of the national security* . . . not limited to . . .

(2) Commission of any act of sabotage, espionage, treason, or sedition, or attempts thereat or preparation therefore, or conspiring with, or aiding or abetting, another to commit or attempt to commit any act of sabotage, espionage, treason, or sedition.

* * *

(4) Advocacy of use of force or violence to overthrow the government of the United States, or of the alteration of the form of government of the United States by unconstitutional means.

An update to DoDI 1325.6, Change 1, February 22, 2012 to DoD Instruction (DoDI) 1325.6 included this guidance:

a. Commanders should remain alert for signs of future prohibited activities. They should intervene early, primarily through counseling, when observing such signs even though the signs may not rise to active advocacy or active participation or may not threaten good order and discipline, but only suggest such potential. The goal of early intervention is to minimize the risk of future prohibited activities.
b. Examples of such signs . . . could include mere membership in criminal gangs and other organizations . . . (are) active participation in prohibited groups by fundraising; demonstrating or rallying; recruiting, training, organizing, or leading members; distributing material; knowingly wearing gang colors or clothing; having tattoos or body markings associated with such gangs or organizations; or

otherwise engaging in activities in furtherance of the objective of such organizations that are detrimental to good order, discipline, or mission accomplishment or are incompatible with military service.

The reality was that Commanders (and other unit leaders) remained alert for signs of bad morale and things that affect the unit mission. They usually didn't see what someone does *off-duty* as something that fell into those categories. The drafters apparently didn't realize that adult gang members were smart enough to conceal their gang affiliation, learning trades they can use to help the gang and using their military experience and exposure to access the logistics pipeline to help drug and weapons trafficking endeavors, and so on.

The military was not designed to be engaged in anything resembling early intervention, or minimizing the risk of future prohibited activities. Those were activities for communities, where there are youth gangs who can be deterred from crime. All military members are adults, and those who were both gang members and military service members, were far past the typical or effective intervention time. The examples of gang behavior in the DoD Instruction do not appropriately represent the breadth, or severity, of gang indicators which should be included in a list of criminal gang offenses. They appeared more like some of the indicators used by state departments of correction and local police departments to confirm gang membership for youth gangs, not the adults with advanced skills brought or honed by military training. The anti-gang strategies supported by that legislation were clearly designed to limit the actions of First Generation Gangs.

MILITARY GANG LAW

Gang members who are in the military must abide by military law, known as the Uniform Code of Military Justice (UCMJ). They must also follow the civilian law in the local jurisdiction when they are off-post. Gang members who are not in the military must follow the civilian law in the jurisdiction where they are. As we look briefly at some of the laws applicable to gang activity, know that I am trying very hard not to include unnecessary legalese. If the topics interest you further than I take them here, I strongly encourage you to go directly to the source.

The Uniform Code of Military Justice

The Uniform Code of Military Justice was established by the United States Congress in accordance with their Constitutional authority. The UCMJ allows for personal jurisdiction over all members of the uniformed services.

Gang members who are in the military must abide by the Uniform Code of Military Justice and civilian law when they are off-post. Source: *iStockPhoto*

There is no definition for "gang" in the UCMJ. In addition to specific and focused legal prohibitions, the following sections of the Uniform Code of Military Justice have been deemed relevant and useful when targeting the actions of MTGMs; they include, but were not limited to:

Article 83—Fraudulent enlistment, appointment, or separation

The crime punishes enlistment in the armed forces by falsely representing, or deliberately concealing, one's qualifications and receiving pay; or (2) procuring one's own separation from the armed forces by false representation or concealing eligibility for that separation. I find it a bit ironic that the punishment for the crime is provided for by a court-martial, as the main "crime" is that the individual was not a legitimate member of the military, and yet the military had the authority to put him on trial. Shouldn't the federal court system be the one to do that? I know that argument is defeated with an example of an illegal alien (we charged someone who had enlisted with that status before that now-unused term became popular), but I said that was ironic, not logical. An example of the crime of fraudulent enlistment would be concealing from the recruiter a criminal record that would otherwise make a recruit ineligible, or providing false identification to enlist in the armed forces.

Article 92, violation or failure to obey lawful general order or regulation

The crime applies to service members who violate a lawful general order or regulation; having knowledge of the lawful order and his/her duty to obey; or being derelict in the performance of his/her duties. A general order is lawful, unless it is contrary to the Constitution, the laws of the U.S., or lawful superior orders. An example of the crime for street gang, OMGs, or DTE group members would be participation in demonstrations or distributions of gang-related literature without approval. Common violations were not commonly punished by court-martial but were generally handled through non-judicial punishment.

Article 116, riot or breach of peace

Riot is a disturbance of the peace by three or more persons with a common purpose to act against anyone who might oppose them. Riots are committed in such a violent and turbulent manner as to cause, or be calculated to cause, public terror.

A breach of the peace is an unlawful disturbance of the peace by someone acting to disturb the public tranquility or impinge upon the peace and good order to which the community is entitled. Engaging in a fight and unlawful discharge of firearms in a public street are examples of conduct which may constitute a breach of the peace. Loud speech and unruly conduct may also constitute a breach of the peace. A speaker may also be guilty if he/she uses language which can reasonably be expected to produce a violent response.

Article 117, provoking speeches or gestures

The charge of provoking speeches or gestures means there is an allegation that the accused made wrongful use of certain words and gestures toward another person; that the words the defendant used or the gestures made by him/her provoked or reproached the other person; and the person against whom the provoking or reproachful words/gestures were used was also covered under the UCMJ.

The words or gestures used should have had a potential to cause a breach of peace in an average person and can elicit a retaliatory turbulent or violent act. Note that the provoking or reproachful words or gestures should have been used in the presence of the person against whom they were directed.

Article 134, general article, specifically, conduct which is prejudicial to good order and discipline

As noted by Eiler, this "catch-all" article criminalized three categories of offenses not covered elsewhere in the UCMJ: offenses to the "prejudice of good order and discipline"; offenses that "bring discredit upon the armed forces"; and offenses involving "noncapital crimes or offenses which violate Federal law."[39] An example of the crime would be a service member violating policy by carrying and concealing a dangerous weapon, or wrongfully influencing, intimidating, impeding, or injuring a witness.

Those laws were the same ones we taught when we gave our briefings to LTC X's unit (and the rest of the military leadership), and they are the examples used today. As it appeared with the military regulations, the military laws available to be used to prosecute gang activity were used primarily to apply to First Generation Gangs. Let's examine some ways to expand the number and types of laws that are available!

Military Use of Civilian Law

Military prosecutors can also use civilian law to prosecute service members for criminal gang activity. The Assimilated Crimes Act, Title 18 of the U.S. Code, Section 13, makes state law applicable to criminal conduct on federal property when the act is not covered by other federal law. Prosecutions under the statute are not an enforcement of the laws of the state, but federal law, the details of which are adopted by reference. The statute has been invoked to cover a variety of crimes, from minor violations to serious criminal offenses like burglary and embezzlement. The Federal law referred to in Article 134 of the UCMJ includes those made applicable through the Federal Assimilative Crimes Act.[40] That made available all the laws of the several states for the prosecution of gang-affiliated military members, even if the military law hasn't caught up with the times. For easy reference, the National Gang Center identifies current gang-related legislation, by state, at https://www.national gangcenter.gov/legislation.

STATE LAW

Lawmakers often create penalty enhancements to show their constituents they are serious about decreasing crime in the community. An examination of State Anti-Gang Statutes by the National Gang Center in their Highlights of Gang-Related Legislation (updated December 2016), showed:

- All fifty states and the District of Columbia (DC) had enacted some form of legislation relating to gangs or gang-related activity.
- Forty-four states and DC had legislation that defines "gang."
- Fifteen states had legislation that defines "gang member."

- Thirty-one states defined "gang crime/activity."
- Twenty-nine states had passed gang-prevention laws.
- Thirty-four states had laws that provided enhanced penalties for gang-related criminal acts.
- Thirty-two of the states had laws against graffiti.
- Twenty-eight states and DC had legislation on gangs and schools.
- Twelve states had enacted laws that dealt with gang-related databases.[41]

By Nevada law, for example, a penalty enhancement does not create a separate offense, but rather it provides an additional penalty for the primary offense. The additional penalty must not exceed the sentence imposed for the underlying crime, and it runs consecutively with the sentence for the crime, as ordered by the court. Nothing requires that prosecutors allege a penalty enhancement or charge a gang crime to use gang evidence. Most cases in which gang evidence was applicable included no specific gang allegation. In those cases, the prosecutor simply explained why the gang evidence should be admitted.

Federal law gives us an example of a penalty enhancement. U.S. federal law defines a criminal street gang as "an ongoing group, club, organization, or association of five or more persons—

1. (A) that has as one of its primary purposes the commission of one or more of the criminal offenses described in subsection (c);
2. (B) the members of which engage, or have engaged within the past five years, in a continuing series of offenses described in subsection (c); and
3. (C) the activities of which affect interstate or foreign commerce." 18 USC § 521(a).

You read that right—five or more persons had to be identified before it's called a gang. That's the definition that Army CID used until FY 2012, when they adopted the standardized definition from the Department of Justice that they use now.

There appear to be two distinct perspectives on gang laws in the United States. Some are focused on the gang-related actions and behavior as it benefits the individual and others are focused on the benefit of the individual's actions to the gang. In Florida, for instance, Section 874.03's "Criminal gang-related activity" means activity committed with the intent to benefit, promote, or further the interests of a criminal gang, or for the purposes of increasing a person's own standing or position within a criminal gang; in which the participants are identified as criminal gang members or associates acting individually or collectively to further any criminal purpose of a criminal gang; activity that is identified as criminal gang activity by a documented reliable informant; or activity that is identified as criminal gang activity by an informant of previously untested reliability and such identification is corroborated by independent information.

Florida's law is individual-oriented, meaning the law focuses on an individual activity to benefit, promote, or further the interests of the gang or increasing a person's standing or position in a gang . . . acting individually or collectively. Kansas (§ 21-4226), South Carolina (§ 16-8-230), and Texas (Fam. Code § 54.0491) are among the states that used a similar application to Florida.

The law in Illinois (§ 740 ILCS 147/10) says gang activity is any criminal activity, enterprise, pursuit, or undertaking directed by, ordered by, authorized by, consented to, agreed to, requested by, acquiesced in, or ratified by any gang leader, officer, or governing or policy-making person or authority, or by any agent, representative, or deputy of any such officer, person, or authority:

- intent to increase gang's size, membership, prestige, dominance, or control in any geographical area; or
- intent to provide the gang with any advantage in, or any control or dominance over, any criminal market sector, or
- intent to exact revenge or retribution for the gang, or any member of the gang; or
- intent to obstruct justice, or intimidate or eliminate any witness against the gang or any member of the gang; or
- intent to otherwise directly or indirectly cause benefit, aggrandizement, gain, profit or other advantage whatsoever to, or for, the gang, its reputation, influence, or membership.

Illinois' law is more group or leader-oriented. It proscribes activity directed by, ordered by, authorized by, consented to, agreed to, requested by, acquiesced in, or ratified by any gang leader, officer, or governing or policy-making person or authority, or by any agent, representative, or deputy of any such officer, person, or authority intent to increase gang's size, membership, prestige, dominance, or control in any geographical area. The laws in states such as Mississippi (§ 97-44-3) and Washington (§ 9.94A.030) tend to follow Illinois.

FEDERAL LAW

The Patriot Act of 2001 expanded the definition of terrorism to include domestic terrorism. That significantly increased the number of activities to which the Patriot Act's expanded law enforcement powers can be applied. That was especially relevant for our purposes, since the term domestic extremism was defined the same as domestic terrorism in Army CID assessments.

In a May 3, 2011, submission of S.867 to the 112th Congress (2011–2012), Senator Robert Menendez [D-NJ] introduced the Fighting Gangs and Empowering Youth Act (FGEYA) of 2011.[42] In it, he proposed grants for innovative approaches to combat gang activity, and designating high-intensity interstate gang activity areas. The FGEYA provided for the reauthorization of programs for combating criminal gangs, including after-school programs and programs for safe and drug-free schools and communities, and expanding the grant program for workplace and community transition training for incarcerated youth offenders (thirty years of age or younger). The bill proposed to amend the Patriot Act to provide funding to hire additional forensic examiners to fight gang activity. It was not further introduced at the time of this writing.

On May 26, 2011, President Obama signed a four-year extension of three key provisions in the Patriot Act: roving wiretaps, searches of business records, and conducting surveillance of individuals suspected of terrorist-related activities, though not linked to terrorist groups. Then, in June 2015, President Obama signed the USA Freedom Act into law. The Act reinstated key counterterrorism laws that had briefly expired and reformed the government's surveillance powers. Three parts of the Patriot Act came back into force. In addition, sweeping surveillance reforms including new restrictions on federal intelligence powers were enacted. The USA Freedom Act ended the National Security Agency's (NSA) bulk collection of Americans' telephone records, limited other ways the government collected large amounts of records and added new transparency measures to the way the government collected information.[43] At the time of this writing, President Donald Trump had yet to identify his intentions regarding either the Patriot Act or the Freedom Act.

Racketeer Influenced and Corrupt Organizations Act (RICO)

RICO was created as Title IX of the Organized Crime Control Act of 1970, which had as its stated goal "the eradication of organized crime." The U.S. Congress determined that organized crime was draining billions of dollars from the U.S. economy annually, and they created legislation to slow that loss. The criminal charges under RICO focused on prohibiting racketeering activity, defined as acts of murder, kidnapping, arson, robbery, bribery, extortion, obstruction of justice, and other crimes.

The FBI has defined significant racketeering activities as those predicate criminal acts that are chargeable under the RICO statute. They were listed in Title 18, Section 1961 (1) of the U.S. Code, and included the following federal crimes:

- Bribery
- Sports Bribery
- Counterfeiting
- Embezzlement of Union Funds
- Mail Fraud
- Wire Fraud
- Money Laundering
- Obstruction of Justice
- Murder for Hire

- Drug Trafficking
- Prostitution
- Sexual Exploitation of Children
- Alien Smuggling
- Trafficking in Counterfeit Goods
- Theft from Interstate Shipment
- Interstate Transportation of Stolen Property[44]

And the following state crimes:

- Murder
- Kidnapping
- Gambling
- Arson

- Robbery
- Bribery
- Extortion
- Drugs[45]

Gangs have increasingly been charged with RICO violations in the past, though it appears that trend may be changing. There are two significant differences between a gang member tried for state violations and one taken to federal court. The first is the significance of the charges—a violation of federal law, not just one state or jurisdiction. The second effect is that prison time in the federal system is typically much longer than what is received in the state system.

Some examples of RICO charges against gang members have included:

- Federal agents in Georgia and Tennessee arrested multiple members and associates of the Gangster Disciples on RICO charges alleging they committed ten murders, twelve attempted murders, two robberies, the extortion of rap artists to force the artists to become affiliated with the Gangster Disciples, and fraud resulting in losses of over $450,000. In addition, the Gangster Disciples trafficked in large amounts of heroin, cocaine, methamphetamine, illegal prescription drugs, and marijuana. The indictment also sought forfeiture of thirty-four different firearms seized as part of the investigation.[46]
- Nine defendants, members of the street gang known as the Hobos, in Chicago were charged with engaging in murders, attempted murders, robberies, and narcotics distribution. The Hobos targeted drug dealers and high-

value targets to rob, retaliate against rival gangs, and prevent witnesses from cooperating with law enforcement.[47]

- Thirty-seven members of the Mara Salvatrucha (MS-13) were indicted by a federal grand jury on racketeering conspiracy charges in the Western District of North Carolina. The gang members committed numerous violent crimes, including armed robberies, assaults, and murders, for the benefit of the criminal enterprise. The defendants were allegedly responsible for numerous criminal acts including drug distribution, armed robberies, extortion, illegal possession of weapons, the assault of individuals suspected of cooperating with law enforcement, and murder.[48]

NON-CRIMINAL SOLUTIONS

Treatment programs are often suggested to show offenders the error of their criminal ways. Most of them apply to street gangs, as they represent the highest number of gang members and are most often the ones to be considered "treatable." Meltzer studied gang-involved adolescent males who were court-mandated to attend a gang reduction program.[49] The program included weekly meetings where speakers from a variety of community and academic areas addressed the group regarding laws, behavior, treatment, and other topics designed to inform their judgment and actions. The primary goals identified for the program were to decrease gang involvement and illegal behavior. Meltzer found an increase in knowledge regarding related laws and an increased concern about the risk and danger of gang association, which was presented by professionals and community representatives.[50] Many of the participants were ready for change when they attended the program and though many of the participants had been involved in gang-related activity, they did not appear to be very deeply involved.[51]

Based on the premise that most gang-affiliated offenders will re-enter society, treatment in prisons is often focused on reducing gang violence.[52] Encouraging dissociation is often the strategy used, especially in prison settings. Treatment in corrections facilities has included programs for gang members who wanted to renounce their gang association.[53] Those programs included interacting with members of other gangs, signing a renunciation form, and cultural awareness training.

The treatment programs that were most likely to reduce recidivism were those that followed the risk-need-responsivity principles.[54] Treatment of gang members with the highest risk of reoffending was most effective. For treatment to be effective, needs that contributed to criminal activities must be assessed, identified, and targeted. The delivery of treatment should be

Gang-free zones and gang injunctions have been used in some communities to limit the negative effects of gangs. Source: iStockPhoto

adjusted to accommodate clients' characteristics to ensure treatment effectiveness. Gang members who wished to change had to perform a delicate balancing act to move away from criminal activities and association, especially in prison.[55]

Gang-free zones and gang injunctions have enjoyed some success in limiting the negative effects of gangs in communities in recent years. In the 1980s, the Los Angeles County district attorney asked for a court order declaring gangs to be a form of quasi-corporate structure, so that each member could be held accountable for the actions of other members.[56] The ruling was sought to enable the community to force gang members to remove their gang's graffiti. Many states had enacted gang-related laws by that time, and thirty-one states had adopted laws like the federal RICO laws. It was thought that the notification requirement of gang members that they were known members of a criminal street gang might contain the seeds for useful deterrence activity.[57] Part of the process for implementing a gang injunction was to notify each individual gang member that there were specific public areas where they were not allowed to be.

Gang scholars Cheryl Maxson, Karen Hennigan, and David Sloane examined the effect and implications of injunctions as policy in California.[58] The report was the first scientific examination regarding the impact of gang injunctions on the community, including the effect on gang presence, gang intimidation, and fear of confrontation with gang members in primary and secondary injunction areas. The authors focused on changes in the quality of life in the neighborhood, rather than the effect on gang members. They found that the gang injunction impacted the level of gang member intimidation and the level of fear of gang members by residents almost immediately.[59] The authors suggested combining injunctions with other strategies offering vocational, educational, or personal growth to expand the positive effect of injunctions.

Gang researchers Malcolm Klein and Cheryl Maxson examined civil gang injunctions and found they resulted in some success with reduced gang member visibility, gang intimidation, and fear of crime by residents. They suggested that a community solution should be the focus and more community involvement should be sought so that innovative strategy can be distinguished from police gang suppression strategy.[60]

Matthew O'Deane, an academic who was also a criminal justice practitioner, examined the effectiveness of gang injunctions at reducing crime in a sampling of jurisdictions in California.[61] O'Deane distinguished his work by examining similar communities, not adjoining ones. He found crime decreased in areas where gang injunctions were implemented. He observed that injunctions should be regularly updated because gangs (membership) change over time, when members die, go to prison, move out of the area, or simply stop being active gang members.[62]

Researchers Eric Fritsch, Tory Caeti, and Robert Taylor evaluated the 1996 anti-gang initiative of the Dallas Police Department.[63] Five targeted areas received overtime-funded officers to implement strategies including saturation patrol, and aggressive curfew and truancy enforcement. They observed that as was seen in earlier studies, undirected saturation patrol did little to reduce crime, but that aggressive enforcement of truancy and curfew laws did reduce gang-related violence in the target areas.[64] They commented that police gang suppression appeared to affect crime and violence committed by gang members, not the conditions that create gangs. The authors noted that the police mission, for which they were designed, organized, staffed, and trained, involved crime, not social services, and to suggest otherwise was naïve and unrealistic.[65]

While gang-free zones have enjoyed success in some communities, the strategy does not appear to be relevant for the military, except perhaps for restrictions in communities on a military installation or for limiting the access of military family members who are affiliated with gangs. The strategies do not appear to have been tried in any military community. They were offered here simply as an example of innovative problem-solving, perhaps to provoke some ideas that might be examined in the future.

DENIAL

Denial is not a recommended response, but it has occurred nonetheless. Denial appears to be a natural response when new problems are encountered.[66] Denial of a street gang, OMG, or DTE presence has occurred at all levels of government and communities.[67] When leaders of large, urban police departments have refused to acknowledge such a presence in their cities, that may not mean street gangs, OMGs, or DTEs are absent. There may simply have been a politically motivated denial because city leaders did not like the idea of acknowledging a street gang, OMG, or DTE problem without a solution.[68] Politics is one of the factors that has made it difficult for police officers to eliminate street gangs, OMGs, or DTEs from their community.[69] Many times, migration and other growth indicators can actually be aided by official denial.[70] Denial by those tasked with investigating criminal activity has allowed street gangs, OMGs, or DTEs to establish strongholds that support narcotic distribution networks and neighborhood drug dealing.[71]

Researchers Knox, McCurrie, Laskey, and Tromanhauser sent a questionnaire to police chiefs in forty-eight states. The questionnaire asked "to what extent do community leaders in your jurisdiction deny the gang problem?" Of those responding, one fifth reported "no gang problem." Of note was that 35 percent of the respondents gave a rating of 6 (of 10) or higher regarding gang denial by community leaders.[72] The researchers estimated that the gang population in the United States in 1996 was approximately 1.5 million.[73]

Examples of Denial

The following comments can be used to engage in denial of a community gang problem. In the absence of verification, they can be used as indicators of denial. The comments are often related to street gangs, as community leaders don't tend to deny the existence of OMGs and DTEs as often.

- These are people who have "overcome mistakes."
  - There is no test for "overcoming mistakes." Both traditional extremists and street gangs tell their people how to "get past" the questions that police, employers, or relatives ask them.
- They thought that the symbol looked cool (regarding graffiti and tattoo).
  - In the gang world, falsely representing membership in a gang by displaying symbols of a gang you are not a member of may result in grievous bodily harm or even death. If a non-gang member tattooed or painted a symbol he/she (and the tattoo artist) would be sought out as a perpetrator by members of the gang that symbol represented. One

of the reasons for this predictable response is what is known as false flagging. False flagging is "throwing a sign" or shouting out a gang slogan to induce or trick a rival gang member into representing his affiliation. As an example, a member of one gang might represent another gang affiliation by "throwing up" that gang's hand sign. When the opposing gang member represents back by "throwing up" the hand sign, he may become the victim of a drive-by shooting or a beating by the offending gang. False flagging accounts for several homicides every year.[74]

- The gang problem is not rampant.
  - As noted previously, waiting until a problem is "rampant" gives the gangs an unnecessary and voluntary head start. In 1999, the FBI rated membership in the military the number three reason for migratory gangs (after formal-corporate employment and informal-laborer employment). Gang presence may not be considered a problem for the military, but how much has it contributed to migration (worldwide) since 1999, as gang-involved military service members return to the civilian communities after their enlistment ends?

An example of the last type of denial, that it's not a "big" problem, was provided shortly after the DoD started acknowledging the gang threat following 9/11. "We recently conducted an Army-wide study, and we don't see a significant trend in this kind of activity, especially when you compare this with a million-man Army," said Christopher Grey, Army CID Public Affairs officer.[75] Note that Grey didn't say how big a problem gangs were in the military. What he did was suggest that it wasn't big enough for an organization with a million or more members to be overly concerned with.

No one has ever found a way to determine how many active gang members are in the military. If it were possible to determine how many gang members were active in the civilian community at the target age of military recruits and compare that number to the same population in the military, it would likely show that a similar percentage of each population has gang ties. This possibility does not excuse the existence of gang members in the military, it simply explains it. As we will discuss in later chapters, numerically, there are far more gang members who have exited the military and now live in the civilian communities than there are active duty military gang members. But for now, the issue is the minimization of the problem, which I do not recommend.

To excuse the existence of gang members in the military would be to say that the military, like McDonald's or Wal-Mart, with over a million youthful employees around the world, understandably draws a few gang members into its ranks from the gang lifestyle.[76] Neither McDonalds nor Wal-Mart runs a background check that rivals the security clearance conducted as standard fare by the military and neither organization trusts their global employees with an issued weapon and ammunition and the authority to engage an armed enemy.

Grey was addressing the results of the first Army-wide assessment of gangs since 9/11, following two gang-related murders in 2005—one in Alaska and the other in Germany. He had not yet polished the command response to inquiries. More recent CID Assessments (since FY 2011) on the gang posture have clearly stated:

> The threat of gangs and DE groups seeking to capitalize on the skill development opportunities provided by the Army is a well-established concern of federal law enforcement agencies and congressional leaders.[77]

In more recent years, Army spokespersons have provided a much more informed view. Neal Carrington, antiterrorism officer for the U.S. Army Garrison Directorate of Plans, Training, Mobilization and Security, said gangs were like terrorists, just "a smaller form of a terrorist organization" intent on holding territory and expanding their beliefs through recruitment and terror-related activities.[78] Carrington advised that gangs recruited heavily from the military because of the tactical and weapons training. As a result, he said some gangs have incorporated military tactics into their crimes.

Wanna-be

Community leaders often respond to the initial appearances of gang-like activity in their communities by referring to those engaged in the activity as wanna-be gang members. Using such a term is a type of denial, or minimization of the problem. Gang researchers Curry and Decker cautioned against using the term wanna-be, as it was counterproductive and allowed gang members to get a head start, without any attention from those who would need to deal with the gang problem in the future.[79] They observed that the term was often used to describe those who operated in the area between core members and those found on the fringe of the gang. Curry and Decker identified the individuals in that category as gang associates.[80]

Using the term wanna-be in an official capacity is not unlike playing the childhood game of hide-and-seek. When the community acts as the seeker, and then looks away, covers their eyes, and counts to 100 or more, they are giving the gang, or gang member, a chance to conceal themselves. If instead of blocking their vision and waiting to respond, they instead started to examine the transition toward genuine gang activity the individuals and groups were making, communities would be much more prepared to deal with the challenges to be faced by a full-blown gang problem. Many gang cops have been heard to ask, when responding to a community leader's dismissal of juvenile gang activity with the term "wanna-be": If a wanna-be gang member shoots a second wanna-be gang member, is he wanna-be dead?

WHAT WORKS

Depending on with whom you are speaking, the list of what "works" and what doesn't is likely to be different. Gang researchers Curry, Decker, and Pyrooz summarized their research by pointing out that while the response to gangs was hardly well-coordinated, it was organized into categories: 1) community organization, 2) social intervention, 3) opportunities provision, 4) suppression, and 5) organizational development and change.[81] Suppression appeared to be the only effective category for the military, so that is the one we will spend the most time on. Many gang scholars will claim to have the best fix for one gang problem or another. What hasn't been discovered, to my knowledge, is a solution to either the adult gang problem or the gang member in the military problem. While there are several good strategies and treatments for the "typical" gang member, we are talking about a select group of people who choose to add or keep a relationship in their lives that is in direct conflict with their sworn and committed primary duty—service to the country and allegiance to it against all enemies, foreign and domestic.

Ultimately, we are looking for a "solution" to the specific gang "problem," so if we agree that solving the gang problem means preventing active gang members from joining, or at least causing them to remain inactive while in the military, we can begin our analysis. I feel that it is critical for the military community to first recognize that there is a problem. The community and its leadership must then mobilize the needed resources and implement solutions which they follow up on regularly. There will be many challenges to this basic strategy—usually based on personal interests and ideologies.

Suppression programs, while popular in the 1970s and 1980s, included such activities as arrest, special prosecution, intensive probation, and incarceration.[82] They tended to be more of a conservative political response and have not enjoyed the same intensity of focus from one executive administration to another, whether at the local, state, or federal level. With the unique dynamic of the military, only the first two activities (arrest and prosecution) were likely to occur, and either was likely to definitively terminate a military career.

Established gang members seek areas where growth would benefit the gang and recruit local residents into the gang.[83] That method is often used to increase the exposure of the gang's criminal enterprise, whether they are engaged in drug trafficking, thefts, forgery, or trafficking in stolen property.[84] Gangs have also used methods that are similar to those used by legitimate business organizations for cultivating and establishing customers, obtaining and distributing products, and providing services.[85] Because of the need for growth, we need to expect changes in gang activity and provide for periodic evaluation in the area of "what works."

Sadly, I don't think there is likely to be a real solution for the existence of gang members in the military community, but we will examine a few successes in other communities. I say this, not because I have a defeatist attitude or because I doubt the ability of policymakers or military leaders, but because I know about the unique nature of the military. In the civilian community, if a person commits a crime and gets caught, the criminal justice system is mobilized to correct the problem, often by running the person through the courts to the corrections system, perhaps by restricting the person's movements to or from a specific area (using probation or injunctions, respectively), and by using an intelligence system to keep tabs on the individual. That process allows the police to get to know the various gang-involved individuals in their community and assists them in determining the best remedies for gang behavior.

The military typically has no such system, at least not for the adult gang member who is also a member of the military. The Military Police have about one shot at learning who is a gang member, and if the military system works there will be no need to do anything further. Given the relatively limited engagement that Military Police have with the community, if a person's behavior is so bad that the police are engaged, that person is not likely to remain a member of the community. Thus, the police are severely restricted from gathering valuable intelligence on embedded and concealed gangs and gang members, and will only interact with the less advanced criminal element.

What Works Elsewhere

In contrast to the approaches taken by the military, some prison systems are using a system of treatment designed to deter recidivism.[86] The process is described as a high intensity cognitive–behavioral (HICB) program. Such studies have provided an opportunity to examine "what works" with those inside the prison system. While prison is clearly not the same as the military, there are a few notable similarities, including the increase in discipline and restriction of freedoms. The basics of the program include using culturally sensitive teaching and therapeutic approaches to address the offenders' needs, providing the offenders with a supportive environment to practice and generalize the new skills; and requiring an exit strategy for the offenders. Overall recidivism was significantly reduced, and for the few who reoffended, the activity was less serious. There was a negative correlation between length of treatment and recidivism, and a longer duration of treatment was related to lower recidivism. The process acknowledged the benefits of isolating gang members from the local community, encouraging them to renounce their gang association and engage in post-treatment analysis.

A version of the HICB treatment used in the military might start with acknowledged gang members seeking to join the military. Instead of simply taking their word that they have desisted from gang activity and continue to do so, the military could assign counselors to debrief the admitted gang member as he enters the military. Working with the recruit, a plan of action could be designed to help him through the stressors and triggers likely to appear during the term of his enlistment. Periodic (quarterly, leading to annually, perhaps) follow-up could be scheduled, to ensure the process is working.

Bill Sanders, a professor and youth gang scholar, suggested the consideration of gangs as a public health issue. He noted that gang-involved youth were at increased risk for incarceration, as well as negative health and social outcomes. Community responses to gangs might improve if they were public health problems, Sanders suggested, as those programs were more defensive and focus on prevention.[87]

A version of the public health application used in the military might be like the suggestion used for the HICB treatment. It would not be unusual for non-criminal directorates to oversee gang and extremist related activities. Medical specialists could categorize and track the progress of enlisted gang members, in coordination with many other administrative and investigative agencies, and report, as needed, to military leadership.

Pioneered in Boston, the approach known as pulling levers was designed to influence the behavior and environment of chronic offenders. The strategy attempted to prevent gang violence by making would-be offenders believe that severe consequences would follow. It was originally named the Boston Gun Project, noting that while gang members made up less than 1 percent of the overall youth population, they accounted for more than 60 percent of youth homicides—often with a handgun.[88] A variation of this strategy was used in programs like Operation Ceasefire, a problem-oriented deterrence program that used a zero-tolerance approach. It involved rounding up offenders and holding a community meeting to explain the consequences of their continued criminal actions (long and arduous prison sentences). Much success has been realized by this approach.[89]

A key element was the delivery of a direct and explicit "deterrence" message regarding what behavior provoked a special response, and what that response was. The basic elements of the approach included:

- Enlisting community support
- Convening an interagency working group
- Placing responsibility on the working group
- Involving researchers
- Developing an effective communication strategy
- Targeting intervention
- Sending the initial message
- Pulling all available enforcement levers
- Continuing communication
- Providing social services and opportunities[90]

A version of the pulling levers approach in the military might also be used with potential gang-affiliated recruits. Instead of trusting the system to "fix" the offender, the approach would entail a similar treatment plan and follow-up to the HICB program. The threat of "brainwashing" posed by drill sergeants of old is not what is being suggested. Instead, a contract with an individual sincerely seeking a way to exit the endless cycle of violence that plagued the gang life is recommended. There should be a long-term commitment on both sides, with checks and balances (perhaps annual psychological evaluations and polygraph examinations) to ensure against a reversion.

CONCLUSION

It may seem a bit unconventional to address potential solutions half way into the book. Most of the books on gangs that I recall reading end with an entire section detailing possible solutions and why each of them will or won't work given the context presented in the book. I will include a few more recommendations as we proceed, but I wanted to do it a bit differently here, as this is genuinely a work in progress. To be clear, I do not know what will work for gang members in the military, and neither does any other gang scholar or expert, or any of the authors of the numerous gang and extremist threat assessments published in recent years. The evidence for that claim is the absence of a working model that has proven successful. The military, depending on with whom you speak, may or may not recognize or acknowledge a problem with gangs and extremists, and rarely is there any mention of a real or viable solution, or even the need for one.

Sadly, when the official reports have mentioned solutions, they have regurgitated the suggestions of a published gang scholar, usually from at least a decade prior, who was addressing a neighborhood gang problem. The majority of gang members in the military have not been members of typical neighborhood gangs—youth from low-income neighborhoods and few marketable skills who turned to gangs to find a sense of belonging and family. They have been individuals who are sophisticated enough to be accepted into the military despite their gang affiliation, or bold enough to choose an additional, criminal vocation or lifestyle after swearing their allegiance to the United States of America. Those guys (and gals) are not going to be deterred by the same strategies that worked for the kids back on the street in Your Hometown, USA.

Although I cannot offer any solid "this works" solutions, I hope to be able to provide a variety of ideas. I have excluded many of the typical solutions and offered those that, in my opinion and experience, have a chance of working with military-trained gang members. Ultimately, those solutions (or a variation of one or more in combination) must be implemented, used, and tested. Communities around the globe often look for a "quick fix," and usually leave empty-handed. There will not be any one solution that fits everywhere.

Chapter Five

Gangs with Members in the Military

In July 2011, active and former Army service members in the DTE group, Forever Enduring Always Ready (FEAR), made plans to destroy a dam and poison several apple orchards in Washington State, set off explosives in a park in Georgia, and assassinate then U.S. president Barack Obama.[1] The group leader, Isaac Aguigui had purchased ninety acres of property in Washington, near where he grew up, and had stockpiled nearly $90,000 worth of military-grade weapons.[2] Aguigui also killed his wife and two others and purchased property and weapons with the $500,000 life insurance policy he received after her death. The existence of the group was apparently known to quite a few unit members, demonstrating what can happen when DTE group members can openly operate so long as they don't "cause problems." The quality of the investigation was also questioned, perhaps demonstrating the problem with waiting to familiarize investigators with those types of groups and waiting to investigate the actions of active military DTE group members until a felony crime has been committed, detected, and reported to authorities.

In the previous chapter, we identified some of the laws, regulations, and strategies used to limit the effect of gangs on the community. As we saw, enacting laws and implementing policies prohibiting and preventing gang activity, or finding "what works" isn't easy. Give some consideration to the effect of the public health style model of high intensity cognitive–behavioral treatment as well as a variation of pulling levers designed especially for the military. Consider the potential for success of those strategies, and others we touched on (or that you are aware of), as we examine the issues in the context of this chapter.

In this chapter, we will look at the potential for a criminal gang presence to be countered with strategic military policy. I have included a relatively short summary of the terms "counterinsurgency" and "cultural awareness" because I think the application of strategies used in both may be useful in the attempt to restrict the negative effects of gang members in the military. It's not something presently being considered by military law enforcement so far as I know, but at the very least, the strategies are worthy of consideration. We will also evaluate the presence of gang members in the military both in recent history and presently and focus on some of the problems inherent in their presence.

There is also an overview and analysis of the compilation of official Army CID annual threat assessments for street gang, OMG, and DTE activity. That analysis includes a summary of the reports from 2005–Present. There was a remarkable shift in reporting and methodology between 2009 and 2010 and the analysis also reflects and identifies that shift. I am not aware of another publication, government or private, that provides such a compilation for analysis. Our concluding focus on the more current problem, from 2012 forward, was intended to reflect what appears to be a settling in the style and focus of reporting by Army CID, which had not been consistent over the previous decade.

COUNTERINSURGENCY AND CULTURAL AWARENESS

The organized response to counterinsurgency was a major adjustment in focus for the U.S. military because of the needed change in focus of the War on Terrorism. Prior to that time, the military's defense posture was tailored to respond to Cold War era threats such as those posed by the former Soviet Union and its allies. Insurgency is not terrorism, nor is it necessarily criminal activity. It is an attempt to push back against the established government control to the extent that real change is affected. Insurgency is best defined as a rebellion against authority, or a political effort, using subversion and violence with a specific aim.

The idea of treating gangs as insurgents is not new. In 1993, retired Army Lieutenant General David Hogg, while finishing graduate school, examined the feasibility of deploying the military against street gangs in the United States. He specifically examined the Crips street gang, and noted that street gangs were considered a "preservationist insurgency."[3] Though street gangs were a threat to the United States, they were deemed neither a military or political threat. So, he concluded the threat of street gangs did not warrant military intervention. Hogg observed the goals of street gangs were making money and providing an environment of security. He noted the violent actions toward other gangs and members of the community amounted to what he called urban terrorism. While it was clear Hogg had sufficiently researched street gangs at the time, it was also clear the gangs he addressed were those in the First Generation. Gangs with military-trained members have far more potential to pose an ongoing and persistent military or political threat.

A counterinsurgency is a coordinated political, security, economic, and informational effort that reinforces governmental legitimacy while reducing the influence of insurgents over the population. Counterinsurgency operations using non-military means are often the most effective as they seek to find the root cause(s) of the insurgency. Central to a counterinsurgency operation (at least in the beginning) is intelligence gathering and analysis.[4] I propose it would make sense to respond to gangs whose members have military training (whether in or out of the military) as if they were insurgents. They represent a more advanced form of gang and gang member and may be more inclined and able to use the government systems, such as community and military infrastructures and logistics, to advance the goals of and acquire assets for their gangs. That would make the recommended approach one of counterinsurgency, right? Even if you think that is a bit of a stretch, try to read the remainder of the book from that perspective, or at least something like it. I think you'll find it is more applicable than you initially thought.

The more advanced contemporary street gangs have been strategically infiltrating our military communities since the late 1980s. At the end of the 1990s, the FBI attributed much of the increase in gang member migration to the military, in addition to civilian job transfers. When acknowledged and active gang members can join the military, they are treated just like other service members. There are no debriefings, no watch lists, and no warnings to local military law enforcement. Is that the right policy for gang members leaving the military?

Gangs are recognized as a coercive force, according to the Army FM on Counterinsurgency, FM 3-24 (MCWP 3-33.5), 2006.[5] As with other groups categorized as such (paramilitary units, tribal militias, and organizational security personnel), gangs should be seriously considered as potential insurgents or adversaries during all military operations—both during peacetime and during conflict. Section 5-42 specifically addressed the connections between street gangs and insurgencies. Criminal organizations such as street gangs, mafias, or cartels may assist insurgent groups in any number of ways, including intimidating government leaders, conducting assassinations and kidnappings, initiating violence, strikes, riots, and smuggling weapons. Section 5-43 noted that many insurgencies degenerate into criminality when primary movements disintegrate or the root cause is addressed. The manual suggested counterintuitively that insurgent disintegration was desirable. It resulted in a downgrade of the threat, since insurgency was a security threat and criminality was (simply) a law-and-order problem.

The typical police perspective, that of law enforcement and order maintenance, tends to be similar to the role filled by our soldiers when conducting counterinsurgency operations. By application, counterinsurgency operations are long-term, and the foundation that is laid during the initial phases must be solid. Only by engaging and interacting with the population in an appropriately respectful manner can a proper foundation for continued relations be laid. The practice of cultural awareness provides for such an engagement.

Part of the counterinsurgency effort involves applying intercultural skills. Air Force Lieutenant Colonel (LTC) Michael Rothstein, while at the Air War College, identified the need to develop intercultural skills in military leadership. He identified intercultural skills as the primary set of skills and knowledge necessary for professional and personal interaction with people of other cultures. He divided intercultural skills into three subsets; cultural awareness, regional understanding, and foreign language competency.[6] He defined cultural awareness as "the ability to understand and appreciate differences among cultures and to be sensitive to the unique challenges cultural differences can create."[7]

LTC Rothstein observed that many Americans do not appreciate the culture of others because they don't understand or appreciate their own. Other military scholars have addressed the importance of cultural awareness by the military, too. Marine Colonel Michael Melillo, a field artillery officer who was the Chief, Operations and Training Branch, at the Security Cooperation Education and Training Center, Quantico, Virginia, noted that Americans had difficulty with cultural awareness because they were part of a culture that ignored the needs of irregular warfare.[8] As a remedy, he suggested transforming the cultural resistance to nontraditional wars. Dr. Max Manwaring, professor of military strategy in the Strategic Studies Institute of the U.S. Army War College, suggested the solution was to avoid the tendency toward "providing traditional military solutions to conventional military problems."[9]

Cultural awareness provides an understanding of the social networks, politics, and traditions of a location; it also provides an understanding of the nuances, behavioral customs, and rules for common interaction. By observing those less-visible subtleties, what was different might be more important to take note of than what was missing. For example, if a certain citizen (Mr. A) was suspected of collaborating with insurgents and he was seen talking to Mr. B, that might be unusual if it occurred in a manner or location where the two would not otherwise meet or converse.

The use of cultural awareness when addressing military-trained gang members (MTGMs) might allow for a better understanding of potential solutions to the problem. It might also result in a relatability between the investigator and the gang member that could prove invaluable for gathering additional intelligence to ensure appropriate anti-gang strategies were in place. The penalty for not applying cultural awareness in a counterinsurgency operation is either the loss of the population's trust or the fostering of an environment in which the insurgent forces can grow.[10] The penalty for not applying cultural awareness in a policing operation involving MTGMs may be the loss of intelligence or the loss of evidence against street gang, OMG, or DTE group members.

I realize it may be considered a radical suggestion, but I also realize what has been tried has not worked. What I am suggesting is that folks who need to understand those street gang, OMG, or DTE group members as part of their job description should take the time to try to understand their adversaries. As the overly quoted ancient master Sun Tzu said about knowing one's adversary, "When the enemy is at ease, be able to weary him; when well fed, to starve him; when at rest, to make him move." Those things are only possible when you know a lot about the adversary. Is there a difference between a property crimes investigator who takes the time to know how a burglar is likely to think and act and a gang cop taking the time to do the same with an MTGM in his or her community?

STREET GANG MEMBERS, OMGs, AND DTEs IN THE MILITARY

The authors of just about every report by the Federal Bureau of Investigation's (FBI) National Gang Intelligence Center (NGIC) have observed "gang members with military training pose a unique threat to law enforcement personnel." The threat posed to law enforcement was even more significant if MTGMs trained other gang members in weapons, tactics, discipline, and planning.[11] Whether trained in combat arms, logistics, finance, or other military occupational specialties, the gang member *with* military experience should be considered more advanced and dangerous than the gang member *without* military experience, and the potential threat MTGMs pose to law enforcement is significant.[12] All facets of the criminal justice system throughout the United States (police, courts, and corrections) at the local, state, and federal level have the potential to encounter MTGMs. Military experience adds a dangerous dimension to the gang member which is not seen in those without military training.

According to the 2015 NGIC report, MTGMs learn combat tactics in the military, then return home to utilize those skills against rival gangs or law enforcement. Military training of individual gang members could ultimately result in more sophisticated and deadly gangs, as well as deadly assaults on law enforcement officers. Additionally, military members' access to weapons and their perceived ability to move easily across international borders may make them ideal targets for recruitment.[13]

I have conducted over a dozen surveys of hundreds of gang investigators over the past few years. I will share more specific results later in the book, but here's a brief look at the method of inquiry. I have simply asked the investigators to what extent they agreed with these statements:

1. *Gang members in my jurisdiction are increasingly using military-type weapons or explosives.*
2. *Gang members in my jurisdiction use military-type equipment (body armor, night-vision, etc.).*
3. *Gang members in my jurisdiction use military-type tactics.*
4. *Gang members in my jurisdiction commit home invasions.*
5. *Gang members in my jurisdiction commit armed robberies.*
6. *There are gang members in my jurisdiction who currently serve in the military.*
7. *There are gang members in my jurisdiction who have served in the military in the past.*
8. *Military representatives advise our department when gang members are discharged.*

Typically, many (about one-third) of the investigators have reported gang members in their jurisdictions were increasingly using military-type weapons or explosives, and about one-fourth report their gang members use military-type equipment like body armor, night-vision devices, and so on. Although many (typically one-fourth to one-half) agree their gang members were using military-type tactics, most (over three-fourths) have reported the gang members in their jurisdictions have committed home invasions and armed robberies.[14] Many, from about one-fourth to one-half, have reported there were gang members in their jurisdiction currently serving, while from one-half to two-thirds have reported they had gang members who had previously served in the military. Most respondents have reported military representatives have not advised their department when gang members were discharged from the military.

I need to make it clear here that I am not suggesting that the military should publicly identify military veterans for being passive or inactive gang members. Without a connection to criminal activity as part of that gang affiliation, no such notification is warranted. In other words, you can report and investigate a person involved in criminal activity, but not someone simply engaged in what is deemed cultural activity. Many local and state gang units must follow and conform to the requirements of federal law, as contained in the Criminal Intelligence Systems Operating Policies of 28 CFR Part 23, a federal regulation that provides guidance to law enforcement agencies when operations are funded under the Omnibus Crime Control and Safe Streets Act of 1968, as amended. As I have pointed out earlier, merely associating with or being in a gang is not a crime. Gang officers must constantly distinguish the *culture* of gangs from the *criminality* of gangs.

Gang members have represented many branches of the military, although the Army has been the most often reported in my surveys, followed by the Marine Corps and the Army Reserve. The Gangster Disciples, Latin Kings, Bloods, Crips, and Vice Lords have been the street gangs typically represented in survey respondents' jurisdictions. Of the OMGs represented by MTGMs, the Outlaws, Hells Angels, and Black Pistons were the most often reported. Sovereign citizens comprised the largest group of DTEs represented by MTGMs, usually followed by white supremacists and racist skinheads. Most survey respondents have reported that under (up to) 10 percent of their gang members had some form of military training.

Enlistees typically bring the gang culture into the military, often unintentionally. Imagine a gang-involved young man in a civilian community who wants to get out of the gang lifestyle. Every day, he sees his fellow gang members getting shot or arrested, and he has had enough. But how does he get out? What is his exit strategy? Often, it is the military. What you may be thinking is, "the military conducts background checks—how can he pass one of those?" They do, that's right, but not all gang members who commit crimes have been arrested, tried, and convicted for those crimes. And for some of those who have, recruiters can provide waivers for "past mistakes."

Whether our gang-involved youth makes the decision on his own, or he encounters a proactive and persuasive military recruiter, he decides to change his ways and turn over a new leaf. He joins the military and starts basic training. A few months later, he is at his first duty assignment. The unit has been to a war zone, but they are not scheduled to return any time soon. Most of what he needs to know is what he learned in basic training. He works the equivalent of an 8–10 hour per day job. He finds that he now has free time, and he decides to expand his social life.

He goes downtown (or somewhere on the military installation) to a club, where he meets some other guys. He realizes they're all getting along well. One of them says something in a way that sounds familiar, like he had some experience on the street, and our previously gang-involved recruit follows up on what the guy said. As it turns out, the other guy was a gang member in a "previous life," too. The two of them have several conversations over the following days and weeks, discussing the many trials and challenges of gang life and adapting to the military. One day, one of them mentions having had a whole bunch of money at one point, or a friend in their unit who was looking for some drugs, or something else that reminds one or both about a favorable experience in their previous life in the gang.

To make a long story short, they make a bad decision and decide to join forces and experiences, and start a new gang in their new location. Imagine now, they begin recruiting fellow service members. The service members they're recruiting have never been in a gang, but they like these guys and they know what it's like to be in an organization that has rank structure. The formerly gang-involved soldiers are fun to hang around and they tell great stories about their life before the military. Regardless of what gets them involved in gang-like activity, they are involved. The makings of a gang are there. While some service members become members of, or affiliate with, gangs after joining the military, others join the military to try to leave a gang, and still others join the military specifically for certain training which would benefit their gang.

I know. I know. That doesn't happen, right? As you will see in this chapter and the following chapter (if you haven't seen already), it does, but I understand your doubt. In fact, one of the early, anonymous reviewers of my proposal neatly summarized the skepticism I often hear—that it was "unrealistic to imagine that strict military regimes would allow sufficient free time for gangbanging." I've heard the same thing from street smart former military members and even former members of some street gangs. But other current and former gang-involved individuals—especially those in the leadership ranks—will likely tell you the military doesn't work to keep folks from gangbanging.

I'll explain with this—a peacetime mission is little more than a typical day job in the location of the military's choosing. The myth that contemporary service members have regimented schedules, in which there is no time for them to live their lives is wrong. It may have been that way when there was a draft in this country, but that was over half a century ago! It's the military, not prison after all. A recruit's schedule may be more regimented and filled in basic training, but after a few weeks of strict control by others, there are years of much more balanced life. This is surely not your grandfather's military!

The Problem with Street Gang Members, OMGs, and DTEs in the Military

The core problem with military-trained street gang, OMG, and DTE group members is they have primary loyalty to the organization, and organization leaders, and not to the military or their military leadership. Additionally, the military training they receive includes tactics they can easily teach others. Finally, this training is a problem because neither military, nor civilian, police officers are typically trained to respond to assaultive military tactics.

Military service members who are also members of one of these groups have an ongoing dilemma—their complete loyalty is expected from both organizations they serve. On the one hand, they are expected to support and defend the Constitution and obey the orders of the president and officers appointed over them.[15] On the other hand, leaders of their gang require a sworn oath to the beliefs and laws of the members of the gang.[16] When scholars have examined the various aspects of gang life, loyalty within the gang organization has received little attention.

The indoctrination phase of the military cannot be accurately compared to those used by gangs. The threat of punishment may be present in both—whether financial, limiting of opportunities, or being ostracized. But the threat of physical injury (as a matter of policy) is present only in the gang. Individuals who hold positions in both the military and a gang clearly present a threat to the security of the military unit and community.[17] While some folks think the military training a recruit receives would break them from, or inoculate them against, the inclination to engage in gang activity or behavior, that is not what I have seen. Yes, the military discipline can be helpful when recruits want to change, but it does not force them to change.

As researchers Alpert, Rojek, Hansen, Shannon, and Decker found in a study funded by the Department of Justice, while the military exerts considerable energy socializing enlisted men and women into their primary role as soldiers, some gang members still hold on to their gang identities. Sadly, the military environment often fails to provide the turning point that placed some individuals on a path away from gang life.[18] As Knox summarized, gang members in the military demonstrate a unique condition of deviance: "someone who literally marches under two sets of colors and to two different drummers, one legitimate (the military) and one illegitimate (the gang)."[19]

The relationship between service in the military and desistance from criminal activity is also an issue. Researchers Galiani, Rossi, and Schargrodsky examined the process of drafting young men into military service in Argentina.[20] They looked at a cohort of males born between 1958–1962 and determined that military service increased the likelihood of developing an adult criminal record, both during peacetime and wartime.[21] They identified positive effects of military service, too. They noted, especially, that military service taught obedience and discipline, which can limit criminality. They suspected that it might improve labor market prospects, too, preventing the inclination to commit property crime. They also observed that military service tended to incapacitate young men from the ability to commit crimes while in the service. Galiani et al. also identified alternative, negative effects of military service, including the delay in entrance into the labor market that it creates, which limits opportunities. They saw it as a negative that military service provides firearms training, reducing the entry costs to crime. And, they suggested that military service provides a social environment that is prone to violent responses.[22]

Researchers Albaek, Leth-Petersen, le Maire, and Tranaes found that military service reduced the likelihood of criminality for those previously disposed to commit crime.[23] In a study of Danish youth who were born in 1964 and drafted into the military while they were between ages 19–22, military service was found to reduce property crime for up to five years. Albaek et al. found no effect on the commission of violent crime from military service and no effect for most draftees.[24] More recently, Teachman and Tedrow, studying external influences for the National Institute of Child Health and Human Development, suggested that voluntary military service did not affect the risk of committing or being convicted of violent crimes.[25] In the first U.S. study to focus on the effect of military service on crime in the twenty-first century, they found voluntary military service reduced the likelihood of contact with the criminal justice system, especially for men with a history of delinquent or criminal behavior prior to enlisting. They studied a cohort of men born between 1980 and 1984, and found voluntary military service significantly reduced the risk of committing or being convicted of non-violent crimes.[26]

On a related topic, family and criminal law professor Michael Boucai made the argument that intentional and active recruitment of criminals would provide a recruitment pool for the military and provide a disciplinary foundation on which individual criminal reform could be attempted.[27] Boucai noted that the military regularly provided waivers for recruits with misdemeanor and felony crimes on their record. Additionally, the enlistment process often depended on the recruit to tell the truth about their criminal history, as juvenile records may be off-limits to the recruiter.[28] As a result, service members were able to enlist with criminal histories and neither requested, nor received, a waiver. Most of those service members did well to avoid committing a crime during the term of their enlistment, Boucai found. Military service has been shown to help reduce an individual's criminal propensity. Why not, then, he wondered, change the informal policy of allowing recruits with criminal history and actively solicit them?[29]

Counting military gang members. Soldiers on a ridge in silhouette demonstrating the difficulty with counting the number of gang members in the military. Source: iStockPhoto

HOW MANY GANG MEMBERS ARE THERE IN THE MILITARY?

While it would be nice to have a solid number or percentage of military service members with gang affiliations, those numbers are as elusive in the military as they are in the civilian community. The easy answer is, it depends on who you ask, and what formula you use. What we know from research supported by funding from the Department of Justice is that there has been no systematic effort to identify how many gang-involved individuals were in the military nor any effort to reasonably measure their related criminal and otherwise disruptive activities.[30]

Per the U.S. Army's long-stated position, gang members represent "less than one percent" of all military members. That number may be intended to represent an insignificant amount, but the attempt at minimization of the issue misses the mark. At any given time, the number of military service members fluctuates, but the military had 1,333,240 active duty service members and 817,384 reservists at the start of 2017. That's a total of 2.15 million.[31] If less than 1/100th of them are gang members, then we only need to be concerned about 21,500 service members who could be simultaneously involved in criminal gangs. While that is a relatively small number if we are considering the size of a city, it represents a sizable number of influential and dangerous individuals. Organizations with which you may be familiar, which also have in the range of 20,000 members, for example, include the Aryan Brotherhood, a nationwide prison gang; the membership of the International Association of Chiefs of Police (IACP); and the student body at Harvard University.

Knox's survey of Illinois National Guard members in Chicago in the early 1990s found:

- 27.9 percent had one, or more, close friends or associates who are gang members.
- 12.8 percent reported having five, or more, such close friends/associates who were gang members.
- 77.8 percent believed gang leaders would have made good soldiers.[32]

The National Guardsmen that were surveyed were asked to estimate, based on their knowledge, what percent of all U.S. military members were gang members. With a mean of 21.5 percent, the lowest estimate was zero, while the highest was 75 percent. The group found the highest percentage of gang members in the National Guard with a mean of 25.6 percent.[33] The survey was conducted at a time when the court system was still finding creative ways to rehabilitate offenders by overtly releasing them to the military in lieu of prosecution. Knox observed that when offenders were paroled to the military, the socialization of the military was useful in reducing recidivism.[34] I don't think the problem has decreased in the last few decades, either. Surveys I have conducted in many parts of the country have shown a range of 18 to 52 percent of the jurisdictions represented had gang members who were currently in the military.

Hunter Glass has suggested there might be more of a problem. He pointed out that many gang members were being released on the streets of America, "trained in arms and combat by the best military in the world." What hits the press is only a small fraction of the problem, he suggested. Many of the extremists feel they are "on a mission . . . these guys are secret agents in their own minds."[35]

THE EFFECT ON MILITARY UNITS

Generally, military rules, publications, and regulations have shown that gang and extremist group membership is inconsistent with military service. Commanders are expected to put policies in place to keep service members from being active gang and extremist group members. Training of military leadership is part of the prevention strategy and gang and extremist activity may occur among military members anyway. In every report to date, street gangs have been more prevalent than either OMGs or DTEs, and yet it often appears that an equal effort is made to investigate members in each category.

A gang-affiliated military member generally must have committed a gang-related crime to be identified as a gang member. Gang affiliation alone will not result in a gang member's discharge from military service. Punitive actions are subject to the discretion of the commander, who may elect not to discipline or discharge a gang-affiliated military member, especially if the member is not considered disruptive or insubordinate. Many criminal and gang-related incidents have been addressed as conduct or administrative matters. To further thwart the possibility of effectively addressing the problem, the frequent turnover of commanders often inhibits implementation of effective enforcement policies. Some of the other complications inherent in the military system include:

- The military demographically reflects American society and has up to 20 percent in annual personnel turnover.
- There is usually a default denial of gang activity and involvement from the military leadership/community.
- There is no military street gang, OMG, or DTE knowledge base, resulting in differences of opinions and definition and a lack of expertise by those who would investigate the crimes committed by group members.
- There are also restrictions on intelligence collection for groups where criminal activity is expected due to the nature of the group.

The following are examples of how a military unit can be affected when there are active members of street gangs, OMGs, or DTEs in the ranks:

- The unit morale suffers, and there is a lack of trust and cohesiveness among unit members, affecting unit readiness. When rival groups operate in a military unit, the whole unit suffers.
- The polarization of those in the involved groups occurs. Those who support one group cannot be expected to work closely with members of another group. The presence of members of street gangs, OMGs, and DTE groups in a military unit undermines the collective confidence of unit members.
- Unit productivity and mission accomplishment can be seriously affected. The unit will not work well together in either the training for or execution of their mission.

The FBI has consistently reported gang members may enlist in the military to escape their current environment or gang lifestyle. Some members may also enlist to receive weapons, combat, and convoy support training; to obtain access to weapons and explosives; or as an alternative to incarceration.[36] There is a growing concern with street gang, OMG, and DTE group members enlisting in the military with the hope of learning the art of war. Upon discharge, or perhaps before, they may employ their military training against law enforcement officials and rivals.[37] Such military training could ultimately result in more organized, sophisticated, and deadly groups, as well as an increase in deadly assaults on law enforcement officers.[38]

THE EFFECT ON CIVILIAN COMMUNITIES

Gang members in the military are involved in the theft and sale of military weapons, ammunition, and equipment, including body armor.[39] According to a conversation recorded by an undercover FBI agent, one U.S. soldier may have stolen military body armor with the intent to supply Chicago gangs with the stolen equipment.[40] Military weapons and supplies have been stolen by both gang-affiliated and by non-gang-affiliated military personnel who sold the weapons to gang members or other criminals on U.S. city streets.[41] Law enforcement officials nationwide have encountered active service members selling or attempting to sell stolen military weapons, supplies, and drugs to civilian gang members and criminals.[42] The FBI noted that U.S. Senate testimony dating back to 1993 revealed that military weapons were being sold at public gun shows, some in their original government packaging.[43] Those weapons obviously ended up in the civilian communities.

As early as the 1980s, *Teen Angels* magazine, the self-described "gang rights activist news organization," regularly encouraged military enlistment.[44] Both active-duty and former military gang-members use their military training, including their knowledge of weapons handling, against rival gang members and law enforcement officers in the community.[45] In 2007, the FBI reported that some law enforcement officials had adjusted their tactics to accommodate MTGMs.[46]

Gus Eyler, a Yale law student, researched the threats posed by MTGMs, examined military policies regarding gang affiliation, and made recommendations for new regulations.[47] Eyler determined that gang members threatened unit order and compromised security and the critical news reports published after reported incidents of military gang activity were a threat to the public perception of the armed services.[48] Moreover, the military justice system was not equipped to prosecute service members who participated in criminal gang activity.

Sazonov, the graduate student at John Jay College of Criminal Justice, conducted interviews of current and former military personnel, male and female, from New York City, Chicago, and San Diego between November 2009 and November 2010.[49] He found some military officers and non-commissioned officers got involved in gang activity and allowed lower ranking gang members to engage in gang activity. One Gangster Disciple stated he personally engaged in weapons theft and battery for which he was never caught. A Crips-affiliated respondent stated that he did not personally engage in weapons theft, but knew of other gang-affiliated personnel who did.[50] Another Gangster Disciples affiliated respondent admitted to shooting an individual and committing a burglary while in the Army. Another respondent, an admitted gang member, engaged in property theft and distribution of marijuana and methamphetamine. If non-gang affiliated personnel observed or reported a gang member, retaliation in the form of assault was likely to follow, he learned. A Gangster Disciples affiliated sergeant said there were several instances of gang-related stabbings that took place on and off the military installation.[51]

HOW DO MTGMs ENLIST?

The increase in gang presence in the military in recent years is not surprising. The economic downturn in the early part of the twenty-first century may have caused some to seek better employment opportunities. Although the average gang member's criminal record and associations might have precluded

Military Enlistment. Gang members can enter the military if they have no criminal record, lie about having one, or get a waiver for one that they have. Source: iStockPhoto

membership in the military, the standards for recruits were lowered since the increase in troop strength following the terrorist attacks of 9/11. Military recruiters typically have had to find recruits that met quite stringent standards. Alvarez, examining military waivers in 2007, learned that less than three-tenths of young people aged seventeen to twenty-four were fully qualified to join the Army, meaning they had a high school diploma, met aptitude test score requirements and fitness levels and would not be barred for other reasons. That struggle to increase recruitment led to increases in waivers which essentially lowered the physical and moral standards of recruits.[52] Moral waivers allowed soldiers with criminal histories to enlist without further restriction. Alvarez noted in 2006 that more than one-tenth of recruits in the U.S. Army had criminal histories.[53]

Most moral waivers have been for serious misdemeanors—often those committed as a juvenile. As Douglas Smith, public information officer for the Army, said, "People make mistakes in their lives and they can overcome those mistakes." Because so few recruits were fully qualified to join, the military increased the number of recruits they were accepting with criminal backgrounds. Without those waivers, the service members would have been barred from service. What clearly wasn't taken into account was that in order for a gang member to get a misdemeanor on their record they often had to commit several felonies. In addition to the chance of being caught each time being low, once there is an arrest, trial, and conviction, there are likely to be strong incentives to plea bargain a felony prosecution to a misdemeanor. Representative Martin Meehan, then chairman of the House Armed Services Subcommittee on Investigations and Oversight, said this about such waivers, "By lowering standards, we are endangering the rest of our armed forces and sending the wrong message to potential recruits across the country."

John Hutson, a former judge advocate general of the Navy, suggested that the military be cautious when deciding to accept recruits with criminal records. There was a reason, he said, why allowing people with criminal histories into the military had long been the exception rather than the rule. "If you are recruiting somebody who has demonstrated some sort of antisocial behavior and then you are a putting a gun in their hands, you have to be awfully careful about what you are doing," Mr. Hutson said. "You are not putting a hammer in their hands, or asking them to sell used cars. You are potentially asking them to kill people."[54]

To see how the moral waivers policy worked in practice, a CBS affiliate in Denver, Colorado, sent a man into a recruiting office, asking the recruiter if it mattered that he was in a gang. At first, the recruiter advised him the Army didn't accept recruits who were gang members. A senior recruiter then interjected that he may have had some gang activity in the past, but that did not disqualify him.[55] The reporter noted that just a few years into the wars in Afghanistan and Iraq, from 2004 to 2005, the number of recruits brought into the Army with serious criminal misconduct waivers had jumped 54 percent, drug and alcohol waivers increased 13 percent, and misdemeanor waivers increased 25 percent.[56]

According to Eyler, moral waivers were granted using a holistic concept of review at the recruiting and enlistment stage.[57] Those reviews considered the severity of the offense(s), the applicant's capacity for reform, and the degree to which the applicant met other Army standards.[58] Army policies directed recruiters to balance competing interests, share information, and give discretion to the individuals most familiar with the applicant when determining whether the applicant should be allowed to enlist. Shortcomings in the execution of those policies undermined good intentions and lent support to critics' claims of lowered standards for recruitment.[59] Sazonov suggested gang members did not present a threat to national security, but the safety of military units, where large numbers of gang members were present, was worrisome.[60] He also learned that generally, the military recruiter's inability to identify gang members allowed them to join the military. Many of the gang members he spoke with reported they lied about their gang affiliation and history.[61]

WHY ARE THEY A PROBLEM?

Gangs are a problem for military communities, much as they are for civilian communities. Those engaging in the gang lifestyle are inherently a security threat to the community and cannot be depended on to support the community. There has been no empirical effort by either the military or gang scholars to examine why gang-involved individuals enlist in the military.[62] Nor has there been much of an effort to examine their effect on the community once they are released from the military. What is known is that the presence of street gangs, OMGs, and DTEs in the military has served to undermine the values, equal opportunity, and legitimate authority of the community.[63]

Manwaring examined gangs from an internal-threat perspective.[64] Though the military has not yet acknowledged different "generations" or "levels" of gang activity, Manwaring clearly identified the various threat levels posed by gangs in the Third Generation. Those gangs did not operate like those that the military (and many of the police departments in our country) are prepared for. They are proactive in their growth, strategic in their operations, and ambitious in their planning. The activity of those gangs generates an annual profit in the billions of dollars.[65] Consequently, they are able to afford to recruit and employ the best—and easily access military training to further their cause.

DATA FROM OFFICIAL REPORTS

The Military Criminal Investigative Organizations (MCIO)—the Army Criminal Investigation Command (CID), Air Force Office of Special Investigations (AFOSI), and Naval Criminal Investigative Service (NCIS)—have identified military personnel with gang membership, or affiliation, in every branch of the military.[66] While military law prohibits active membership in such "extremist" groups, street gangs, OMGs, and DTE groups all have members who have enlisted. Group members and associates who joined the military may have joined to get away from the lifestyle and the criminal temptations associated with it. They may also have been trying to acquire military training and access to weapons and sensitive information.[67] The Army's annual threat assessments have been regularly requested and obtained as part of the research for this book.

Most of the Army's annual threat assessments (identified now as U.S. Army Gang and Domestic Extremist Activity Threat Assessments, or GDEATA), since their inception in 2005, have reported an increase in both gang-related investigations and incidents over previous years. The most commonly reported gang-related crime has been drug trafficking, which has encompassed most of the gang-related offenses reported in all assessments for all organization types (street gang, OMG, DTE).[68] Assaults, homicides, and robberies have also frequently been reported as gang-related crimes.[69] Official inquiries by other branches have yielded much the same results.[70,71]

In 2010 and 2014, the Army experienced a slight decrease in all gang-related criminal investigations and an overall decrease in felony investigations with an Army connection. There was no satisfactory explanation for the decreases, which were followed the next year by significant increases in both gang-related and all felony investigations, enough to support the observation that gang activity in the military was consistently increasing, at least based on the Army's investigative reporting. There were also fewer overall felony investigations year to year in 2007, 2009, and 2015, as well, yet no mention was made of those changes, and the number of gang investigations increased in those years. The authors of the assessments speculated that the decrease might be attributed to the continued awareness of gangs and extremists by commanders or the elimination of identified members from the Army. The changes might also have been correlated to the decrease in all CID felony investigations, they suggested. The decrease in all crimes was not explained further.

Nowhere in any of the CID reports was there information regarding the number of gang members who had been prosecuted or otherwise removed from the military, nor was any mention made regarding notification of law enforcement in the civilian community that received the discharged gang member. Recently, the Army started distinguishing street gangs from OMGs and DTE groups in their annual reports. No explanation was made for the change. Typically, Army CID GDEATAs have identified most subjects of gang-related activity as enlisted, single males, between the ages of 18–24. That fit the official description of an average Army soldier.[72]

The NGIC has included MTGMs in their periodic reports on gangs and recently found that known or suspected gang members in over 100 responding jurisdictions had sought, or obtained, employment in the military or a public criminal justice field in the previous two years. Employment with the U.S. military was the most common, followed by corrections. Army CID recently became more involved in collecting data on MTGMs nationwide and expanding the focus of the NGIC questionnaire. In the 2015 NGIC survey, the following military-trained gang-related questions were added for the first time:

- Within the past two years, have gang members in your jurisdiction applied for, or gained, employment in any of the following fields (check all that apply)? Potential Responses were Law Enforcement, Corrections, Judiciary/ Courts, Military.
- In your jurisdiction, do you ask street gang members about their military affiliation or related employment (Active Duty, Reserves, National Guard, Dependent Family Member, Government Civilian Employee, or Government Contractor)? Yes and No were the only options offered. In follow-up, the next line states: If yes, please indicate who you notify if a gang member is affiliated with the military.
- Approximately what percentage of street gangs in your jurisdiction have current or former military experience or display behavior indicative of military training? Choices were 0 (none or less than 1 percent), 1–10 percent, 11–20 percent, 21–30 percent, 31–40 percent, 41–50 percent, and over 50 percent.

You'll note some similarities to the survey I designed, the Modified Military Gang Perception Questionnaire (MMGPQ). That was a result of several conversations with the (now former) CID Command Intelligence Analyst. I also adjusted the MMGPQ survey after collaborating with her and the analysts for the other military branches. Answers to those questions will help law enforcement at all levels ensure they and their communities are prepared for the effects of MTGMs. None of the responses to the 2015 NGIC Survey questions regarding MTGMs were published.

MTGMs IN STREET GANGS, OMGs, AND DTEs

The Army CID (and other branch MCIOs) have been reporting on gang-related investigations since 2005. The CID has published an assessment annually, with varying degrees of detail and analysis, apparently dependent on the authors' focus. There were a total of 1,598 reports, both Reports of Investigation/Law Enforcement Reports (ROI/LERs) and Criminal Intelligence (CRIMINTEL), identified from 2002–2015. Of that, 374 were felony criminal investigations by CID. An additional 1,224 cases did not rise to that standard, but were nonetheless investigated to some extent.

In the early years of the renewed, post-9/11 interest in gangs in the military, Army CID found that typically street gangs were the major problem, so much so that the reports counted all gang activity together, apparently because the statistics from OMGs and DTEs were relatively insignificant. That occurred through 2009 and included a summary of the incidents recorded Army-wide. There was a different layout and substantially different depth of analysis up to that point, as well.

The annual reports have differentiated between ROI, recently changed to LER and CRIMINTEL. The primary difference between the two is the severity of the crime. Army CID investigates mostly serious felony crimes, for which an ROI is often the chosen reporting mechanism. If a reported crime does not qualify as a serious felony, it will usually be referred to another agency—often the Military Police. CRIMINTEL reports are used for investigations with CID interest, but not investigative responsibility, or when simply documenting information that did not amount to the reporting of criminal activity. Those reports may include investigations by the Military Police or civilian law enforcement, or simply the results of undeveloped information received by a CID agent. Done properly, proactive investigations such as those involving criminal gang activity can be conducted as CRIMINTEL until a felony is identified.

In the 2005 assessment, a report summarizing the number of gang crimes, when there was no intense official focus on them from the Command level, there were ten gang-related ROIs, out of a total of over 10,000 ROIs Army-wide, and thirteen gang-related CRIMINTEL reports. There were twenty-six subjects identified and most of the incidents appeared to involve the Gangster Disciples and Crips. The report noted that the crimes involving Gangster Disciples were more sophisticated than the crimes perpetrated by other gangs. It was observed that in 2005, there was an increase in gang crimes over the previous years, with no effort made to determine the cause of the increase.

The number of gang-related crimes seemed to somewhat trend with the size of the installation, though little mention of that was made as an explanation. The highest number of gang-related investigations was at Fort Hood, Texas, with four, followed by Fort Leonard Wood, Missouri, and Grafenwoehr/Hohenfels, Germany, tied with three. Fort Wainwright, Alaska, tied with Iraq/Kuwait and Japan with two gang-related investigations each. Assaults, to include aggravated assault, attempted murder, and murder, were the most frequently listed crimes, followed by drugs.

In 2006, there were sixteen gang-related ROIs, out of a total of over 10,000 ROIs Army-wide, and forty-four CRIMINTEL reports identified in the assessment. There were twenty-seven subjects and most of the incidents appeared to involve the Gangster Disciples and a group called Street Military. It was observed that again in 2006 there was a significant increase in gang crimes over the previous years, with no effort made to determine the cause of the increase.

The number of gang-related crimes continued to trend with the size of the installation, though little mention of that was made as an explanation. The highest number of gang-related investigations was at Fort Hood with nine, followed by Fort Campbell with eight, and Fort Lewis with six. Fort Leonard Wood followed with five, and Ansbach, Germany, tied with Fort Bragg, Fort Drum, New York, and Fort Richardson, Alaska, with four apiece. Assaults, to include attempted murder, murder, and sexual assaults, were the most frequently listed with six, followed by drug crimes with five and robbery, with two incidents.

In the 2007 assessment, there were seventeen gang ROIs, out of a total of over 8,000 ROIs army-wide, and sixty-two CRIMINTEL reports. There were twenty-nine subjects and most of the incidents appeared to involve the Gangster Disciples and the Latin Kings. While the number of ROIs did not increase significantly, as a proportion of overall ROIs there was a significant increase over the previous years, yet no effort was made to determine the cause of the increase.

The highest number of gang-related investigations were at Fort Lewis with ten, then Fort Sill, Oklahoma, and Fort Campbell with five, followed by Fort Hood with four. Fort Leonard Wood followed with five, and Ansbach, Germany, tied with Fort Jackson, South Carolina, Fort Bliss, and Fort Richardson, Alaska, at three apiece. Assaults (including homicides) were tied with drug-related crime, with a total of six investigations, followed by theft, one of which was reported.

In 2008, there were twenty-seven gang ROIs, out of a total of over 8,000 ROIs Army-wide, and ninety-two CRIMINTEL reports. There were sixty-three subjects and most of the incidents appeared to involve the Bloods (nine incidents), followed by the Gangster Disciples (four incidents). It was observed that again in 2008 there was a noteworthy increase in gang crimes over the previous years, with no effort made to determine the cause of the increase. The report noted that the crimes involving the Bloods gang members were more sophisticated than the others and the Crips gang was more prevalent within the Army environment from previous years. If that were the case, the reports did not adequately reflect it, although the observation may be considering the number of self-identified gang members, not those who were caught in the commission of a crime.

The number of gang-related crimes continued to trend with the size of the installation, though inconsistent identification of that variable was made. The highest number of gang-related investigations was at Fort Lewis with eighteen, and Fort Hood with fourteen. Fort Meade, Maryland, reported thirteen, and Fort Bragg and Fort Irwin, California, each had five. The report noted that Fort Bliss, Fort Bragg, and Schofield Barracks, Hawaii, had shown consistent increases for the last three fiscal years, but noted those were larger installations with larger troop populations. Assaults, to include attempted murder, murder, and sexual assaults, were the most frequently listed with twelve, followed by drug crimes with five, and robbery, with three reported incidents.

In 2009, there were thirty-four gang ROIs, out of a total of over 8,000 ROIs army-wide, and 109 CRIMINTEL reports. There were sixty-three subjects, and most of the incidents appeared to involve the Bloods with nine, and the Latin Kings, Crips, and the Juggalos tied for a distant second. There was again a remarkable increase in gang crimes over the previous years, with no effort made to determine the cause of the increase. The number of gang-related crimes continued to trend with the size of the installation, though little mention of that was made as an explanation. The highest number of gang-related investigations was at Fort Hood with nine, followed by Fort Campbell with eight and Fort Lewis with six. Fort Leonard Wood followed with five, and Ansbach tied with Fort Bragg, Fort Drum, and Fort Richardson with four apiece. Assaults, to include attempted murder, murder, and sexual assaults, were tied with drug crimes for the most frequently listed with eleven, followed by housebreaking/larceny (burglary), with five incidents.

It took some back-and-forth (negotiation) discussions to get the 2010 and 2011 CID threat assessments when I requested them, and when they were sent they reflected a quite abbreviated report. The assessments have little to contribute to a contemporary analysis and were limited enough in substance and information to represent a noteworthy transition in report-writing styles. Due to the dated information, I figured there was no need to attempt to obtain a more comprehensive report. While FY 2010 saw a decrease in gang-related investigations as noted elsewhere, FY 2011 brought enough gang-related investigations to make up the difference. There was none of the detail of individual incidents seen previously, although it appeared in 2010 that an attempt to explain year-to-year changes might soon occur. The sparse amount of information in 2011 and the following years proved otherwise.

MTGMs in Street Gangs

In the most recently examined U.S. Army CID GDEATAs, from FY 2012–2015, ninety-four total felony reports of investigation involved members of street gangs. Drugs were the focus of forty-eight of the investigations; fourteen were homicide-related; and ten were sex crime-related. The remaining cases were comprised of various offenses such as robbery, assault, extortion, larceny, and failure to obey. There were ninety subjects identified, fifty-eight of them were soldiers, forty-eight of whom were active duty. Most of the street gang subjects were African American males who were 20–24 years old, single, and junior enlisted (E1–E4).[73]

In addition to the investigations, there were 147 CRIMINTEL reports associated with street gangs from 2012–2015. Within the CRIMINTEL reports, 209 individuals were identified as having suspected affiliation with street gangs. There were 114 soldiers, of whom 105 were active duty. The remaining individuals included seventy-six with no DoD affiliation and sixteen otherwise DoD-affiliated persons.

While the CID has stopped providing case summaries, a sampling from excerpts in FY 2012 was enlightening, and representative of the gang investigations conducted:

- A Fort Bliss soldier was in possession of Crip gang documentation and blue bandanas, which were located during a search. The soldier admitted to being a Crip prior to enlisting in the Army. The commander was briefed on the soldier's gang involvement and indicated the soldier would be involuntarily released from the military.
- Three Fort Campbell soldiers were involved in an on-post shooting. One of the soldiers was identified as a member of the Crips and had tattoos of a six-pointed star (symbolic of the Folk Nation) and "Thug Life." The shooting investigation was determined to be non-gang related. The unit commander was briefed on the soldier's apparent involvement in a gang.

MTGMs in Outlaw Motorcycle Gangs (OMG)

In the FY 2012–2015 GDEATAs, twenty-five of the felony investigations involved OMGs with twenty-eight subjects, and all but one of them were active duty soldiers. The investigations involved the offenses of murder, wrongful distribution of drugs, assault, fraud, and failure to obey. Most subjects in the felony OMG investigations were white males who were 20–24 years old and senior enlisted (E5–E9).

There were an additional 356 CRIMINTEL reports associated with OMGs from 2012–2015. Within the CRIMINTEL reporting, 473 subjects were suspected of affiliation with OMGs. There were 297 soldiers, 264 of whom were on active duty. The remaining individuals included ninety-two with no DoD affiliation and ninety otherwise DoD-affiliated persons. The 2015 Assessment reported the number of OMG investigations more than doubled. It was suggested that the increase was due to greater awareness and improved tracking and reporting by CID offices.

While the CID has stopped providing case summaries, a sampling from FY 2012 is considered enlightening and representative of the OMG investigations conducted:

- A Fort Carson soldier was arrested for first degree murder for the shooting of a civilian after a fight at the Sin City Deciples clubhouse. On February 13, the soldier was convicted of manslaughter and was acquitted on the first-degree murder and robbery charges.
- Two U.S. Army Fort Bragg soldiers were identified as members of the Ruff Ryders MC. Those two members were involved in a common robbery and assault case against a civilian at a night club adjacent to Ramsey Street, Fayetteville, North Carolina.

MTGMs in Domestic Terrorist Extremist (DTE) Groups

While street gang and OMG members clearly commit crimes as part of their membership, DTE members were more likely to be political. The Department of Justice does not publish or maintain a list of DTE organizations. That was partly due to First Amendment concerns.[74] The NGIC identified three main types of DTEs: Black separatist extremists, sovereign citizen extremists, and white supremacist extremists.[75]

From 2012–2015, there were twenty-two DTE investigations by Army CID. The DTE investigations involved drug-related offenses, murder, assault, communicating a threat, provoking speech or gestures, threats, and failure to obey. Four investigations involved members of white supremacist groups, two involved militia groups, and one involved an anti-government group. There were fifteen subjects identified, with twelve soldiers, all on active duty. Most DTE-related subjects were white males who were 20–24 years of age, single, and junior enlisted (E1–E4).[76]

There were an additional sixty-five CRIMINTEL reports associated with DTEs from 2012–2015. Within the CRIMINTEL reporting, seventy-six subjects were suspected of affiliation with DTEs. There were forty-one soldiers, thirty-four of whom were on active duty. The remaining individuals included seven with no DoD affiliation and twenty-seven otherwise DoD-affiliated persons. The 2015 Assessment by CID also included an increase in DTE cases. No attempt to explain the increase was made.

While the CID has stopped providing case summaries, a sampling from FY 2012 is considered enlightening and representative of the gang investigations conducted:

- A Fort Sill, Oklahoma, soldier was charged with provoking speeches or gestures after being found in possession of a KKK recruiting card and making racial slurs.
- Four soldiers from Fort Stewart, Georgia, were involved in the deaths of two civilians. Both victims were located at an off-post location with apparent gunshot wounds to their heads. One of the soldiers assembled the group under the name "FEAR" (Forever Enduring Always Ready) with the eventual intention of overthrowing the U.S. government and committing various crimes and bombings on Fort Stewart. One of the victims was initially part of the group; however, he was murdered because he attempted to terminate affiliation with the group. The second victim was murdered because she was with the other victim when he was killed. Many of the soldiers have been convicted in civilian court.[77]

THE FY 2015 GDEATA

The FY 2015 CID Assessment was included in the above numbers, but there were certain parts that were noteworthy.

- The CID continued to focus on identifying a "threat level." For the current year, the threat posed by gangs and DTEs on and off Army installations was *low*. The threat level was determined by comparing the number of gang and DTE investigations to the total of CID investigations for the year. The threat level was first used in the FY 2005 assessment, but the measurements were not articulated until the FY 2007 assessment. The level as initially calculated was: low—up to 5 percent; medium—6 percent, and high—11 percent and up. The only rationale for it has been the percentage of total cases, not potential for increase in numbers or increase in dangerousness. The current rating scale was: negligible—0 percent; low—0.1

percent; medium—3.1 percent, and high—6.1 and up. That rating was first seen in the FY 2012 assessment, with no information regarding the logic for a change of the scale. The current report observed that the threat level was designed in response to numerous media articles referring to gang problems in the military without a corresponding standard to identify how much crime must exist before there is a problem.[78]

- Also noteworthy in the 2015 assessment was the continued absence of a longitudinal analysis of the data. Many assessments have compared one year to the next, and in the early years there were multiple years identified. Never has there been an explanation for significant increases in gang-related activity, and the explanations for the infrequent decreases have had no basis in actual research on causation or claim thereof. In recent years, the assessments appeared to be no more than a benchmark analysis. If there were an actual focus on limiting gang activity in the military, there would be a measured increase or decrease, accompanied by the identification of ongoing or discontinued attempts to address the issue or success stories shared with other law enforcement agencies. As the official reports may not contain all the relevant information, it was hoped that those communications were being made both internally and externally, though with the randomness of the observations, that was doubtful.[79]

- An increased focus in the potential effect of gang involvement on security clearances was first seen in 2012. Among the recommendations for FY 2015 was that commanders, MPI, and CID report soldiers' gang and DTE affiliation confirmed by other law enforcement agencies (presumably in a CRIMINTEL report) to the unit security officer.[80] I believe the effects of gang affiliation and alliance are a major concern, and if gang-affiliation was tolerated of recruits, either expressly or implicitly, it should be limited to recruits filling those military positions where access to classified material is seriously limited.

CONCLUSION

Though many reports were focused on the commission of crime by gang members, it was important to remember the gang lifestyle, when contradictory to that of the community, can lead to social conflict. Crime does not need to occur, be detected, or be reported for there to be problems with street gangs, OMGs, and DTE group members in the military. Dual membership pits the loyalty and responsibilities a member has for the criminal group in regular conflict with the loyalty and duties to the military.[81] That conflict exists even for those gang members who are not "active."[82] McVeigh,

Burmeister, and Apodaca are all well-known examples of the dangers that resulted from dual membership in groups with diametrically opposed views. The good news is the required summaries of investigations were being generated over ten years after the order was given in 2005. The bad news is that there continues to be limited and useless analysis and even less justification or support for the recommendations in each report.

The summaries have consistently shown the concerns expressed by elected officials, military lawyers, law students, and others are legitimate. The recent focus on subcategories of gang members serves to identify which of the gang types are being identified. It doesn't necessarily show which types are a bigger problem for the military. Clearly there have been problems with gang members committing crimes while in the military and that seemed to be a continuing problem. What wasn't clear was the level of commitment, or strategy, of military or government leaders. If there is ever a concerted effort to limit the ability of gang-involved recruits to join the military, the annual assessments will provide a solid foundation for that effort. If you would like to see the above data in table form, check out the website for the book—http://www.gangsandthemilitary.com.

Chapter Six

Military-Trained Gang Members in Civilian Communities

On July 7, 2016, military veteran Micah Johnson shot fourteen police officers in Dallas, Texas. Five of the officers died. Johnson was in the Army Reserve from 2009–2015 and had served in Afghanistan from 2013–2014. Johnson had been a member of the Houston chapter of the New Black Panther Party, a group that believed Black Americans should have their own nation and advocated violence against whites.[1] Johnson had stated he wanted to kill white people, especially white police officers. Detectives found bomb-making materials, ballistic vests, rifles, ammunition, and a personal journal of combat tactics. Johnson tried to take refuge in a parking garage and exchanged gunfire with police. Johnson died when the police used a bomb disposal remote control robot to blow him up after negotiations for his surrender failed.[2] The attack caused the highest number of police deaths since 9/11. The incident demonstrated the dangerousness of MTGMs in the civilian community, especially those that espoused DTE beliefs.

As we saw in the previous chapter, Army CID has conducted annual gang threat assessments since the two gang-related deaths of soldiers occurred in 2005. Military-trained gang members, the vast majority of whom are adults, have been reported in all branches of the military since then. While there have been changes in substance and format, and only limited analysis and reporting, the data provided in the annual CID assessments have been useful. It has shown that despite an apparent lack of commitment to address the entirety of the problem, especially with respect to the effect on the civilian community, the inadvertent detection of gang members while they are in the military is being tracked.

In this chapter, we will examine street gang, OMG, and DTE members who have transitioned from the military back to the civilian community.

As I have stated previously, I believe this is the biggest issue, and the only issue that can be addressed without assistance coming from the military. Veterans without gang affiliations often have a difficult time getting reacquainted with the civilian community. To add the potential for bias against gang-involved veterans to the list of hurdles to overcome is asking too much. The problem is obviously bigger than the military, but that's where the solution should start.

TRANSITION TO MILITARY-TRAINED GANG MEMBERS IN THE COMMUNITY

Originally, the focus for those of us who were investigating the issue was on gangs in the military, or more properly stated, gang members in the military. The problem was ongoing and there never seemed to be enough interest by the military leadership to design and implement effective prohibitions to limit gang membership. It seemed like no gang member ever caused enough of a problem while serving in the military and the military leadership never felt like the military was being infiltrated or overcome, despite the events of 1995 and 2005.

As I mentioned previously, in 2007, I stopped talking about *gangs in the military* and started talking about *military trained gang members* in the civilian community. I had been doing the former for about fifteen years, and I had seen relatively few changes in the way the issue was handled above the installation level. With reports from the U.S. Army CID, Air Force OSI, and the FBI's National Gang Intelligence Center during that time, and the later report by Navy NCIS, many civilian criminal investigators have since realized that gang members with military training were bringing that training back to the civilian communities and local police officers would need to be able to deal with it.

With the wars in Iraq and Afghanistan in the past, or so we thought at the time, fewer people sincerely thought that gang members with military training were going to arbitrarily cease being a concern. In fact, more were concerned because they brought their training and gangbanging back to our civilian communities, requiring local police officers to be able, and equipped, to deal with an increased threat, often without advanced warning. For civilian law enforcement, the focus began to shift from a passing interest in gang members in the military to a focused study of gang members with military training who had returned to their civilian communities or, as we identify the issue in the title of this book, gangs *and* the military.

An anonymous service member in Germany throws up gang hand signs when asked by a police officer, according to Detective Hunter Glass. Source: *Hunter Glass*

HOW MANY MILITARY-TRAINED GANG MEMBERS ARE THERE IN THE UNITED STATES?

The short answer is I don't know, but my best estimate is that based on official counts and estimates there are between 20,000 (about 1 percent of the estimated number of gang members in the country) and 200,000 (about 10 percent of the estimated number of gang members in the country). There's more to the analysis than that, but that's the ballpark, "official" figure. If there are around 200,000, that represents about 4,000 per state, just to put it into perspective. Let's look at the long version of the best answer to the question. A few years back, in 2012, there were an estimated 850,000–1.4 million gang members in the U.S. according to reports by the two primary gang-focused government research organizations. For all intents and purposes, those numbers were both 1) inaccurate and 2) the best we have. Here's why.

The National Gang Center (NGC) is jointly funded by the U.S. Department of Justice's (DOJ) Office of Juvenile Justice and Delinquency Prevention (OJJDP) and the Bureau of Justice Assistance (BJA). The NGC has surveyed law enforcement agencies annually since 1995 regarding the number of active gang members in their jurisdictions. During the most recent survey year

(2012), there were approximately 850,000 gang members.[3] That represented an 8.6 percent increase in gangs, which was accompanied by an 11 percent increase in gang members from 2011 to 2012 (the latest years in which data was available at the time of publication). Over the past decade, annual estimates of the number of gang members by the NGC have averaged around 770,000 nationally. There hasn't been such a tally since then, but if there was a 10 percent increase in gang members in each year since (based on the increase from 2011 to 2012), that would mean there were 935,000 in 2013, 1,131,350 in 2015, and 1,368,933 in 2017.

The National Gang Intelligence Center (NGIC) was started in 2005 by the FBI, part of the DOJ, at the direction of Congress. About every two years since then, the NGIC has asked law enforcement around the country about the gang members in their jurisdictions. The 2009 and 2011 surveys identified estimates of 1 million and 1.4 million gang members, respectively, across the country. The 2013 survey was unable to provide an estimate due to "inconclusive reporting and lack of confidence in estimates." The 2015 report did not include any estimates of gang members in the United States, either. Had the number in 2013 continued growing as it had for the previous two years, it might have been closer to 1.9 million and well over 2 million by 2015. By 2017, then, the number of gang members might have exceeded 2.5 million, and by 2019, perhaps close to 3 million. Of course, all the numbers furnished since 2011 are speculation, but I submit that they are infinitely better than the numbers (not) provided by the federally run or supported research organizations tasked with providing numbers. And, as we will see below, they may even be too low. It's important to note that both adult and juvenile gang members are calculated in the estimates of the NGC and NGIC.

While the NGC and the NGIC tried to identify the number of gang members in the United States by asking police officers about the people in their jurisdictions, other researchers have suggested those estimations were significantly lower than research indicates. Gang researchers David Pyrooz and Gary Sweeten recently suggested there were significantly more young people involved with gangs. They used a combination of the National Longitudinal Survey of Youth and the Census to produce a national estimate of gang membership. They estimated there were 1,059,000 juvenile gang members, representing 2.0 percent (about one of every fifty) of persons between the ages five to seventeen years in the U.S. population.[4] For every 401,000 who joined, another 378,000 juveniles exited gangs each year. They found that most who joined a gang left it long before adulthood.

Most Gang Members are Adults

Do you remember the early gangs in Boston and New York? They were all adults, some with groups of juveniles that supported their activities. Most of the gangs since then have been adults, as well, and recent research has shown that is still the case. There have been more adult gang members than juveniles in the United States since at least 1996. The organization known then as the National Youth Gang Center (NYGC—now the NGC) has over fifteen years of gang-related data collected by the annual National Youth Gang Survey of 2,500 U.S. law enforcement agencies. NYGC researchers have found a progressive increase in adult gang members for almost every year since 1996. In 1996, the percentage of gang members was reported to be 50 percent juvenile and 50 percent adults. In 2006, the distribution was 36.5 percent juvenile and 63.5 percent adult. In every year since then, the proportion of adults in the tally has been much higher than the proportion of juveniles.[5] In the last reported year, 2011, 35 percent of the gang members in the United States were juveniles and 65 percent were adults.

In a multi-site study covering 1998–1999, researchers Charles Katz and Vincent Webb examined the police response to gangs to identify the factors that led to the creation of a gang unit, alternative responses to community gang problems, and the relevant beliefs held by gang unit officers.[6] The researchers chose Albuquerque, New Mexico; Inglewood, California; Las Vegas, Nevada; and Phoenix, Arizona, based on their likeliness of response to their existing gang problems and variety of organizational configurations. Most (79 percent and up) of the gang members in Albuquerque, Las Vegas, and Phoenix were young adults between eighteen and thirty-six years old.[7] Age data were not available for Inglewood.

In 2007, the New Jersey State Police (NJSP) Street Gang Bureau collected information about gang activity and analyzed gang trends. In their summary of recent NJSP Gang Surveys, analysts found that most (60 percent) gang members in 2001 were adults. In 2004, 53 percent of the reported gang members were adults. Though that represented a decrease, the number of adult gang members still exceeded the number of juvenile gang members.[8]

The Florida Department of Law Enforcement (FDLE) 2007 Statewide Gang Survey indicated 56.5 percent of the state gang population were adults. The focus of the research was clearly on youth gangs, and the authors of the report noted an average 38.4 percent of gang members were between fifteen and seventeen years of age. The results of the study showed that over half of the gang members were adults.[9]

The Adjusted Count of Gang Members in the United States

So, if Pyrooz and Sweeten's estimates that there were over 1 million juvenile gang members were accurate, there would be no less than an additional 1.1 million adult gang members (if the lower adult-juvenile percentage of 53:47 found by the New Jersey State Police is accurate) to as much as 5.6 million (if the higher adult-juvenile percentage of approximately 85:15 found in one of the studies by Katz and Webb is accurate).[10] That would mean there were actually at least 2.1 million gang members in the United States when the last recorded NGIC tally was conducted in 2011. It could also mean that there were close to 2.6 million in 2013, 2.8 million in 2015, and as many as 3.5 million and 4 million gang members in the United States in 2017 and 2019, respectively, if those numbers continued to climb. And those numbers don't reflect the thousands of OMGs and DTEs in the country!

The 2011 NGIC report observed that there were 44,000 OMG members in 3,000 gangs.[11] The NGIC reported OMGs members represented 2.5 percent of gang members in the United States. The NGIC estimated there were 1.4 million gang members in that report, so 2.5 percent of that was 35,000.[12] In the most recent (2015) report, the NGIC noted that the International Outlaw Motorcycle Gang Investigator's Association (IOMGIA) estimated that for every one OMG member there were an additional ten OMG associates who supported the gang in its legal and illegal activities.[13] No organization has estimated the total number of OMGs to the extent that the number of street gangs has been tallied. The Southern Poverty Law Center has estimated there were 892 Hate (Supremacist) groups and 998 Patriot (often Separatist) groups in the United States at the end of 2016.[14] No organization has estimated the total number of DTEs, but David Pyrooz, Scott Decker, and other gang researchers recently studied the similarities of street gang and DTE group members. They found the average age was 19 and 34 years old for street gang and extremist group members, respectively. They also learned close to 5 percent of street gang members and about 20 percent of DTEs had been in the military.[15] Those estimations are very different than the findings of the 1996 Army-wide task force!

The Adjusted Count of MTGMs in the United States

In my first MTGM surveys of gang cops (in 2009–2010), survey respondents reported roughly 10 percent of their jurisdiction's gang members were MTGMs. In 2014 and 2015, the average (mean) ranged from 6 percent in the northwest United States to 10 percent in the southern United States. In recent surveys, I have simply asked whether the respondents thought the percentage of gang members was 1–10 percent, 11–20 percent, or over 20 percent. On a related note, when asked whether their gang members were currently in the military, the percentage of respondents that acknowledged having active duty MTGMs has ranged from 20–30 percent. When asked whether their gang members were formerly in the military, typically 40–50 percent of respondents have said that they had some of those. Said another way, it appears that about 50 percent of the jurisdictions represented by respondents I have surveyed have MTGMs in their jurisdictions with some form of military training, often because they are, or have been, in the military.

Let's apply this new information about MTGMs in the community with a conservative 7.5 percent estimation of the number of gang members in the United States to the last (2011) tally by the NGIC:

- If 7.5 percent of gang members had military training, and there were an estimated 2.1 million gang members identified by Pyrooz and Sweeten, with an adjusted NGIC count (using a ratio of 53:47 as found by the New Jersey State Police), that would mean there were 147,500 MTGMs in the U.S. in 2017. That number represents the population of a relatively large city in just about every state in the country!
- If the higher adjustment were correct (approximately 85:15 by Katz and Webb), there would be 6.6 million gang members, which would mean there were 495,000 MTGMs in the U.S. in 2017. That's roughly the population of Wyoming!

I know some will criticize the estimations and want to use a more conservative percentage like the long-used estimate by the Army CID that "less than one percent" of service members are gang members. One problem with such a low estimate is that those numbers were based on the number of gang members known by police. As criminologists and criminal justice students everywhere can tell you, the police are not aware of all the criminals in their jurisdictions—only those who have been caught! If what the IOMGIA suggested about OMGs was also true for street gangs or DTEs, there could be a much bigger problem than anyone has imagined. Another problem with that number was that with approximately 22 million veterans among the 316 million people in the United States, that would still mean we had 220,000 MTGMs at any given time. And the number of MTGMs representing 1 percent of the military could be increasing in the civilian community as that number cycles out of the military. Imagine an extra 3,500 MTGMs added to the numbers every year!

WHAT DO THE GANG COPS
AND CORRECTIONS OFFICIALS SAY?

In surveys of gang cops in 2014 and 2015, I asked a lot of questions about how they perceived the problem with MTGMs in their communities. A modified version of the Military Gang Perception Questionnaire (MGPQ) was used to collect data. The MGPQ was designed using current literature, interviews with gang investigators and MTGMs and my own practical experience as a guide.[16] Subject matter experts (retired high-ranking military leaders, university professors with professional experience in gang investigations and

Gang cops work the streets to engage with gang members in a variety of situations. They were asked questions about their perceptions. Source: *iStockPhoto*

activities, and law enforcement officials who were gang specialists) assisted with development and refinement of the survey for length, format, scope, and content validity. Finally, a pilot test was conducted to further validate and assess the reliability of the MGPQ.[17] In the years since, the same methods have been applied to improve upon the questionnaire. The current survey, the Modified Military Gang Perception Questionnaire (MMGPQ), contains questions designed to identify the respondents' perceptions of the presence of MTGMs in their jurisdictions.

The survey asks for responses to questions using a Likert scale to assess the level of agreement with the statement/question (Strongly Disagree, Disagree, No Opinion, Agree, and Strongly Agree). The survey questions specifically refer to the respondents' perception of use of military weapons, equipment, and tactics by gang members in their jurisdictions. Questions are asked to assess indicators of MTGMs, whether they directly obtained the training or training was passed on by someone else who received the training directly, and the knowledge and sources of knowledge regarding MTGMs in the respondents' jurisdictions. Limited demographic and employment-related questions are asked.

Eight primary perception questions and twelve secondary perception, awareness, and demographic questions are asked of respondents. The primary questions are designed to determine the perception of the respondents regarding the presence of MTGMs in his or her community. The current questions, rationale for the questions, and responses are as follows:

1. *Gang members in my jurisdiction are increasingly using military-type weapons or explosives.*

The question is asked to determine the perceived prevalence of military-type weapons or explosives use by gang members. Gang members with military type (assault) weapons and explosives can be a security threat to the community because they may endanger citizens when they conduct drive-by shootings of rival gang members and may be more likely to initiate or engage in potentially deadly confrontations with police.

Several gang members have been found in possession of improvised explosive devices (IEDs), destructive devices, or components. Thankfully, the threat of IEDs and other explosives posed by street gangs remains minimal in the United States.[18] Gang members in some jurisdictions have been found in possession of military explosive hardware and ammunition.[19] A follow-up question asks about the source of the weapons or explosives, if known.

2. *Gang members in my jurisdiction use military-type equipment (body armor, night-vision, etc.).*

The question is asked to determine the perceived prevalence of military-type equipment use by gang members. Gang members with military equipment can be a security threat to the community because they may be able to employ technology-enhanced activities with additional protection against bullets and the ability to see and attack targets in the dark.

The presence of gang members with military-type equipment poses a serious threat to the communities and law enforcement, as they may be more likely to initiate or engage in potentially deadly confrontations with police.[20] A follow-up question is asked about the source of the military-type equipment, if known.

3. *Gang members in my jurisdiction use military-type tactics.*

The question is used to determine the perception of gang use of military tactics by respondents. Advanced combat tactics have become more available to gang members in civilian communities. MTGMs introduce military tactics and training to local gang members, creating an increase in the level of gang violence within the community.[21]

4. *Gang members in my jurisdiction commit home invasions.*

The question is used to determine if respondents naturally considered the movements of participants in a home invasion as military tactics. In a classic home invasion robbery, two or more gang members forcefully enter a residence armed with weapons to control the actions of the occupants with the goal of stealing property and committing other opportunistic crimes. A gang home invasion may appear like the action of police executing a no-knock warrant or raiding a drug house. It also has similarities to the military tactic of breaching and clearing a dwelling as part of close-quarters combat tactics.

5. *Gang members in my jurisdiction commit armed robberies.*

The question is also used to clarify the responses from the previous question, to determine if respondents naturally considered the actions of armed robbery a military tactic. In an armed robbery, the offender typically threatens the victim with a weapon (whether a knife, gun, or other object), in any number of locations (like a bank, on the street, or in another public area), and demands some form of property (such as a car, money, or jewelry). The offender may have only threatened to use a weapon, may have actually used a weapon, or may have only pretended to use a weapon for the charge to be used. Armed robbery entails the offensive use of a weapon, and all military service members are trained with a variety of weapons, both offensively and defensively.[22]

6. *There are gang members in my jurisdiction that currently serve in the military.*

Active gang members adversely affected the military in a variety of distinct ways. The 1998 study after the Fort Bragg murders reported that while there was no official accounting of the scope and nature of the problem, leaders of the individual branches of the military thought the problem was significant.[23] The study found recruiters and other relevant personnel needed better guidance on gang identifiers and the policies that guided decisions to allow gang members to enlist. The goal was to eliminate the possibility that gang members could enlist in the military.[24] Department of Defense (DOD) Instruction 1325.06 more recently designated active participation in extremist groups and gangs as prohibited activities and provided commanders the authority to take administrative and disciplinary actions for that participation.[25] Pyrooz and Decker's research reported 5 percent of the street gang members and 20 percent of the DTEs had been in the military.[26]

7. *There are gang members in my jurisdiction that have served in the military in the past.*

The authors of many of the NGIC assessments have observed "gang members with military training posed a unique threat to law enforcement personnel."[27] The threat posed to law enforcement was even more significant if MTGMs trained other gang members in weapons, tactics, and planning.[28] Whether trained in combat arms, logistics, finance, or other military occupational specialties, the gang member with military experience should be considered more advanced and dangerous than the gang member without military experience, and the potential threat to law enforcement is significant.[29] The threat to communities increases because all MTGMs were, or will be, discharged from the military at some point, either due to inappropriate activity (i.e., conduct contrary to military discipline, criminal actions) or because their commitment to military service was satisfied.[30]

8. *Military representatives advise our department when gang members are discharged.*

Regulations direct MCIOs to ensure that within their area of responsibility there is close coordination and mutual exchange of criminal intelligence between their unit and other military and civilian law enforcement agencies on matters of common interest. Criminal intelligence about an individual may be disseminated outside law enforcement channels only to those persons whose official duties create a definite and identifiable need for them to have access.[31] The question was included to gauge perception of a need and not to grade a public service. The author was aware of the manpower commitment that would be necessary for the described process to occur. Additionally, the hurdles caused by legal and regulatory requirements that distinguish a known or suspected gang member from a service member who has committed a crime can be confusing. In fact, unless the gang member is suspected of committing crimes, the conversation should not occur in the first place. The question was related to a follow-up question, which asked, "Does your department/organization have a working relationship with military investigative authorities?"

The following is a summary of many of the surveys I have done to help analyze the threat to the community brought by the presence of MTGMs. I summarized the key points gathered in the surveys without going into too much depth for those interested only in basic information. While the below are in narrative form, if you would like to see the data in table form, check out the website for the book—http://www.gangsandthemilitary.com.

MTGMs IN THE MIDWEST

Illinois

In October 2014, I surveyed gang cops in northern Illinois at a conference. I asked 152 of them to answer the questions and received responses from seventy-one of them who answered all or almost all the questions on the survey. The response rate provided a 95 percent confidence level and an 8.52 percent margin of error. Many respondents reported gang members in their jurisdictions were increasingly using military-type weapons or explosives (36 percent), as well as military-type equipment like body armor, night-vision devices, and so on (24 percent). Although few (24 percent) agreed that gang members were using military-type tactics, a majority (over 87 percent) reported gang members committed home invasions and armed robberies. Many (29 percent) reported that there were gang members in their jurisdiction currently serving, while 47 percent reported they had gang members who had previously served in the military. Most of the respondents (77 percent) did not believe that military representatives advised their department when gang members were discharged from the military.

Gang members in their jurisdictions represented many branches of the military, although the Army was the most often reported, followed by the Marine Corps and the Army Reserve. The Gangster Disciples, Latin Kings, and Vice Lords were the street gangs represented most by the MTGMs in survey respondents' jurisdictions. Of the OMGs represented by MTGMs, the Outlaws, Hells Angels, and Black Pistons were most reported. Sovereign citizens comprised the largest group of DTEs represented by MTGMs, followed by white supremacists and racist skinheads. Most survey respondents (74 percent) reported that fewer than 10 percent of their gang members had some form of military training, and most (45 percent) respondents reported the MTGMs in their jurisdiction received military training directly.

MTGMs IN THE SOUTH

Alabama

In May 2014, I handed out surveys to cops from all over the state of Alabama who were meeting in Birmingham. Of the seventy I asked to complete the survey, forty-nine participants answered all or almost all of the questions on the survey, resulting in a 95 percent confidence level and a 7.72 percent margin of error. Many respondents reported gang members in their jurisdictions were increasingly using military-type weapons or explosives, but few reported their gang members were using military-type equipment (body armor, night-vision, etc.). Although only one in three (31 percent) agreed that gang members were using military-type tactics, a majority (over 80 percent) reported gang members committed home invasions and armed robberies.

Many reported that gang members in their communities demonstrated military-type leadership and 22 percent reported that there were gang members in their jurisdiction currently serving, while 41 percent reported they had gang members who had previously served in the military. Most of the respondents believed active gang members should not be allowed to join the military. Most of the respondents (71 percent) did not believe that military representatives advised their department when gang members were discharged from the military. Survey respondents reported an estimated 11 percent of their gang members had some form of military training.

Tennessee

In August 2014, I asked gang cops in Tennessee to complete the survey. Of the 164 folks who were asked, seventy participants answered all or almost all the questions on the survey. That response rate provided a 95 percent confidence level and 8.9 percent margin of error. Many respondents reported gang members in their jurisdictions were increasingly using military-type weapons or explosives (51 percent), as well as military-type equipment like body armor, night-vision devices, and so on (30 percent). Although few (24 percent) agreed that gang members were using military-type tactics, a majority (over 90 percent) reported gang members committed home invasions and armed robberies. Many (46 percent) reported that there were gang members in their jurisdiction currently serving, while 64 percent reported they had gang members who had previously served in the military. Most of the respondents (66 percent) did not believe that military representatives advised their department when gang members were discharged from the military.

Gang members in the respondents' jurisdiction represented many branches of the military, although the Army was the most often reported, followed by the Army National Guard and the Marine Corps. The Bloods, Crips, Gangster Disciples, Vice Lords, and Mara Salvatrucha were the street gangs represented most by the MTGMs in survey respondents' jurisdictions. Of the OMGs represented by MTGMs, the Outlaws, Hells Angels, and Black Pistons were most reported. White supremacists comprised the largest group of DTEs represented by MTGMs, followed by sovereign citizens and racist skinheads. Most survey respondents (43 percent) reported that fewer than 10 percent of their gang members had some form of military training, and most (44 percent) respondents reported the MTGMs in their jurisdiction received military training directly.

MTGMs IN THE NORTHWEST

In May 2014, I surveyed gang cops from Idaho, Montana, Oregon, and Washington while in Spokane, Washington. I asked 305 of them to complete the survey, and 166 of them did. That response rate provided a 95 percent confidence level and a 5.14 percent margin of error. Many respondents reported gang members in their jurisdictions were increasingly using military-type weapons or explosives (27 percent), as well as military-type equipment like body armor, night-vision devices, and so on (19 percent). Although few (14 percent) agreed that gang members were using military-type tactics, a majority (over 65 percent) reported gang members committed home invasions and armed robberies. Many reported that gang leaders in their communities demonstrated military-type leadership, and 18 percent reported that there were gang members in their jurisdiction currently serving, while 33 percent reported they had gang members who had previously served in the military. Most of the respondents believed active gang members should not be allowed to join the military. Most of the respondents (79 percent) did not believe that military representatives advised their department when gang members were discharged from the military.

Gang members in the respondents' jurisdiction represented many branches of the military, although the Army was the most often reported, followed by the Army National Guard and the Army Reserve. The Crips, 18 Street, Bloods, Gangster Disciples, and Mara Salvatrucha were the street gangs represented most by the MTGMs in survey respondents' jurisdictions. The OMGs and DTEs represented by MTGMs were not separately recorded. Survey respondents estimated a mean of 6 percent of their gang members had some form of military training.

MTGMs IN THE SOUTHWEST

Arizona

In June 2014, I surveyed ninety-seven Arizona gang cops while in Tempe. I received responses from thirty-one participants, providing a 95 percent confidence level and a 14.59 percent margin of error. Most respondents reported gang members in their jurisdictions were increasingly using military-type weapons or explosives (55 percent), as well as military-type equipment such as body armor and night-vision devices (52 percent). Although only one in three (36 percent) agreed that gang members were using military-type tactics, a majority (over 80 percent) reported gang members committed home invasions and armed robberies.

Many reported that gang leaders in their communities demonstrated military-type leadership, and 26 percent reported that there were gang members in their jurisdiction currently serving, while 49 percent reported they had gang members who had previously served in the military. Most of the respondents believed active gang members should not be allowed to join the military. Most of the respondents (61 percent) did not believe that military representatives advised their department when gang members were discharged from the military. Survey respondents reported an estimated 9 percent of their gang members had some form of military training.

Gang members in the respondents' jurisdiction represented many branches of the military, although the Army was the most often reported, followed by the Marine Corps and the Air Force. The Bloods, Crips, Gangster Disciples, Vice Lords, and Latin Kings were the street gangs represented most by the MTGMs in survey respondents' jurisdictions. The OMGs and DTEs represented by MTGMs were not separately recorded. Survey respondents estimated a mean of 9 percent of their gang members had some form of military training.

Nevada

In April 2015, I passed out the survey to Nevada gang cops in Las Vegas. There were 305 of them, and 114 answered all or almost all the questions on the survey. That response rate provided a 95 percent confidence level and a 7.28 percent margin of error. Most respondents reported gang members in their jurisdictions were increasingly using military-type weapons or explosives (56.6 percent), as well as military-type equipment like body armor, night-vision devices, and so on (46.3 percent). Although several (39.6 percent) agreed that gang members were using military-type tactics, a majority (over 85 percent) reported gang members committed home invasions and armed robberies.

Most (51.8 percent) reported that there were gang members in their jurisdiction currently serving in the military, while 62.3 percent reported they had gang members who had previously served in the military. Almost half of the respondents (49.1 percent) did not believe that military representatives advised their department when gang members were discharged from the military.

Gang members in the respondents' jurisdiction represented many branches of the military, although the Air Force was the most often reported, followed by the Army and the Marines. The Sureños, Bloods, and Crips were the street gangs represented most by the MTGMs in survey respondents' jurisdictions. Of the OMGs represented by MTGMs, the Hells Angels, Mongols, and Vagos were most reported. Sovereign citizens comprised the largest group of DTEs represented by MTGMs, followed by white supremacists and racist skinheads. Most survey respondents (67.1 percent) reported that fewer than 10 percent of their gang members had some form of military training, and most (79.7 percent) respondents reported the MTGMs in their jurisdiction received military training directly.

California

In October 2014, I passed out the survey questionnaire to California gang cops in Redwood City. Of the 255 there, 121 participants completed the survey, for a 95 percent confidence level and a 6.47 percent margin of error. Most respondents reported gang members in their jurisdictions were increasingly using military-type weapons or explosives (66 percent), as well as military-type equipment like body armor, night-vision devices, and so on (56 percent). Although few (33 percent) agreed that gang members were using military-type tactics, a majority (over 84 percent) reported gang members committed home invasions and armed robberies.

Many (31 percent) reported that there were gang members in their jurisdiction currently serving, while 51 percent reported they had gang members who had previously served in the military. Most of the respondents (53 percent) did not believe that military representatives advised their department when gang members were discharged from the military.

Gang members in the respondents' jurisdiction represented many branches of the military, although the Army was the most often reported, followed by the Marine Corps and the Army Reserve. The Norteños, Sureños, and Mara Salvatrucha (MS-13) were the street gangs represented most by the MTGMs in survey respondents' jurisdictions. Of the OMGs represented by MTGMs, the Hells Angels, Mongols, and Vagos were most reported. Sovereign citizens comprised the largest group of DTEs represented by MTGMs, followed by white supremacists and racist skinheads. Most survey respondents (51 percent) reported that fewer than 10 percent of their gang members had some form of military training, and most (32 percent) respondents reported the MTGMs in their jurisdiction received military training directly.

Utah

In April 2015, I surveyed 550 Utah cops, educators, and community workers in Salt Lake City. The 205 who completed the survey provided a 95 percent confidence level and a 5.43 percent margin of error. Some respondents reported gang members in their jurisdictions were increasingly using military-type weapons or explosives (29.3 percent), as well as military-type equipment like body armor, night-vision devices, and so on (22.1 percent).

Although only a few (22.5 percent) agreed that gang members were using military-type tactics, a majority (over 80 percent) reported gang members committed home invasions and armed robberies. Many (36.9 percent) reported that there were gang members in their jurisdiction currently serving in the military, while 44.6 percent reported they had gang members who had previously served in the military. More of the respondents (37.7 percent) did not believe that military representatives advised their department when gang members were discharged from the military.

Gang members in the respondents' jurisdiction represented many branches of the military, although the Army was the most often reported, followed by the Marines, the Army Reserve, and the Army National Guard. The Sureños, Norteños, Crips, Bloods, 18th Street, MS-13, and Gangster Disciples were the street gangs represented most by the MTGMs in survey respondents' jurisdictions. Of the OMGs represented by MTGMs, the Mongols, Bandidos, and Hells Angels were most reported. White supremacists comprised the largest group of DTEs represented by MTGMs, followed by sovereign citizens and racist skinheads. Most survey respondents (74.9 percent) reported that fewer than 10 percent of their gang members had some form of military training, and most (69.8 percent) respondents reported the MTGMs in their jurisdiction received military training directly.

Wyoming

In August 2015, I passed out surveys to a variety of folks in Rock Springs, Wyoming. Of the sixty in attendance on that day, thirty answered all or almost all the questions on the survey. That response rate provided a 95 percent confidence level and a 12.76 percent margin of error. Few respondents reported gang members in their jurisdictions were increasingly using military-type weapons or explosives (6.7 percent), and none reported gang members were using military-type equipment like body armor, night-vision devices, and so on. Although some (8.3 percent) agreed that gang members were using military-type tactics, a majority (over 50 percent) reported gang members committed home invasions and armed robberies.

Many (46.7 percent) reported that there were gang members in their jurisdiction currently serving in the military, while 50 percent reported they had gang members who had previously served in the military. A few of the respondents (13.3 percent) did not believe that military representatives advised their department when gang members were discharged from the military.

Gang members in the respondents' jurisdiction represented many branches of the military although the Marine Corps was the most often reported, followed by the Army and the Army National Guard. The Norteños, Sureños, Bloods, and Crips were the street gangs represented most by the MTGMs in survey respondents' jurisdictions. Of the OMGs represented by MTGMs, the Sons of Silence were the only group reported. Sovereign citizens comprised the largest group of DTEs represented by MTGMs, followed by white supremacists. Most survey respondents (93.3 percent) reported that fewer than 10 percent of their gang members had some form of military training, and most (61.5 percent) respondents reported the MTGMs in their jurisdiction received military training directly.

As you can see, each jurisdiction has their own street gang, OMG, and DTE problems and their own MTGM problems. For readability, I did not include charts and graphs in this book. If you would like to see a state-by-state breakdown of the data, check out the website for the book—http://www.gangsandthemilitary.com.

MTGMs IN JAILS AND PRISONS

The study of MTGMs in Corrections is something I am also interested in, as it represents a logical extension of the community for MTGMs. Kathryn Tierney, a graduate student of Wiskoff's, examined self-identified gang members in military prisons. The interviews focused on reasons the gang members enlisted in the military and included: truthfulness with recruiters regarding prior arrests and criminal convictions, links to gangs and extremist groups, and reasons for lack of assimilation and acculturation in the military.[32] The top reason (37.1 percent) given for enlisting was to get a better life or get out of the current environment. Other reasons included avoiding death or jail because of the gang lifestyle, providing for family, and getting job experience.[33] None of the military gang members seemed to have had patriotism among their reasons for enlisting in the military.

Regarding their truthfulness with recruiters regarding prior arrests, many of the interviewees (over 50 percent) reported they had prior arrests, including those sealed by juvenile courts. Others reported that their recruiter encouraged them to conceal their arrest record. For those who had criminal records, a moral waiver was sought and granted. Many of the interviewees without criminal records admitted to pre-service involvement in criminal activity which was undetected by law enforcement. Most of the interviewees were incarcerated for a crime that was not considered gang-related.[34]

Gang members often spend time in prison because of the activities of the gang. Military-trained gang members who are in prison can be especially dangerous for the corrections officers and fellow inmates alike. Source: iStockPhoto

For most of the interviewees, links to gangs began before enlistment. Several of the interviewees reported family members were extensively involved in gangs, with many of those family members in prison for gang-related crimes. Other interviewees had friends who were gang members. Reasons for lack of assimilation and acculturation in the military were not specifically identified, though many of the interviewees had characteristics that combined to form profiles of military members who had problems adjusting to military life.[35] Tierney, as well as Flacks and Wiskoff, recommended an expanded study of the connections between gang membership and military acculturation and an effort to determine the impact of gangs and extremist groups on the military. Areas in which Tierney recommended additional focus included access to the juvenile records of potential enlistees, the process used by recruiters to obtain moral waivers, the conscientiousness of recruiters regarding concealment of enlistees' criminal records, screening procedures to identify potential enlistees with gang histories, and clarification of policies regarding active duty gang members serving in the military. While the scope of the book was mostly limited to MTGMs in the traditional community, here's a glimpse of their activity and presence in the jails.

In August 2015, I surveyed jail administrators meeting at the Tennessee Corrections Institute (TCI) FTO training conference in Pigeon Forge,

Tennessee. Of the 274 attending the conference, 242 participants answered all or almost all the questions on the survey. That response rate provided a 95 percent confidence level and a 2.16 margin of error. It should be noted that while the respondents worked in county jail facilities, many of their responses include their perception of the presence of gang members and MTGMs in the civilian community. There were no mechanisms in place to differentiate between the community and the jail. Many respondents reported gang members in their jurisdictions were using military-type weapons or explosives (39 percent), and some (22 percent) reported gang members were using military-type equipment like body armor, night-vision devices, and so on.

Although many (32.4 percent) agreed that gang members were using military-type tactics, a majority (over 65 percent) reported gang members committed home invasions and armed robberies. Many (22.5 percent) reported that there were gang members in their jurisdiction currently serving in the military, while more (47.1 percent) reported they had gang members who had previously served in the military. Many of the respondents (49.5 percent) did not believe that military representatives advised their department when gang members were discharged from the military.

Gang members in the respondents' jurisdiction represented many branches of the military, although the Army was the most often reported, followed by the Army National Guard and the Army Reserve. The Bloods, Crips, Vice Lords, and Gangster Disciples were the street gangs represented most by the MTGMs in survey respondents' jurisdictions. Of the OMGs represented by MTGMs, the Outlaws, Hells Angels, and Pagans were the main groups reported. Sovereign citizens comprised the largest group of DTEs represented by MTGMs, followed by white supremacists and racist skinheads. Most survey respondents (80.3 percent) reported that fewer than 10 percent of their gang members had some form of military training, and most (56.4 percent) respondents reported the MTGMs in their jurisdiction received military training directly.

Another Perspective

Steve Lucero worked in corrections and intelligence with the Colorado Department of Corrections for many years and has seen his share of military-trained gang members. He shared this about MTGMs in prison.

> There have always been guys that come from military backgrounds to the hood and then to prison. Three major things they possess is education, loyalty and training in wartime tactics. They will always rise to the top or gain respect from that group for what they know and how they have protected our country, but also what they can do for the gang or neighborhood. They hold many of the same values as a dedicated gangster, like loyalty. They will work hard to prove

themselves. Shot callers look for those that have a military background and possess these traits to help further their cause inside the prison system. They have learned that ex-military have a different mindset and are more structured and ready to continue their soldier life inside the walls. Their thinking is more militant and based on wartime training.

When they walk the yard, they are more observant than most and have learned in the military what to look for in their surroundings. All inmates are more observant than most because of their surroundings, but the military minded who have been in combat or have trained for combat are more intense and teach others what they have learned and how to prepare for that type of life. They understand the importance of delegation and training to do just that. They learn to plant weapons for easy access in time of battle and assign others to be security and monitor not only the enemy but correctional staff.

They are watching you watching them. If they know a battle is about to take place they might assign each gangster an opponent, an individual they are responsible for. Should that person not handle his assignment in battle they know who is responsible. This makes it easier to track who is doing their job. Those that don't carry out their assignment are usually violated. Military minds always learn where the blind spots are available for hits or other illicit activity.

Their loyalty is what they are very proud of and many times push on others. They can spot those who are not loyal by testing others to do violations or beat downs often telling those they assign they are finding out where their heart is, making everyone put in work (doing tasks for the gang). This could be anything from an introduction of drugs into the system to murder.

In the training that they learned in the military they look for the crime committed by their homies, the time they are doing and reputation they already have and nurture that. They teach and program theirs not to jump the gun in situations. Teach the difference between logic and emotion, to use their head not their feelings, and to pay attention to the smallest detail.

Most leaders and those that are military-trained read books like *The 48 Laws of Power* by Robert Greene, *The Art of Seduction*, *The 50th Law*, Sun Tzu's *The Art of War*, and *The Book of the 5 Rings*. Training is a part of being programmed to believe what you are fighting for, to develop a mindset for the cause. To be knowledgeable about the skills being practiced on the yard, the cell block and the politics of gang structure in prison. Many like the Norteños or Nuestra Familia are taught to teach of their ancient culture.

I have talked to many gang members in prison that were in a gang and ex-military. One Crip gang member told me that the military is like a gang to many, and they join for stability. They think the gangs can give them financial stability through illegal gain, usually drugs, they think the Marines can give them that also. They want to be loved, to be part of something. Protection, a lot of people think that by being taught how to kill and do things like that you'd be able to protect yourself better and people won't bother you. It's the same concept, and most of the reasons why they joined the military were why they joined the gangs. They learn in boot camp about battle and loyalty. It's embedded in you.

In my experience military-trained gang members usually rise to the top. They already have the educated experience, they are already structured, trained, and many have already been in battle that can result in death. They become teachers to the gang in and outside of a prison setting. Good leadership will recognize all these values and utilize them to the best interest of that gang. It is part of the evolution of the gang lifestyle to be better at violence. Violence is the language of a true Gangster. It helps them communicate with their enemies as well as their prospect's. In some cases, they become the Drill Sergeants of their gang.

One inmate said that the Gang members in the military are throughout the ranks but once they get to an E-5, E-6, or E-7 area there is not much going on illegally with them because they are more into a career. As they get older they began to ride the back seat as not a lot is required of them by the gang. He went on to say that CID, Military Police and Naval intelligence, and other MCIOs have little effective training on gangs and how to recognize the problems. The highest ranking Gangster Disciple he knew was a Lieutenant Colonel.

I have been told that gang members in the military stationed at Fort Carson would try to steal ammo or weapons. In Colorado, it was said that some African American gangs in Colorado Springs traded grenades and other weapons to the Sureños in Pueblo who had the drug connections. Fort Carson Army base in Colorado Springs was about forty-three miles away from Pueblo, Colorado. In the Colorado Prison system, some gangs encouraged some street gang members to join the military to enhance the gang member's knowledge of structure, weapons and organized violence.

Also, according to one of my sources, the Gangster Disciples are the most organized. They mimic the military so much that they use ranks, and everything is war. They have a Chief of Security, foot soldiers, Captains, Lieutenants and ranks like that. This source told me that when Colorado Department of Corrections started hiring staff without college credits, Gangster Disciples (GDs) started telling some of their people to try to get hired. He said they focus on the private prisons like Corrections Corporation of America (CCA). They enticed the applicant by telling them we have people there that will pay all your bills. They were trying to set up mules for drugs. No names were given. Gangs have evolved into organized crime and prisons are the Harvard training for gangs, from the Mexican Mafia, that has major influence in Colorado and other parts of the western U.S., to the Gangster Disciples from Chicago, IL.

Steve Lucero, Lieutenant
Intelligence Officer (Retired)
Colorado Department of Corrections

CONCLUDING THOUGHTS

Individuals end up with joint membership in gangs and military service in a variety of ways. Theories explaining those phenomena are different from those explaining typical gang membership. Gang members with military connections extend back through the history of our country. Members of street gangs, OMGs, and DTE groups have served in the U.S. military in each wartime era and they are serving today. They all leave the service, and as many as 10 percent of a community's street gang members may have military training. Some gang members have entered the military because of the lowered recruiting standards and the process of granting waivers or simply overlooking many disqualifying factors. Increased awareness and examination of the presence of gang members in the military is important to limit the effect on the military.

Civilian communities have seen increases in recent years regarding gang member use of military-type weapons and equipment, as well as gang members committing home invasions and armed robberies. More communities have reported their gang members were currently in the military or had military training. I believe former gang members deserve a chance at military service, but not if they have yet to give up their criminal gang lifestyles, associates, and behavior. If the Army is going to recruit and accept current or former gang members, it should also work to make sure those people successfully get out of and stay away from the gangs. If we get folks who're clean enough and dedicated enough to join the military, great! But the military needs to track them and check up on them regularly to ensure they stay out of the gang life. Army officials have said they recognize and are concerned about gangs infiltrating the ranks. They have also said the problem was not a major threat and leaders and criminal investigators are trained to monitor and identify possible gang activity.

A Strategy for the Military in the Future

Is a definitional change needed? Are the groups we have been discussing best referred to as "gangs"? Should those groups be called Urban or Domestic Terrorists? Could a term be used that would refer to all those groups without missing any? How about Security Threat Group (STG)? The term Security Threat Group for military-trained gang members in the military was patterned after the term used by various states' departments of corrections (DOC).

A Security Threat Group is typically identified as a:

Formal or informal ongoing groups, gangs, organizations or associations consisting of two or more members who have a common name or common identifying signs, colors, or symbols . . . whose members/associates engage in a pattern of gang activity or violation of laws/regulations.

When we called those groups gangs, extremists, and so on, many in military and government leadership expressed only passing interest, especially when they were not aware of a "problem." When we used the term Security Threat Group, all those groups suddenly become identified under ONE definition and the term accurately described the focus of their activity.

Gang Intelligence

I have taught several Criminal Justice classes and I have typically asked students to consider what a first-time offender is. They often say it's the first time somebody committed a crime and that the judge will usually give them an opportunity to "repent from their evil ways" and to fix their life. They realize soon that it was a "trick" question. The reality of first time offenders is that it's usually the first time those people got caught doing whatever it was that they were doing. Lest there be doubters, did you get caught speeding the first time you accelerated your car past the posted speed limit? Less than one percent of the people I have asked that question to have said that happened.

Consider, then, someone identified as a gang member in the military. It's likely the first time they were identified as a gang member in the military was not the first time that they were "gang-banging," but rather it was simply the first time the police, unit commander, or other leader happened to be there at the same time and noticed. If we let those people out of the military and they have more advanced training, they already know how to avoid being caught. They're going to be in "stealth mode." They've been fighting, or trained to fight, in war and they know how to evade the enemy who is trying to kill them. They've practiced being able to avoid detection as a gang member while in the military, too, where a higher percentage of people are "in your business" than in the typical civilian community. Surely they can evade the police who are just trying to see if they're doing anything wrong!

I think civilian police would be better able to investigate the issue of MTGMs in the community if the military would do a proper hand-off of the information they have. Many times in the military, a person who was identified in the military as a criminal, but not convicted, was moved as part of their military assignment. For intelligence purposes, the information obtained by the CID in their former community can be passed on to the CID in the community to which the soldier was being transferred. Army CID can send an alert to the police in the new community relatively quickly.

If it's another unit in another location that the individual moved to, they'll tell the CID in that area "Hey you've got a known gang-banger and here's who his associates are, here's what he does, here's what we think he's involved in." That's how intelligence works. Well let's do that with the police when we're releasing them to "Your Town, USA!" Let's contact the police department there and say "Hey we had a guy in the military that was arrested (or suspected) for this-or-that gang-related activity and he's coming to your town. He's been trained in explosives, he's been trained in leadership, or he can dismantle chemical weapons, and we thought you might want to know." The military doesn't do that. That's not on their list of priorities, so the civilian police don't have that opportunity. They end up with a guy who was trained in the military and all they know was that he wore a uniform and so he's coming out with training they may never know about. And he could train other people, the other members of the gang, how to do what he can do!

The presence of gangs in a military unit influences the members of that unit at all levels. The commander typically chooses to either acknowledge or deny the presence of a gang member once he or she has learned of their existence. Depending on what degree of acknowledgment they give, they may or may not have the support and respect of the members of their command. The morale of the company may be in jeopardy, because the commander was likely the last one to find out there was a gang problem in the unit, and a bunch of junior and mid-level managers, leaders, commissioned and non-commissioned officers, and sergeants have known for quite a while. The real soldiers in the units and the real sailors and the real marines, the ones that are actually there to serve their country and be loyal to their unit and do what they are there to do, their morale goes right in the toilet when there's a gang member in the unit and no one's doing anything about it.

Recommendations. The following basic recommendations have been offered to military and police leaders based on the responses to the surveys, research, and experience of the author. Some have evolved with progressive (albeit minimal) response by the military. Others are very much like what I have recommended for twenty-five years.

a. Commanders should ensure there are designated persons in, or accessible to, their unit to screen new personnel for potential gang membership. New unit members who have gang affiliation may tattoo their bodies with gang symbols and wear clothing of a certain style, or color, to represent their group or they may be more advanced gang members, who cannot be so easily identified. Unit representatives and Military Police have public access to many resources so they can learn basic gang knowledge (see http://www.gangsandthemilitary.com and More Gang Training for examples). More advanced and current gang training is available for military law enforcement and criminal intelligence personnel by coordinating with their state and regional gang investigators' association or other source of reliable gang training (see http://www.gangsandthemilitary.com and More Gang Training for sources).

b. Military leadership should continuously examine the activities of all suspected military gang members to identify active gang affiliation for retention or discharge purposes while evaluating the degree or extent of any gang affiliation for security clearances. Current policy guidance, specifically DoD Instruction 1325.6, prohibits military service members from active gang membership, yet the primary determination of such activity appears to be the presence of a criminal record. That was a systemic weakness, as not all gang members are detected and arrested by law enforcement each time they commit a crime. For service members requiring a security clearance, any identified gang affiliation in the recent past should be considered as potential grounds for disqualification, even passive or associate membership, unless accompanied by a complete and public renunciation of the gang and follow-up evaluation by representatives of the appropriate medical and criminal justice authority.

c. Responsible military investigative units should coordinate and liaise with local law enforcement gang specialists and ensure they are aware of MCIO and DoD policies and contacts regarding the identification of gang members in or connected to the military. Regulations direct that ongoing liaison and cooperation will be maintained with civilian and military law enforcement and investigative agencies and military intelligence activities to ensure that criminal investigative, or other information of mutual interest, is exchanged or disseminated.[36] The MCIOs encourage federal, state, and local law enforcement agencies to report information concerning military personnel in their communities who have suspected gang affiliations.[37] MCIOs should ensure they report similar information to the supported communities. When able, information reports should be submitted to the local law enforcement agency when a known or suspected gang member is discharged from the military.

d. Commanders and responsible investigative units should be aware that MTGMs might seek access to military-type weapons, ammunition, and explosives, as well as equipment. Periodic audits of inventory may limit access of those items to gang members. Enhanced security may serve to verify the trustworthiness of unit members.

e. Commanders and MCIOs should use the term Security Threat Group (STG) to describe the groups identified.[38] A typical STG is a group of three (3) or more persons with recurring threatening or disruptive behavior including but not limited to gang crime or gang violence.[39] By identifying them as an STG, any recognition they may draw from publicity about their group or its activities was limited or eliminated. Also, the term clearly and accurately describes how those groups can impact the security of military operations and law and order.

f. MCIOs should also recognize that although there has been a tradition of stating that "less than 1%" of military members are involved in gangs, that number increases exponentially with the cumulative total of former military members in the civilian community. If it were possible to determine how many gang members were active in the civilian community at the target age of military recruits, and compare that number to the same population in the military, it might show that a similar percentage of each population has gang ties. That possibility does not excuse the existence of gang members in the military, it simply explains it. Thus, the presence of gang members in the military should be aggressively examined, questioned, and reported. Instead of accepting the existence of gang members in the military community, the goal should be to limit opportunities to join and be retained and subsequently released to the civilian community.[40]

g. Civilian law enforcement and corrections professionals should ensure they play an active role in contacting and maintaining communication with MCIOs responsible for investigating criminal activity in their jurisdictions. Individuals assigned to military law enforcement units may change job assignments (locations) more frequently than civilian law enforcement, making it necessary for the organizations with continuity and institutional knowledge—local law enforcement—to be responsible for maintaining the connection and intelligence regarding MTGMs.

Consider the Points

Before we finish, let me propose one more thing for your consideration. Civilian police in many locations have a process for identifying gang members called the "points system." It was designed to make the process of determining whether someone has gang membership as objective as possible. Presumably, even someone with little in the way of training or familiarity regarding gangs could consider the available information and determine whether someone was gang-affiliated. That's the best sort of process to use when it comes to the legal system. Here's how it works.

The investigator determines whether the suspected gang member has a number of indicators, whether he or she has admitted gang involvement; been identified by a parent, guardian, or reliable informant as a gang member; whether he or she resides in an area known to be populated by gang members, adopts the gang lifestyle or dress, uses gang hand signs, has gang tattoos, or associates with known gang members; is identified and corroborated as a gang member; has been arrested more than once in the presence of known gang members; or has been identified as a gang member by physical evidence. Each of the indicators is assigned a point value, and the investigator tallies up the points. If the total exceeds a certain number, they have validated that person as a gang member.

Use of the point system for identifying suspected gang members allows investigators to objectively quantify indicators of gang membership. Additionally, prosecutors, judges, and jurors are better able to understand how the investigator reached the conclusion that the accused was a gang member. I suggest that investigators show more than the minimum required number of points so there is even less likelihood of a claim of bias or subjectivity.

Why would they go through all that trouble, you ask? Because many jurisdictions provide enhancement penalties for gang association, and those penalties can add time to the sentence a convicted gang member receives. The added penalties can be quite burdensome, too. In Tennessee, for instance, a criminal gang offense committed by a defendant who was a criminal gang member at the time of the offense is punished one classification higher than the offense committed. A criminal gang offense committed by a non-gang affiliated defendant who committed the offense to fulfill an initiation or other requirement for joining a criminal gang is punished one classification higher the offense committed. And, a criminal gang offense committed by a defendant who was a criminal gang leader or organizer at the time of the offense is punished two classifications higher than the offense committed.

Objections to the points system include the claim that the system is too limiting and doesn't take certain behavior into account. Also, it can be argued that allowing an expert witness to present proof of a gang member's pattern of criminal activity—from various sources by various officers—violates the Sixth Amendment's confrontation clause, which established the defendant's right to cross-examine each witness against him or her. Some will argue that self-admission as a gang member is different from "admits to criminal gang involvement," the words used in the law. Finally, it has been argued and upheld that using what amounts to hearsay for assigning points to determine someone's gang affiliation is not constitutional.[41] Testimonial statements of witnesses absent from trial have been admitted only where the declarant is unavailable and only where the defendant has had a prior opportunity to cross-examine. But the majority of the points system seems to work well and is used by many agencies to determine gang involvement.

Consider Using Steps

Some may prefer to use an alternative to the points system. For those, I recommend using indicators not as a checklist but as a type of scale, to help determine priorities for further investigation as resources become available. Use the collected information or intelligence as a weighting program, not unlike the intelligence-based approach in use by police and other government agencies worldwide. It may be easiest to try using steps, indicating degrees or likelihood of gang involvement. They would not be the same as points, as they are articulable factors used to reach the conclusion that the individual was a gang member. The collection process can take each step into account, perhaps equally weighted. If the number of indicators keeps climbing and resources are available, the organization can choose to devote time to cultivate more intelligence or determine an appropriate strategy. If prioritization of investigations is needed due to heavy workload, the steps system could easily provide the way.

That's the extent of my recommendations for fixing the system. If the military implements a concerted effort to managing street gang, OMG, and DTE group members while they are in the military, I suspect some variation of one or more of these recommendations will be used. If that doesn't happen, perhaps military law enforcement, commanders, or community leaders can implement some of the ideas I have shared here. If you are in one of those groups, or are aware of that being done, please let me know. I doubt this is the last you will hear about gangs and the military, so let's keep in touch!

Afterword

When Gangs and the U.S. Military Collide: Two Cases, One Installation

Two incidents at one of America's largest and busiest military installations serve to illustrate what can happen when gang-related activity intersects with the U.S. military.

As the commanding officer of the U.S. Army Criminal Investigation Command battalion responsible for felony investigations at Fort Bragg, North Carolina, from 1996–1998, I can attest to the extent to which we devoted an inordinate amount of time and resources to both cases. They were anything but routine investigations. Standard practices and day-to-day operations were insufficient to the task of rooting out these types of organized criminal enterprises. These types of cases required the dedication of significant assets and specialized expertise, none of which were available at the outset. In both cases, Army officials were slow to discern the extent of criminal activity that was underway providing an opportunity for destructive subcultures to take root.

The first incident of note occurred in December 1995, when three white soldiers assigned to the famed 82nd Airborne Division conspired to murder two African-American citizens of Fayetteville, North Carolina. The victims were not targeted because of involvement in an ongoing criminal enterprise, but were selected at random merely because they happened to come into the path of an alcohol-fueled young soldier and his accomplices, who were determined to earn a spider web tattoo, which had meaning in some white-supremacist circles. Their first intention was to attack a synagogue in the local community, but when they had difficulty locating one, they drove around an otherwise quiet neighborhood until they observed hapless targets of opportunity. While the driver waited in the car, two others, one armed with a privately owned 9mm pistol, approached the unsuspecting couple from behind. When a series of shots rang out, the driver panicked and drove away leaving the shooter and an accomplice to find their way home on foot. They

209

shared an off-post trailer where they were later apprehended. Feeling guilty about leaving his comrades, the driver circled the area and eventually came to the attention of police officers who were securing the crime scene. Upon questioning the driver, he stated that he was alarmed when he heard the shots because he really didn't think they would carry through with the plan. He turned state's evidence and assisted in the prosecution of the other two who received life sentences for premeditated murder.

As investigations go, the murder case was not particularly difficult to solve. It was fairly evident early on who did what and why. Army criminal investigators worked closely with local detectives to build a strong case that was prosecuted by the local district attorney. More troubling and difficult to resolve were the questions that arose during and after the investigation. It became apparent the three soldiers were part of a neo-Nazi subculture that had emerged on an American military installation. The signs were there long before the murders, but the chain of command either did not recognize them, or ignored them. It was known that there were some skinhead bars in the community, which were patronized by military personnel. It was also known that one of the soldiers admired Adolf Hitler and displayed a Nazi flag in his barracks room. It was not until the murders, however, that action was taken to determine the full scope of the problem. Eventually twenty-two soldiers were identified as having some ties to white-supremacist activity. Some were merely counseled and others were administratively discharged depending on their level of involvement.

The case prompted some significant introspection including an Army-wide study directed by the Secretary of the Army. How could it be that in an organization designed to protect American citizens, one that prided itself as the most racially diverse in the nation, could produce a number of soldiers who were willing to kill their own just because of the color of their skin? Commanders and spokesmen from Fort Bragg classified the crime as an anomaly which was not representative of American soldiers, while watchdog agencies and the press contended the incident was indicative of deeper unresolved racial tensions. Perhaps in an attempt to foster additional racial tension, a white supremacist group rented a billboard near the installations that proclaimed, "Take back Amerika" and provided a 1-800 number. Those who called the number heard a racist message. Policies were changed to tighten prohibitions on hate group membership. Before this event, a soldier could be a member of a recognized hate group, as long as they did not engage in group-related activities. It was possible before the murders to walk through the Post Exchange in clothing that was representative of affiliation with a racist extremist group without being accosted. That changed in the aftermath of the murders. Tattoo inspections were ordered and sensitivity to the signs of hate group activity increased significantly. Command presence in the barracks after hours was significantly increased. At Fort Bragg, all new company commanders received briefings from the CID office on racial and ethnic extremism indicators as part of a standing pre-command course of instruction. Efforts were made to increase the level of information sharing between equal opportunity offices, chaplains, and other organizations that might come across signs of extremist activity. Liaison was established between military officials and nongovernmental organizations such as the National Association for the Advancement of Colored People (NAACP). Intelligence about hate groups from local law enforcement and the FBI was almost nonexistent, but partnerships with human rights organizations such as the Anti-Defamation League and the Southern Poverty Law Center uncovered a treasure-trove of troubling, yet useful information.

The Army learned, perhaps for a brief period of time, what to look for and how to intervene to prevent, or militate, against the establishment of extremist organizations. It also learned about those who may not be actual members of a hate group, but are influenced by their ideology. None of the soldiers who participated in the Fayetteville murders could be identified as members of a particular hate group, yet searches of their off-post residence turned up large quantities of white supremacist literature. Since the Army experiences a high personnel turnover rate, the level of expertise associated with identifying and dealing with extremism is likely higher than it was in 1995, but lower than it was immediately following the murders. The policies that were changed in the wake of the case remain in effect, even if the high degree of sensitivity around the issue has decreased. A study of the policy history of the Department of Defense's treatment of extremism indicates a rather episodic approach. After a major event triggers public outrage, a burst of policy activity takes place followed by long periods of relative inattention.

The murders in Fayetteville represented a high impact, but infrequent type of occurrence. The second case from the same installation illustrates a more common problem whereby criminal gangs establish a presence on, or near, military installations. In the second case, a soldier from Chicago returned home after his enlistment in the Army and apparently made a case to the Gangster Disciples that the Fayetteville community represented an opportunity for expansion of their criminal enterprises. The soldier's time in uniform was unremarkable and without evidence of criminal activity. As a civilian, he used connections with military associates to foster drug trafficking and other crimes on and off of the military installation. He also became an organizing entity for soldiers who had a propensity for the gangster lifestyle. Some were gang affiliated before entering the military while others who might have been marginalized, or unfulfilled, in their units sought a more unsavory affiliation.

Local police began to notice increasingly troubling signs of gang activity. Gang related graffiti, drive-by shootings, an increase in drug trafficking, and the sporting of gang signs and symbols were in evidence. On post, some charged with monitoring the barracks as Charge of Quarters reported being intimidated out of their checks by gang members. Some soldiers reported that gang members had taken over certain basketball courts on post designated for common use. Intelligence, aided by network link analyses, pointed to the Gangster Disciples under the direction of the former soldier who was careful about avoiding direct involvement in criminal acts. One soldier who was involved in a gang-related drive-by shooting was brazen enough to proclaim his gang affiliation on the door to his barracks room with a label of the inscription, "GD to da bone." As with the extremism case, the chain of command did not recognize or respond to the declaration.

Once it became apparent that the Gangster Disciples were active in the area, a multi-jurisdictional approach was warranted. The United States Attorney's office brought in a group of attorneys with a long history and experience in prosecuting Gangster Disciple cases. They provided insights and tips that were adopted by military and civilian prosecutors. Military Deputy Assistant U.S. Attorneys and local prosecutors compared notes. They derived a coordinated approach to vigorous prosecution in both federal and local courts.

The beginning of the end for the gang occurred when members attempted to co-opt young African American family members into cashing stolen checks at the PX in exchange for some of the proceeds. Alerted to the scam, CID agents advised cashiers to be on the lookout for those cashing checks who fitted a particular profile. Upon notification, agents responded not to the cashier's cage, but to the parking lot where low-level gang members were waiting for their payoff. Facing a number of federal offenses, including The Racketeer Influenced and Corrupt Organizations Act (RICO), well-informed investigators, and aggressive prosecutors, the gang members readily provided information useful in dismantling the criminal franchise. The former soldier who charted the territory for the Gangster Disciples as the local "OG" disappeared and was never seen again, leading some to believe that he was eliminated by the organization for messing up what promised to be a lucrative expansion.

Both of the cases profiled above involved an ongoing association of three or more people involved in criminal acts as a primary activity. Thus, they can rightly be designated as gang activity. They were different in several respects. The extremism case, which resulted in murders off of the military installation, involved soldiers with no prior known association to hate groups or activities. They went from marginal performers to criminals in a relatively short period of time of about nine months. The three soldiers, who were to some degree marginalized in their own units due to poor performance, found each other and bonded around a racist ideology that was inimical to military service. The murders touched off a public firestorm that embarrassed the U.S. Army and launched a spate of policy changes that impacted the entire Department of Defense. For years after the murders, the installation was hypersensitive to indicators of racist activity. It would be an overstatement to suggest that such activity was eliminated, but at the very least it was driven underground.

The case involving the Gangster Disciples prompted no headlines or policy changes, but it did result in a very productive partnership between Military Criminal Investigative Organizations, local law enforcement, and both federal and local prosecutors. In both cases, the signs of gang activity were there for all to see, but they were not recognized as an organized threat worthy of intervention until significant criminal activity had occurred. The strength of the prevailing narrative of a successfully integrated and mission-driven organization served to blind officials to evidence that there were some who were not on board with the espoused values of the organization. Inattention, complacency, and moribund leadership combined to provide a fertile environment for the growth of criminal organizations.

George E. Reed, PhD
Colonel, U.S. Army (Retired)
Dean and Professor, School of Public Affairs
University of Colorado—Colorado Springs
Former Director of Command and Leadership Studies, U.S. Army War College
Author of *Tarnished: Toxic Leadership in the U.S. Military*

Notes

CHAPTER 1. THE HISTORY OF GANGS
AND THE MILITARY CONNECTION

1. Egan, Timothy. (February 3, 1993). "Military Base Jarred by Specter of Gang Killings." *The New York Times*. Retrieved from http://www.nytimes.com/1993/02/03/us/military-base-jarred-by-specter-of-gang-killings.html.

2. Egan, Timothy. (February 3, 1993). "Military Base Jarred by Specter of Gang Killings." *The New York Times*. Retrieved from http://www.nytimes.com/1993/02/03/us/military-base-jarred-by-specter-of-gang-killings.html.

3. National Gang Intelligence Center (NGIC) (2009). *National gang threat assessment—2009*. Washington, DC: National Gang Intelligence Center.

4. Pearson, G. (1983). *Hooligan: A history of respectable fears*. London, England: Macmillan.

5. Pearson, G. (1983). *Hooligan: A history of respectable fears*. London, England: Macmillan.

6. Haskins, J. (1974). *Street gangs: Yesterday and today*. New York, NY: Hastings House.

7. Haskins, J. (1974). *Street gangs: Yesterday and today*. New York, NY: Hastings House.

8. Haskins, J. (1974). *Street gangs: Yesterday and today*. New York, NY: Hastings House.

9. Bell, J.L. (November 12, 2011). Blog Post - Ebenezer Mackintosh, Captain of the South Enders. Boston 1775 History, analysis, and unabashed gossip about the start of the American Revolution in Massachusetts. Retrieved from http://boston1775.blogspot.com/2011/11/ebenezer-mackintosh-captain-of-south.html.

10. Sante, L. (1991). *Low life: Lures and snares of old*. New York: Vintage Books.

11. Asbury, H. (1927). *The gangs of New York: An informal history of the underworld*. New York, NY: Vintage Books.

12. Sante, L. (1991). *Low life: Lures and snares of old*. New York: Vintage Books.

13. Sante, L. (1991*). Low life: Lures and snares of old*. New York: Vintage Books.

14. Rothert, Otto A. (1924). *The outlaws of Cave-in-Rock: Historical accounts of the famous highwaymen and river pirates who operated in pioneer days upon the Ohio and Mississippi Rivers and over the old Natchez trace*. Cleveland, OH: Arthur H. Clark.

15. Weiser, K. (2013). "Mississippi Legends: Samuel 'Wolfman' Mason Takes on the Natchez Trace." *Legends of America*. Retrieved from http://www.legendsof america.com/we-samuelmason.html.

16. Rothert, Otto A. (1924). *The outlaws of Cave-in-Rock: Historical accounts of the famous highwaymen and river pirates who operated in pioneer days upon the Ohio and Mississippi Rivers and over the old Natchez trace*. Cleveland, OH: Arthur H. Clark.

17. Rothert, Otto A. (1924). *The outlaws of Cave-in-Rock: Historical accounts of the famous highwaymen and river pirates who operated in pioneer days upon the Ohio and Mississippi Rivers and over the old Natchez trace*. Cleveland, OH: Arthur H. Clark.

18. Rothert, Otto A. (1924). *The outlaws of Cave-in-Rock: Historical accounts of the famous highwaymen and river pirates who operated in pioneer days upon the Ohio and Mississippi Rivers and over the old Natchez trace*. Cleveland, OH: Arthur H. Clark.

19. Rothert, Otto A. (1924). *The outlaws of Cave-in-Rock: Historical accounts of the famous highwaymen and river pirates who operated in pioneer days upon the Ohio and Mississippi Rivers and over the old Natchez trace*. Cleveland, OH: Arthur H. Clark.

20. Rothert, Otto A. (1924). *The outlaws of Cave-in-Rock: Historical accounts of the famous highwaymen and river pirates who operated in pioneer days upon the Ohio and Mississippi Rivers and over the old Natchez trace*. Cleveland, OH: Arthur H. Clark.

21. Rothert, Otto A. (1924). *The outlaws of Cave-in-Rock: Historical accounts of the famous highwaymen and river pirates who operated in pioneer days upon the Ohio and Mississippi Rivers and over the old Natchez trace*. Cleveland, OH: Arthur H. Clark.

22. Coates, R. M. (2010 [1930]). *The outlaw years: The history of the land pirates of the Natchez Trace*. Gretna, LA: Pelican Publishing.

23. Asbury, H. (1936). *The gangs of New Orleans: An informal history of the French Quarter underworld*. London, England: Arrow Books.

24. Weiser, K. (2013). "Mississippi Legends: Samuel 'Wolfman' Mason Takes on the Natchez Trace." *Legends of America*. Retrieved from http://www.legendsof america.com/we-samuelmason.html.

25. Coates, R. M. (2010[1930]). *The outlaw years: The history of the land pirates of the Natchez Trace*. Gretna, LA: Pelican Publishing.

26. Weiser, K. (2013). "Mississippi Legends: Samuel 'Wolfman' Mason Takes on the Natchez Trace." *Legends of America*. Retrieved from http://www.legendsof america.com/we-samuelmason.html.

27. Coates, R. M. (2010 [1930]). *The outlaw years: The history of the land pirates of the Natchez Trace.* Gretna, LA: Pelican Publishing.

28. Rothert, Otto A. (1924). *The outlaws of Cave-in-Rock: Historical accounts of the famous highwaymen and river pirates who operated in pioneer days upon the Ohio and Mississippi Rivers and over the old Natchez trace.* Cleveland, OH: Arthur H. Clark.

29. Rothert, Otto A. (1924). *The outlaws of Cave-in-Rock: Historical accounts of the famous highwaymen and river pirates who operated in pioneer days upon the Ohio and Mississippi Rivers and over the old Natchez trace.* Cleveland, OH: Arthur H. Clark.

30. Weiser, K. (2013). "Mississippi Legends: Samuel 'Wolfman' Mason Takes on the Natchez Trace." *Legends of America.* Retrieved from http://www.legendsof america.com/we-samuelmason.html.

31. Weiser, K. (2013). "Mississippi Legends: Samuel 'Wolfman' Mason Takes on the Natchez Trace." *Legends of America.* Retrieved from http://www.legendsof america.com/we-samuelmason.html.

32. Allen, J. W. (April 30, 1964). "Colonel Plug and his wooden plugs." *The Southeast Missourian.* Retrieved from https://news.google.com/newspapers?nid=1893&dat= 19640430&id=waAtAAAAIBAJ&sjid=eNcEAAAAIBAJ&pg=923,2652251&hl=en.

33. Rochester Daily Advertiser (January 29, 1830). "The Boat-Wreckers—Or Banditti of the West" (Rochester, NY). *Jon's Southern Illinois History Page.* Retrieved from http://www.illinoishistory.com/plug.html.

34. Rochester Daily Advertiser (January 29, 1830). "The Boat-Wreckers—Or Banditti of the West" (Rochester, NY). *Jon's Southern Illinois History Page.* Retrieved from http://www.illinoishistory.com/plug.html.

35. Rochester Daily Advertiser (January 29, 1830). "The Boat-Wreckers—Or Banditti of the West" (Rochester, NY). *Jon's Southern Illinois History Page.* Retrieved from http://www.illinoishistory.com/plug.html.

36. Allen J. W. (April 30, 1964). "Colonel Plug and his wooden plugs." *The Southeast Missourian.* Retrieved from https://news.google.com/newspapers?nid=1893&dat= 19640430&id=waAtAAAAIBAJ&sjid=eNcEAAAAIBAJ&pg=923,2652251&hl=en.

37. Asbury, H. (1936). *The gangs of New Orleans: An informal history of the French Quarter underworld.* London, England: Arrow Books.

38. Asbury, H. (1936). *The gangs of New Orleans: An informal history of the French Quarter underworld.* London, England: Arrow Books.

39. Rochester Daily Advertiser (January 29, 1830). "The Boat-Wreckers—Or Banditti of the West" (Rochester, NY). *Jon's Southern Illinois History Page.* Retrieved from http://www.illinoishistory.com/plug.html.

40. Allen J. W. (April 30, 1964). "Colonel Plug and his wooden plugs." *The Southeast Missourian.* Retrieved from https://news.google.com/newspapers?nid=1893&dat= 19640430&id=waAtAAAAIBAJ&sjid=eNcEAAAAIBAJ&pg=923,2652251&hl=en.

41. Allen J. W. (April 30, 1964). "Colonel Plug and his wooden plugs." *The Southeast Missourian.* Retrieved from https://news.google.com/newspapers?nid=1893&dat= 19640430&id=waAtAAAAIBAJ&sjid=eNcEAAAAIBAJ&pg=923,2652251&hl=en.

42. Asbury, H. (1936). *The gangs of New Orleans: An informal history of the French Quarter underworld.* London, England: Arrow Books.

43. Asbury, H. (1927). *The gangs of New York: An informal history of the underworld.* New York, NY: Vintage Books.

44. Asbury, H. (1927). *The gangs of New York: An informal history of the underworld.* New York, NY: Vintage Books.

45. Anbinder, T. (2001). *Five Points: The 19th century New York City neighborhood that invented tap dance, stole elections, and became the world's most notorious slum.* New York, NY: Free Press/Simon & Schuster.

46. Anbinder, T. (2001). *Five Points: The 19th century New York City neighborhood that invented tap dance, stole elections, and became the world's most notorious slum.* New York, NY: Free Press/Simon & Schuster.

47. Asbury, H. (1927). *The gangs of New York: An informal history of the underworld.* New York, NY: Vintage Books.

48. Asbury, H. (1927). *The gangs of New York: An informal history of the underworld.* New York, NY: Vintage Books.

49. Sante, L. (1991). *Low life: Lures and snares of old.* New York: Vintage Books.

50. Sante, L. (1991). *Low life: Lures and snares of old.* New York: Vintage Books.

51. Asbury, H. (1927). *The gangs of New York: An informal history of the underworld.* New York, NY: Vintage Books.

52. Asbury, H. (1940). *The gangs of Chicago.* New York, NY: Perseus Books.

53. Asbury, H. (1940). *The gangs of Chicago.* New York, NY: Perseus Books.

54. Stringham, E. (2015). "San Francisco's Private Police Force: The City by the Bay has a second, private police force . . . with a better record than the government cops." *Reason.* Retrieved from http://reason.com/archives/2015/07/21/san-franciscos -private-police.

55. Browning, P. (1998). *San Francisco/Yerba Buena: From the beginning to the gold rush.* Lafayette, CA: Great West Books.

56. Van Meter, L. A. (2007). *Yerba Buena.* New York, NY: Infobase Publishing.

57. Mullen, K. (February 1, 1996). "Gangs once ruled Frisco." SF Gate. Retrieved from http://www.sfgate.com/news/article/Gangs-once-ruled-Frisco-3159206.php.

58. Asbury, H. (1933). *The gangs of San Francisco: An informal history of the San Francisco underworld.* London, England: Arrow Books.

59. Eldredge, Z. S. (1912). *The beginnings of San Francisco: From the expedition of Anza, 1774 to the city charter of April 15, 1850.* New York, NY: John C. Rankin Company.

60. Eldredge, Z. S. (1912). *The beginnings of San Francisco: From the expedition of Anza, 1774 to the city charter of April 15, 1850.* New York, NY: John C. Rankin Company.

61. Eldredge, Z. S. (1912). *The beginnings of San Francisco: From the expedition of Anza, 1774 to the city charter of April 15, 1850.* New York, NY: John C. Rankin Company.

62. Eldredge, Z. S. (1912). *The beginnings of San Francisco: From the expedition of Anza, 1774 to the city charter of April 15, 1850.* New York, NY: John C. Rankin Company.

63. Soulé, F., Gihon, J. H., and Nisbet, J. (1855). *The annals of San Francisco.* Retrieved from http://www.sfgenealogy.com/sf/history/hbann3-1.htm.

64. Asbury, H. (1933). *The gangs of San Francisco: An informal history of the San Francisco underworld.* London, England: Arrow Books.

65. Eldredge, Z. S. (1912). *The beginnings of San Francisco: From the expedition of Anza, 1774 to the city charter of April 15, 1850.* New York, NY: John C. Rankin Company.

66. Richards, R. (2008). *Mud, blood, and gold: San Francisco in 1849.* San Francisco, CA: Heritage House Publishers.

67. Richards, R. (2008). *Mud, blood, and gold: San Francisco in 1849.* San Francisco, CA: Heritage House Publishers.

68. Richards, R. (2008). *Mud, blood, and gold: San Francisco in 1849.* San Francisco, CA: Heritage House Publishers.

69. Asbury, H. (1933). *The gangs of San Francisco: An informal history of the San Francisco underworld.* London, England: Arrow Books.

70. Richards, R. (2008). *Mud, blood, and gold: San Francisco in 1849.* San Francisco, CA: Heritage House Publishers.

71. Richards, R. (2008). *Mud, blood, and gold: San Francisco in 1849.* San Francisco, CA: Heritage House Publishers.

72. Bureau of Labor Statistic's annual Consumer Price Index (CPI). (2016). Retrieved from http://www.in2013dollars.com/1863-dollars-in-2016?amount=300.

73. Asbury, H. (1927). *The gangs of New York: An informal history of the underworld.* New York, NY: Vintage Books.

74. Asbury, H. (1927). *The gangs of New York: An informal history of the underworld.* New York, NY: Vintage Books.

75. Asbury, H. (1927). *The gangs of New York: An informal history of the underworld.* New York, NY: Vintage Books.

76. Perkins, U. E. (1987). *Explosion of Chicago's black street gangs: 1900 to present.* Chicago, IL: Third World Press.

77. Lindberg, R. C. (2016). *Gangland Chicago: Criminality and lawlessness in the Windy City.* Lanham, MD: Rowman and Littlefield.

78. Howell, J. C., and Moore, J. P. (May 2010). *History of street gangs in the United States.* National Gang Center Bulletin No. 4. Bureau of Justice Assistance.

79. Howell, J. C., and Moore, J. P. (May 2010). *History of street gangs in the United States.* National Gang Center Bulletin No. 4. Bureau of Justice Assistance.

80. Howell, J. C., and Moore, J. P. (May 2010). *History of street gangs in the United States.* National Gang Center Bulletin No. 4. Bureau of Justice Assistance.

81. Howell, J. C. (2015). *The history of street gangs in the United States: Their origins and transformations.* Lanham, MD: Lexington Books.

82. Thrasher, F. M. (1927). *The gang: A study of 1,313 gangs in Chicago.* Chicago, IL: University of Chicago Press (reprinted 2000).

83. Allender, D. (2001). "Gangs in Middle America." *FBI Law Enforcement Bulletin, 70* (12).

84. History.com (2015). "This Day in History: Outlaw Frank James Born in Missouri." A+E Networks. Retrieved from http://www.history.com/this-day-in-history/outlaw-frank-james-born-in-missouri.

85. Clark, J., and Palattella, E. (2015). *A history of heists: Bank robbery in America.* Lanham, MD: Rowman & Littlefield.

86. Clark, J., and Palattella, E. (2015). *A history of heists: Bank robbery in America.* Lanham, MD: Rowman & Littlefield.

87. Clark, J., and Palattella, E. (2015). *A history of heists: Bank robbery in America.* Lanham, MD: Rowman & Littlefield.

88. History.com (2015). *This day in history. Outlaw Frank James born in Missouri.* A+E Networks. Retrieved from http://www.history.com/this-day-in-history/outlaw-frank-james-born-in-missouri.

89. Haskins, J. (1974). *Street gangs: Yesterday and today.* New York, NY: Hastings House.

90. Haskins, J. (1974). *Street gangs: Yesterday and today.* New York, NY: Hastings House.

91. Haskins, J. (1974). *Street gangs: Yesterday and today.* New York, NY: Hastings House.

92. Miller, Walter B. (1975). "Violence by Youth Gangs and Youth Groups as a Crime Problem in Major American Cities." Washington, DC:. U.S. Department of Justice.

93. Hagedorn. John M. (n.d.) Hagedorn's Working Definition. Retrieved from http://gangresearch.net/GangResearch/Seminars/definitions/hagdef.html.

94. National Gang Intelligence Center [NGIC]. (2013). *National gang report, 2013.* Washington, DC: National Gang Intelligence Center.

95. Allender, D. M., and Marcell, F. (2003). "Career criminals, security threat groups, and prison gangs: An interrelated threat." *FBI Law Enforcement Bulletin,* 72(6), 8–12.

96. Tornabene, R. (2005). *Gangs 101 for school personnel.* G.A.T.E. America Inc.

97. Sheldon, R. G., Tracy, S. K., and Brown, W. B. (2001). *Youth gangs in American society* (2nd ed.). Stamford, CT: Wadsworth/Thomson Learning.

98. Ruble, N. M., and Turner, W. L. (2000). "A systemic analysis of the dynamics and organization of urban street gangs." *The American Journal of Family Therapy,* 28(2), 117–32.

99. Ruble, N. M., and Turner, W. L. (2000). "A systemic analysis of the dynamics and organization of urban street gangs." *The American Journal of Family Therapy,* 28(2), 117–32.

100. Ruble, N. M., and Turner, W. L. (2000). "A systemic analysis of the dynamics and organization of urban street gangs." *The American Journal of Family Therapy,* 28(2), 117–32.

101. Ruble, N. M., and Turner, W. L. (2000). "A systemic analysis of the dynamics and organization of urban street gangs." *The American Journal of Family Therapy,* 28(2), 117–32.

102. Ruble, N. M., and Turner, W. L. (2000). "A systemic analysis of the dynamics and organization of urban street gangs." *The American Journal of Family Therapy,* 28(2), 117–32.

103. Ruble, N. M., and Turner, W. L. (2000). "A systemic analysis of the dynamics and organization of urban street gangs." *The American Journal of Family Therapy,* 28(2), 117–32.

104. Sullivan, J. P., and Bunker, R. J. (2007). Third Generation Gang Studies: An Introduction. *Journal of Gang Research,* 14(4), 1–10. National Gang Crime Research Center: Chicago.

105. Valdez, A. (2007). *Gangs across America: History and sociology.* LawTech Custom Publishing: San Clemente, CA.

106. Valdez, A. (2007). *Gangs across America: History and sociology.* LawTech Custom Publishing: San Clemente, CA.

107. Tuckman, B. (1965). "Developmental sequence in small groups." *Psychological Bulletin, 63,* 384–99.

108. Sullivan, J. P., and Bunker, R. J. (2007). "Third Generation Gang Studies: An Introduction." *Journal of Gang Research,* 14(4), 1–10. National Gang Crime Research Center: Chicago.

109. Sullivan, J. P., and Bunker, R. J. (2007). "Third Generation Gang Studies: An Introduction." *Journal of Gang Research,* 14(4), 1–10. National Gang Crime Research Center: Chicago.

110. Sullivan, J. P., and Bunker, R. J. (2007). "Third Generation Gang Studies: An Introduction." *Journal of Gang Research,* 14(4), 1–10. National Gang Crime Research Center: Chicago.

111. Sullivan, J. P., and Bunker, R. J. (2007). "Third Generation Gang Studies: An Introduction." *Journal of Gang Research,* 14(4), 1–10. National Gang Crime Research Center: Chicago.

112. Sullivan, J. P., and Bunker, R. J. (2007). "Third Generation Gang Studies: An Introduction." *Journal of Gang Research,* 14(4), 1–10. National Gang Crime Research Center: Chicago.

113. Sullivan, J. P., and Bunker, R. J. (2007). "Third Generation Gang Studies: An Introduction." *Journal of Gang Research,* 14(4), 1–10. National Gang Crime Research Center: Chicago.

114. Sullivan, J. P., and Bunker, R. J. (2007). "Third Generation Gang Studies: An Introduction." *Journal of Gang Research,* 14(4), 1–10. National Gang Crime Research Center: Chicago.

115. Sullivan, J. P., and Bunker, R. J. (2007). "Third Generation Gang Studies: An Introduction." *Journal of Gang Research,* 14(4), 1–10. National Gang Crime Research Center: Chicago.

116. Sullivan, J. P., and Bunker, R. J. (2007). "Third Generation Gang Studies: An Introduction." *Journal of Gang Research,* 14(4), 1–10. National Gang Crime Research Center: Chicago.

117. Skolnick, J. T., Navarro, C. E., and Rabb, R. (1990). "The Social Structure of Street Drug Dealing." *American Journal of Police* 9(1): 1-42.

118. Skolnick, J. T., Navarro, C. E., and Rabb, R. (1990). "The Social Structure of Street Drug Dealing." *American Journal of Police* 9(1): 1–42.

119. Sheldon, R. G., Tracy, S. K., and Brown, W. B. (2001). *Youth gangs in American society* (2nd ed.). Stamford, CT: Wadsworth/Thomson Learning.

120. Curry et al. (2002). "Strategies to deal with youth gangs" (November 2000). *Organized Crime Digest,* 21(21), 6.

121. National Gang Intelligence Center [NGIC]. (2013). *National gang report, 2013.* Washington, DC: National Gang Intelligence Center.

122. National Gang Intelligence Center [NGIC]. (2015). *National gang report, 2015.* Washington, DC: National Gang Intelligence Center.

123. U.S. Department of Justice (2016). Retrieved from https://www.justice.gov/criminal-ocgs/gallery/outlaw-motorcycle-gangs-omgs.

124. National Gang Intelligence Center [NGIC]. (2015). *National gang report, 2015.* Washington, DC: National Gang Intelligence Center.

125. National Gang Intelligence Center [NGIC]. (2015). *National gang report, 2015.* Washington, DC: National Gang Intelligence Center.

126. Deciples is a linguistic blend of the words decibels and disciples.

127. National Gang Intelligence Center [NGIC]. (2015). *National gang report, 2015.* Washington, DC: National Gang Intelligence Center.

128. National Gang Intelligence Center [NGIC]. (2015). *National gang report, 2015.* Washington, DC: National Gang Intelligence Center.

129. Title 18, U.S. Code, Section 2331[5].

130. Department of Homeland Security (DHS) (2011). *Domestic terrorism and homegrown violent extremism lexicon.* Office of Intelligence and Analysis, Homeland Counterterrorism Division, Homegrown Violent Extremism Branch. DHS.

131. Department of Homeland Security (DHS) (2011). *Domestic terrorism and homegrown violent extremism lexicon.* Office of Intelligence and Analysis, Homeland Counterterrorism Division, Homegrown Violent Extremism Branch. DHS.

132. U.S. Department of Justice (2014). *Domestic terrorism.* U.S. Attorneys, Priority Areas, National Security. Retrieved from https://www.justice.gov/usao/priority-areas/national-security/domestic-terrorism.

133. Martin, G. (2013). *Understanding terrorism* (4th ed.). Thousand Oaks, CA: SAGE.

134. Southers, E. (2013). *Homegrown Violent Extremism.* Waltham, MA: Anderson Publishing.

135. Martin, G. (2013). *Understanding terrorism* (4th ed.). Thousand Oaks, CA: SAGE.

136. Bjelopera, J. P. (May 15, 2012). *The domestic terrorist threat: Background and issues for Congress.* 7-5700. Retrieved from www.crs.gov R42536. Congressional Research Service.

137. Department of Homeland Security (DHS) (2011). *Domestic terrorism and homegrown violent extremism lexicon.* Office of Intelligence and Analysis, Homeland Counterterrorism Division, Homegrown Violent Extremism Branch. DHS.

138. Federal Bureau of Investigation (2017). *What are known violent extremist groups?* Retrieved from https://cve.fbi.gov/whatare/?state=domestic.

139. National Gang Intelligence Center (NGIC). (2009). *National gang threat assessment—2009*. Washington, DC: National Gang Intelligence Center.

140. Smith, C. F., and Doll, Y. (2012). "Gang investigators perceptions of military-trained gang members." *Critical Issues in Justice and Politics*, 5(1), 1–17.

141. Sutherland, E. H. (1940). "White-Collar Criminality." *American Sociological Review,* 5(1) 1. doi:10.2307/2083937.

142. Sutherland, E. H. (1940). "White-Collar Criminality." *American Sociological Review*, 5(1) 1. doi:10.2307/2083937.

143. Glaser, D. (1956). "Theories and behavioral images." *The American Journal of Sociology*, 61(5) 433–44. doi:10.1086/221802.

144. Glaser, D. (1956). "Theories and behavioral images." *The American Journal of Sociology,* 61(5) 433–44. doi:10.1086/221802.

145. Knox, G. W. (2006). *An Introduction to Gangs*. 6th ed. Peotone, IL: New Chicago School Press.

146. Knox, G. W. (2006). *An Introduction to Gangs*. 6th ed. Peotone, IL: New Chicago School Press.

147. Sanchez-Jankowski, M. (1991). *Islands in the Street: Gangs and the American Urban Society*. Berkeley, CA: University of California Press.

148. Sanchez-Jankowski, M. (1991) *Islands in the Street: Gangs and the American Urban Society*. Berkeley, CA: University of California Press.

149. Levitt, S., and Venkatesh, S. (2000). "An Economic Analysis of a Drug-Selling Gang's Finances." *The Quarterly Journal of Economics*. August. 755–89.

150. Levitt, S., and Venkatesh, S. (2000). "An Economic Analysis of a Drug-Selling Gang's Finances." *The Quarterly Journal of Economics*. August. 755–89.

151. Heim, Michael (2007). *Exploring Indiana highways*. Wabasha, MN: Travel Organization Network Exchange, p. 68.

152. Rosenthal, L. (2000). "Gang loitering and race." *Journal of Criminal Law & Criminology*, 91(1), 99–160.

153. "Youth gangs mature into high-risk crimes" (2002, August). *Crime Control Digest,* 36(33), 2.

154. Zatz, M. S., and Portillos, E. L. (2000). "Voices from the barrio: Chicano/a gangs, families, and communities." *Criminology,* 38(2), 369–401.

155. Howell, J. C. (2006). *The impact of gangs on communities*. National Youth Gang Center, Office of Juvenile Justice and Delinquency Prevention.

156. Howell, J. C. (2006). *The impact of gangs on communities*. National Youth Gang Center, Office of Juvenile Justice and Delinquency Prevention.

157. Padilla, F. M. (1996). *The gang as an American enterprise*. New Brunswick, NJ: Rutgers University Press; Allender, D. M., and Marcell, F. (2003). "Career criminals, security threat groups, and prison gangs: An interrelated threat." *FBI Law Enforcement Bulletin,* 72(6), 8–12; Sheldon, R. G., Tracy, S. K., and Brown, W. B. (2001). *Youth Gangs in American Society* (2nd ed.). Stamford, CT: Wadsworth/Thomson Learning.

158. Padilla, F. M. (1996). *The gang as an American enterprise*. New Brunswick, NJ: Rutgers University Press; Decker, S. H., and Van Winkle, B. (1996). *Life in the gang: Family, friends and violence*. New York: Cambridge University Press; Decker,

S. H., Bynum, T. S., and Weisel, D. L. 1998. "A tale of two cities: Gangs as organized crime groups." *Justice Quarterly* 15:395–423.

159. Decker, S. H., Bynum, T. S., and Weisel, D. L. (1998). "A tale of two cities: Gangs as organized crime groups." *Justice Quarterly* 15:395–423.

160. Sheldon, R. G., Tracy, S. K., and Brown, W. B. (2001). *Youth Gangs in American Society* (2nd ed.). Stamford, CT: Wadsworth/Thomson Learning; Scott, G. (2001). "Broken windows behind bars: Eradicating prison gangs through ecological hardening and symbol cleansing." *Corrections Management Quarterly,* 5(1), 23.

161. Knox, G. W. (2005). *The problem of gangs and security threat groups (STG's) in American prisons today: Recent research findings from the 2004 prison gang survey.* National Gang Crime Research Center. Available at http://www.ngcrc .com/corr2006.html.

162. Klein, M. W. (1995). *The American street gang: Its nature, prevalence, and control.* New York: Oxford University Press.

163. Decker, S. H., and Van Winkle, B. (1996). *Life in the gang: Family, friends and violence.* New York: Cambridge University Press; Sheldon, R. G., Tracy, S. K., and Brown, W. B. (2001). *Youth Gangs in American Society* (2nd ed.). Stamford, CT: Wadsworth/Thomson Learning.

164. Decker, S. H., and Van Winkle, B. (1996). *Life in the gang: Family, friends and violence.* New York: Cambridge University Press; Scott, G. (2001). "Broken windows behind bars: Eradicating prison gangs through ecological hardening and symbol cleansing." *Corrections Management Quarterly,* 5(1), 23.

165. Katz, C. M. (2001). "The establishment of a police gang unit: An examination of organizational and environmental factors." *Criminology,* 39(1), 37.

166. Maxson, C. L., Hennigan, K. M., and Sloane, D. C. (2005). "It's getting crazy out there: Can a civil gang injunction change a community?" *Criminology & Public Policy,* 4(3), 577–605; Kakar, S. (1998). "Schools: Criminal activity and security measures administration." *Journal of Security Administration,* 21(2), 55–73.

167. Howell, J. C. (2006). *The Impact of Gangs on Communities.* National Youth Gang Center, Office of Juvenile Justice and Delinquency Prevention.

168. Evans, D. G., and Sawdon, J. (October 2004). "The Development of a gang exit strategy: The youth ambassador's leadership and employment project." *Corrections Today, 66*(6), 78–81.

169. McCormick, J. (February 5, 1996). "The 'Disciples' of drugs—and death." *Newsweek*; Spergel, I. A. (1995). *The youth gang problem.* New York, NY: Oxford University Press.

170. McCormick, J. (February 5, 1996). "The 'Disciples' of drugs—and death." *Newsweek*; Howell, J. C. (2006). *The impact of gangs on communities.* National Youth Gang Center, Office of Juvenile Justice and Delinquency Prevention.

171. Forman Jr., J. (2004). "Community Policing and youth as assets." *Journal of Criminal Law & Criminology,* 95(1), 1–48.

172. Forman Jr., J. (2004). "Community Policing and youth as assets." *Journal of Criminal Law & Criminology,* 95(1), 1–48.

173. Levitt, S., and Venkatesh, S. A. (2000). "An Economic Analysis of a Drug-Selling Gang's Finances." *Quarterly Journal of Economics* 13(4): 755–89.

174. Decker, S. H., and Van Winkle, B. (1996). *Life in the gang: Family, friends and violence.* New York: Cambridge University Press.

175. Sassen, S. (2007). "The global city: One setting for new types of gang work and political culture?" *Gangs in the global city,* Hagedorn, J. M. (ed.). Chicago: University of Illinois Press.

176. Levitt, S., and Venkatesh, S. A. (2000). "An Economic Analysis of a Drug-Selling Gang's Finances." *Quarterly Journal of Economics* 13(4): 755–89.

177. Sassen, S. (2007). "The global city: One setting for new types of gang work and political culture?" *Gangs in the global city,* Hagedorn, J. M. (ed.). Chicago: University of Illinois Press.

CHAPTER 2. THE EMERGENCE OF GANGS IN THE MILITARY

1. Fainaru, S. (April 3, 2005). "In Mosul, a Battle Beyond Ruthless—Onetime Gang Member Applies Rules of Street." *Washington Post.* Retrieved from http://www.washingtonpost.com/wp-dyn/articles/A48017-2005Apr12.html.

2. Hanson, N. (2010). *Monk Eastman: The gangster who became a war hero.* New York, NY: Alfred A. Knopf

3. Asbury, H. (1927). *The gangs of New York: An informal history of the underworld.* New York, NY: Vintage Books.

4. Hanson, N. (2010). *Monk Eastman: The gangster who became a war hero.* New York, NY: Alfred A. Knopf

5. Asbury, H. (1927). *The gangs of New York: An informal history of the underworld.* New York, NY: Vintage Books.

6. Asbury, H. (1927). *The gangs of New York: An informal history of the underworld.* New York, NY: Vintage Books.

7. Asbury, H. (1927). *The gangs of New York: An informal history of the underworld.* New York, NY: Vintage Books.

8. Asbury, H. (1927). *The gangs of New York: An informal history of the underworld.* New York, NY: Vintage Books.

9. Lewis, Alfred Henry. *The Apaches of New York.* New York: G. W. Dillingham Company, 1912 (pp. 89–116)

10. Asbury, H. (1927). *The gangs of New York: An informal history of the underworld.* New York, NY: Vintage Books.

11. Dash, M. (2008). *Satan's circus: Murder, vice, police corruption, and New York's trial of the century.* New York, NY: Random House.

12. Davis, J. R. (1982). *Street gangs: Youth, biker and prison gangs.* Dubuque, IA: Kendall Hunt.

13. Howell, J. C. (2015). *The history of street gangs in the United States.* Lanham, MD: Lexington Books.

14. Howell, J. C. (2015). *The history of street gangs in the United States.* Lanham, MD: Lexington Books.

15. Davis, J. R. (1982). *Street gangs: Youth, biker and prison gangs.* Dubuque, IA: Kendall Hunt.

16. Thrasher, F. M. (1927). *The gang: A study of 1,313 gangs in Chicago.* Chicago, IL: University of Chicago Press.

17. Howell, J. C. (2012). *Gangs in american communities.* Thousand Oaks, CA: SAGE, p. 24.

18. Moore, J. W. (1998). *Understanding youth street gangs: Economic restructuring and the urban underclass.* In Watts, M. W. (ed.). *Cross-cultural perspectives on youth and violence.* Stamford, CT: JAI Press.

19. Curry, G. D., and Decker, S. H. (2003). *Confronting gangs: Crime and community.* Los Angeles, CA: Roxbury Publishing Company.

20. Allender, D. (2001). "Gangs in Middle America." *FBI Law Enforcement Bulletin,* 70 (12).

21. Valdemar, R. (October 25, 2007). "Criminal Gangs in the Military: Although the military may deny it, gang members do infiltrate the ranks—and bring newly acquired tactical skills back to our streets." *PoliceOne.* Retrieved from http://www .policemag.com/blog/gangs/story/2007/10/criminal-gangs-in-the-military.aspx.

22. Valdemar, R. (October 25, 2007). "Criminal Gangs in the Military: Although the military may deny it, gang members do infiltrate the ranks—and bring newly acquired tactical skills back to our streets." *PoliceOne.* Retrieved from http://www .policemag.com/blog/gangs/story/2007/10/criminal-gangs-in-the-military.aspx.

23. Dunn, J. (1999). "Poverty & Prejudice: Gangs of All Colors. EDGE—Ethics of Development in a Global Environment." Retrieved from https://web.stanford.edu/ class/e297c/poverty_prejudice/gangcolor/lacrips.htm.

24. Valdez, Al. (2007). *Gangs across America: History and sociology.* LawTech Custom Publishing: San Clemente, CA.

25. Valdez, Al. (2007). *Gangs across America: History and sociology.* LawTech Custom Publishing: San Clemente, CA.

26. Valdez, Al. (2007). *Gangs across America: History and sociology.* LawTech Custom Publishing: San Clemente, CA.

27. Valdez, Al. (2007). *Gangs across America: History and sociology.* LawTech Custom Publishing: San Clemente, CA.

28. Valdez, Al. (2007). *Gangs across America: History and sociology.* LawTech Custom Publishing: San Clemente, CA.

29. Harrison, A. (Ed.) (1991). *Black exodus: The great migration from the American South.* Jackson, MS: University Press of Mississippi,

30. Cureton, S. R. (2009). "Something wicked this way comes: A historical account of Black gangsterism offers wisdom and warning for African-American leadership." *Journal of Black Studies,* 40, 347–61.

31. Valdemar, R. (October 25, 2007). "Criminal Gangs in the Military: Although the military may deny it, gang members do infiltrate the ranks—and bring newly acquired tactical skills back to our streets." *PoliceOne.* Retrieved from http://www .policemag.com/blog/gangs/story/2007/10/criminal-gangs-in-the-military.aspx.

32. Valdemar, R. (October 25, 2007) "Criminal Gangs in the Military: Although the military may deny it, gang members do infiltrate the ranks—and bring newly acquired tactical skills back to our streets." *PoliceOne*. Retrieved from http://www.policemag.com/blog/gangs/story/2007/10/criminal-gangs-in-the-military.aspx.

33. "Bio" (2016). *Frank Lucas biography*. Retrieved from http://www.biography.com/people/frank-lucas-253710.

34. "Bio" (2016). *Frank Lucas biography*. Retrieved from http://www.biography.com/people/frank-lucas-253710.

35. Johnson, M., and Quinones Miller, K. E. (2008). *Harlem Godfather: The rap on my husband, Ellsworth "Bumpy" Johnson*. Philadelphia, PA: Oshun Publishing Company.

36. "Bio" (2016). *Frank Lucas biography*. Retrieved from http://www.biography.com/people/frank-lucas-253710.

37. "Bio" (2016). *Frank Lucas biography*. Retrieved from http://www.biography.com/people/frank-lucas-253710.

38. Lucas, F., with King, Aliya S. (2010). *Original gangster: The real life story of one of America's most notorious drug lords*. New York, NY: St. Martin's Griffin.

39. "Bio" (2016). *Frank Lucas biography*. Retrieved from http://www.biography.com/people/frank-lucas-253710.

40. Associated Press (January 21, 2008). "'American Gangster' is more fiction than fact: Movie is 99 percent Hollywood, says former narcotics prosecutor." *NBC News—Today.com*. Retrieved from http://www.today.com/id/22716542/ns/today-today_entertainment/t/american-gangster-more-fiction-fact/#.V2mbHVc3eTk.

41. Associated Press (January 21, 2008). "'American Gangster' is more fiction than fact: Movie is 99 percent Hollywood, says former narcotics prosecutor." *NBC News—Today.com*. Retrieved from http://www.today.com/id/22716542/ns/today-today_entertainment/t/american-gangster-more-fiction-fact/#.V2mbHVc3eTk.

42. Associated Press (January 21, 2008). "'American Gangster' is more fiction than fact: Movie is 99 percent Hollywood, says former narcotics prosecutor." *NBC News—Today.com*. Retrieved from http://www.today.com/id/22716542/ns/today-today_entertainment/t/american-gangster-more-fiction-fact/#.V2mbHVc3eTk.

43. Reed, G. E. (2003). "Determining the scope and nature of racial and ethnic extremism in the United States Army." Unpublished doctoral dissertation, Saint Louis University.

44. Southern Poverty Law Center (SPLC) (July 7, 2006). *Extremism and the military: A timeline*. Retrieved 1 August 2006, from http://www.splcenter.org/intel/news/item.jsp?sid=23.

45. California Department of Justice (CDJ) (November 2005). *Gang Members in the Military—Part 1*. Retrieved from http://img2.tapuz.co.il/forums/1_90024783.pdf.

46. California Department of Justice (CDJ) (November 2005). *Gang Members in the Military—Part 1*. Retrieved from http://img2.tapuz.co.il/forums/1_90024783.pdf.

47. California Department of Justice (CDJ) (November 2005). *Gang Members in the Military—Part 1*. Retrieved from http://img2.tapuz.co.il/forums/1_90024783.pdf.

48. California Department of Justice (CDJ) (November 2005). *Gang Members in the Military—Part 1.* Retrieved from http://img2.tapuz.co.il/forums/1_90024783.pdf.

49. Smith, C. F. (2011). "View from the field: The early days of military gang investigating." *Journal of Gang Research* (Summer 2011), 18(4), 46–52.

50. Smith, C. F. (2011). "View from the field: The early days of military gang investigating." *Journal of Gang Research* (Summer 2011), 18(4), 46–52.

51. U.S. Army Criminal Investigations Command (2006). *Summary report gang activity threat assessment fiscal year 2006: A review of gang activity affecting the Army.*

52. "Demolition Man Quotes—IMDB" (1993). Retrieved from http://www.imdb.com/title/tt0106697/quotes.

53. SPLC (July 7, 2006). *Extremism and the military: A timeline.* Retrieved August 1, 2006, from http://www.splcenter.org/intel/news/item.jsp?sid=23.

54. SPLC (July 7, 2006). *Extremism and the military: A timeline.* Retrieved August 1, 2006, from http://www.splcenter.org/intel/news/item.jsp?sid=23.

55. SPLC (July 7, 2006). *Extremism and the military: A timeline.* Retrieved August 1, 2006, from http://www.splcenter.org/intel/news/item.jsp?sid=23.

56. Vista, G. (July 24, 1995). "Gangstas in the Ranks." *Newsweek,* p. 48.

57. Vista, G. (July 24, 1995). "Gangstas in the Ranks." *Newsweek,* p. 48.

58. Knox, G. W. (2006). *An introduction to gangs* (6th ed.). Peotone, IL: New Chicago School Press.

59. Knox, G. W. (2006). *An introduction to gangs* (6th ed.). Peotone, IL: New Chicago School Press.

60. Knox, G. W. (2006). *An introduction to gangs* (6th ed.). Peotone, IL: New Chicago School Press.

61. Egan, Timothy. (February 3, 1993). "Military Base Jarred by Specter of Gang Killings." *The New York Times.* Retrieved from http://www.nytimes.com/1993/02/03/us/military-base-jarred-by-specter-of-gang-killings.html.

62. Egan, Timothy (February 3, 1993). "Military Base Jarred by Specter of Gang Killings." *The New York Times.* Retrieved from http://www.nytimes.com/1993/02/03/us/military-base-jarred-by-specter-of-gang-killings.html.

63. Vista, G. (July 24, 1995,). "Gangstas in the Ranks." *Newsweek,* p. 48.

64. McMaster, K. J. (1994). "An analysis of the 'our gang' syndrome on a military base community and implications for educational leaders." Unpublished doctoral dissertation, The University of Arizona.

65. McMaster, K. J. (1994). "An analysis of the 'our gang' syndrome on a military base community and implications for educational leaders." Unpublished doctoral dissertation, The University of Arizona.

66. Associated Press, (December 1, 1994). "U.S. Marine Sentenced to Life in Killing of Fellow Marine." Retrieved from http://www.apnewsarchive.com/1994/U-S-Marine-Sentenced-to-Life-in-Killing-of-Fellow-Marine/id-d7e3963727d6a3d8cdccd23b280d250c.

67. SPLC (July 7, 2006). *Extremism and the military: A timeline.* Retrieved August 1, 2006, from http://www.splcenter.org/intel/news/item.jsp?sid=23.

68. Rimer, S., and Bennett, J. (April 24, 1995). "Terror in Oklahoma: The Brothers 2 Who See Government As an Intrusive Authority." *New York Times.* Retrieved from http://www.nytimes.com/1995/04/24/us/terror-in-oklahoma-the-brothers-2-who-see -government-as-an-intrusive-authority.html.

69. Vista, G. (July 24, 1995). "Gangstas in the Ranks." *Newsweek,* p. 48.

70. Vista, G. (July 24, 1995). "Gangstas in the Ranks." *Newsweek,* p. 48.

71. McFadden, R. D. (May 4, 1995). "Terror in Oklahoma: John Doe No. 1—A special report. A Life of Solitude and Obsessions." *New York Times.* Retrieved from http://www.nytimes.com/1995/05/04/us/terror-oklahoma-john-doe-no-1-special-re port-life-solitude-obsessions.html.

72. McFadden, R. D. (May 4, 1995). "Terror in Oklahoma: John Doe No. 1—A special report. A Life of Solitude and Obsessions." *The New York Times.* Retrieved from http://www.nytimes.com/1995/05/04/us/terror-oklahoma-john-doe-no-1-special-re port-life-solitude-obsessions.html.

73. McFadden, R. D. (May 4, 1995). "Terror in Oklahoma: The suspect. One Man's Complex Path to Extremism. *The New York Times.* Retrieved from http://www.ny times.com/1995/04/23/us/terror-in-oklahoma-the-suspect-one-man-s-complex-path -to-extremism.html?pagewanted=1.

74. Rimer, S. (May 28, 1995). "The Second Suspect—A special report. With Extremism and Explosives, A Drifting Life Found a Purpose." *New York Times.* Retrieved from http://www.nytimes.com/1995/05/28/us/second-suspect-special-report -with-extremism-explosives-drifting-life-found.html.

75. Nichols, N. (2003). *Domestic terrorism 101—Terry Lynn Nichols (Misfit #2).* Retrieved from http://web.archive.org/web/20031207133144/http://eyeonhate.com/ mcveigh/mcveigh9.html.

76. Barrett, S. (December 18, 1995). "DoD Emphasizes Policy on Supremacist Groups." American Forces Press Service, Washington, DC. Retrieved from http:// archive.defense.gov/news/newsarticle.aspx?id=40488.

77. Smith, C. F. (2011). "View from the field: The early days of military gang investigating." *Journal of Gang Research* (Summer 2011), 18(4), 46–52.

78. Hudson, W. M. (March 1999). "Racial Extremism in the Army." *Military Law Review.* DA Pam 27-100-159.

79. Barrett, Stephen (December 18, 1995). "DoD Emphasizes Policy on Suprema-cist Groups." American Forces Press Service, Washington, D.C. Retrieved from http://archive.defense.gov/news/newsarticle.aspx?id=40488.

80. Hudson, W. M. (March 1999). "Racial Extremism in the Army." *Military Law Review.* DA Pam 27-100-159.

81. Hudson, W. M. (March 1999). "Racial Extremism in the Army." *Military Law Review.* DA Pam 27-100-159.

82. Hudson, W. M. (March 1999). "Racial Extremism in the Army." *Military Law Review.* DA Pam 27-100-159.

83. *The Secretary of the Army's task force on extremist activities.* U.S. De-partment of Defense [DoD], 1996, para. 16. Retrieved from https://www.hsdl. org/?view&did=28893.

84. Smith, C. F. (2011). "View from the field: The early days of military gang investigating." *Journal of Gang Research* (Summer 2011), 18(4), 46–52.

85. Donegan, C. (April 26, 1996). "New military culture." *CQ Researcher*, 6, 361–84. Retrieved from http://library.cqpress.com/cqresearcher/cqresrre1996042600.

86. Barrett, S. (December 18, 1995). "DoD Emphasizes Policy on Supremacist Groups." American Forces Press Service, Washington, D.C.. Retrieved from http://archive.defense.gov/news/newsarticle.aspx?id=40488.

87. Barrett, S. (December 18,1995). "DoD Emphasizes Policy on Supremacist Groups." American Forces Press Service, Washington, D.C.. Retrieved from http://archive.defense.gov/news/newsarticle.aspx?id=40488.

88. Donegan, C. (April 26, 1996). "New military culture." *CQ Researcher*, 6, 361–84. Retrieved from http://library.cqpress.com/cqresearcher/cqresrre1996042600.

89. *The Secretary of the Army's Task Force on Extremist Activities.* U.S. Department of Defense [DoD], 1996, para. 16. Retrieved from https://www.hsdl.org/?view&did=28893.

90. Vista, G. (July 24, 1995). "Gangstas in the Ranks." *Newsweek*, p. 48.

91. Eyler, G. (2009). "Gangs in the Military." *The Yale Law Journal.* 118: 696–742.

92. Quintanilla v. United States (March 30, 2010). *Petition for Extraordinary Relief.* Retrieved from http://www.jag.nay.mil/courts/documents/archive/2010/QUNITANILLA,%20J.A.pdf.

93. SPLC (July 7, 2006). *Extremism and the military: A timeline.* Retrieved August 1, 2006, from http://www.splcenter.org/intel/news/item.jsp?sid=23.

94. Associated Press (January 11, 1999). "Soldier accused of ordering murders." *Amarillo Globe-News.* Retrieved from http://amarillo.com/stories/1999/01/11/tex_LD0639.001.shtml#.V2McmVc3eTk.

95. *U.S. v. Billings,* ARMY 9900122, Retrieved from https://www.jagcnet.army.mil/Portals%5CFiles%5CACCAOther.nsf/OD/FA47861329FA617D85256D44004B9A04/$FILE/oc-billings,j%20.pdf.

96. Logan, S. (February 16, 2012). *A profile of Los Zetas: Mexico's second most powerful drug cartel.* Combating Terrorism Center. Retrieved from https://www.ctc.usma.edu/posts/a-profile-of-los-zetas-mexicos-second-most-powerful-drug-cartel.

97. Logan, S. (February 16, 2012). *A profile of Los Zetas: Mexico's second most powerful drug cartel.* Combating Terrorism Center. Retrieved from https://www.ctc.usma.edu/posts/a-profile-of-los-zetas-mexicos-second-most-powerful-drug-cartel.

98. U.S. State Department (2016). *Narcotics rewards program—Target information.* Retrieved from http://www.state.gov/j/inl/narc/rewards/c27667.htm.

99. Logan, S. (February 16, 2012). *A profile of Los Zetas: Mexico's second most powerful drug cartel.* Combating Terrorism Center. Retrieved from https://www.ctc.usma.edu/posts/a-profile-of-los-zetas-mexicos-second-most-powerful-drug-cartel.

100. National Gang Intelligence Center (NGIC). (2011). *National gang threat assessment—2011.* Washington, DC: National Gang Intelligence Center.

101. National Gang Intelligence Center (NGIC). (2015). *National gang report—2015.* Washington, DC: National Gang Intelligence Center.

102. Womer, S., and Bunker, R. J. (2010). "Sureños gangs and Mexican Cartel Use of Social Networking Sites." *Small Wars & Insurgencies.*

103. Flacks, M., and Wiskoff, M. (1998). *Gangs, extremists groups, and the military: Screening for service.* Retrieved from www.dtic.mil/cgi-bin/GetTRDoc?AD =ADA359551.

104. Flacks, M., and Wiskoff, M. (1998). *Gangs, extremists groups, and the military: Screening for service.* Retrieved from www.dtic.mil/cgi-bin/GetTRDoc?AD =ADA359551.

105. Flacks, M., and Wiskoff, M. (1998). *Gangs, extremists groups, and the military: Screening for service.* Retrieved from www.dtic.mil/cgi-bin/GetTRDoc?AD =ADA359551.

106. Flacks, M., and Wiskoff, M. (1998). *Gangs, extremists groups, and the military: Screening for service.* Retrieved from www.dtic.mil/cgi-bin/GetTRDoc?AD =ADA359551.

107. Flacks, M., and Wiskoff, M. (1998). *Gangs, extremists groups, and the military: Screening for service.* Retrieved from www.dtic.mil/cgi-bin/GetTRDoc?AD =ADA359551.

108. Flacks, M., and Wiskoff, M. (1998). *Gangs, extremists groups, and the military: Screening for service.* Retrieved from www.dtic.mil/cgi-bin/GetTRDoc?AD =ADA359551.

109. Smith, C. F. (2011). "View from the field: The early days of military gang investigating." *Journal of Gang Research* (Summer 2011), 18(4), 46–52.

110. Geranios, N. K. (February 7, 2003). "FBI: Couple had top-secret chemical, nuclear information." *The Seattle Times.* Retrieved from http://community.seattle times.nwsource.com/archive/?date=20030207&slug=webespionage07.

111. Alvarez, L. (February 14, 2007). "Army Giving More Waivers in Recruiting." *The New York Times.* Retrieved from http://www.nytimes.com/2007/02/14/us/14military.html

112. Smith, C. F. (2011). "View from the field: The early days of military gang investigating." *Journal of Gang Research* (Summer 2011), 18(4), 46–52.

113. White, J., and Glod, M. (November 11, 2009). "Muhammad is executed for sniper killing." The Breaking News Blog. *The Washington Post.* Retrieved from http://www .washingtonpost.com/wp-dyn/content/article/2009/11/10/AR2009111001396.html.

114. White, J., and Glod, M. (November 11, 2009). "Muhammad is executed for sniper killing." The Breaking News Blog. *The Washington Post.* Retrieved from http://www .washingtonpost.com/wp-dyn/content/article/2009/11/10/AR2009111001396.html.

115. Guffey, M. (January 25, 2005). "Hood soldier guilty in gang-related trial." *The Killeen Daily Herald.* Retrieved from http://kdhnews.com/news/hood-soldier -guilty-in-gang-related-trial/article_89d6c512-b905-5ff8-a00a-8b6a3b4ee9b4.html.

116. Savelli, L. (December 14, 2011). "Gangs in the Military: A Dangerous Combination for America's Law Enforcement." SFGATE. Retrieved from http://www .gtitraining.org/news_121411.htm.

117. Savelli, L. (December 14, 2011). "Gangs in the Military: A Dangerous Combination for America's Law Enforcement." Retrieved from http://www.gtitraining. org/news_121411.htm.

118. DeFao, J. (January 16, 2005). "Marine who killed cop linked to gang activity: Family members dispute account by investigators." SFGATE. Retrieved from http://

www.sfgate.com/bayarea/article/CERES-STANISLAUS-COUNTY-Marine-who
-killed-cop-2738399.php.

119. Mraz, S. (May 13, 2007). "Sgt. Juwan Johnson: His death and what it's
meant for a gang." *Stars and Stripes.* Retrieved from http://www.stripes.com/news/
sgt-juwan-johnson-his-death-and-what-it-s-meant-for-a-gang-1.63944.

120. Mraz, S. (May 13, 2007). "Sgt. Juwan Johnson: His death and what it's
meant for a gang." *Stars and Stripes.* Retrieved from http://www.stripes.com/news/
sgt-juwan-johnson-his-death-and-what-it-s-meant-for-a-gang-1.63944.

121. Mraz, S. (May 13, 2007). "Sgt. Juwan Johnson: His death and what it's
meant for a gang." *Stars and Stripes.* Retrieved from http://www.stripes.com/news/
sgt-juwan-johnson-his-death-and-what-it-s-meant-for-a-gang-1.63944.

122. Mraz, S. (May 13, 2007). "Sgt. Juwan Johnson: His death and what it's
meant for a gang." *Stars and Stripes.* Retrieved from http://www.stripes.com/news/
sgt-juwan-johnson-his-death-and-what-it-s-meant-for-a-gang-1.63944.

123. Mraz, S. (May 13, 2007). "Sgt. Juwan Johnson: His death and what it's
meant for a gang." *Stars and Stripes.* Retrieved from http://www.stripes.com/news/
sgt-juwan-johnson-his-death-and-what-it-s-meant-for-a-gang-1.63944.

124. Associated Press. (August 28, 2005). "3 soldiers indicted in fatal shooting." *JuneauEmpire.com.* Retrieved from http://juneauempire.com/stories/082805/
sta_20050828011.shtml#.V2MaQlc3eTk.

125. U.S. Army Criminal Investigations Command (2006). *Summary report
gang activity threat assessment fiscal year 2006: A review of gang activity affecting the Army.*

126. Fisher, C. (March 10, 2008). "Petty Officer gets bad-conduct discharge but
no jail." *Stars and Stripes.* Pacific Edition.

127. U.S. Army Criminal Investigations Command. (2006). *Summary report
gang activity threat assessment fiscal year 2006: A review of gang activity affecting the Army.*

128. Kugler, S. (September 21, 2006). "Former soldier accused of smuggling
machine guns from Iraq." Associated Press. Retrieved from http://www.accessmy
library.com/.

129. Coryell, L. (April 11, 2011). "Vet sentenced to 3-years probation for selling
guns. *NJ.com.* Retrieved from http://www.nj.com/mobile/paper2.ssf?/news/times/
regional/index.ssf?/base/news-22/130336472386201.xml&coll=5.

130. U.S. Government Accountability Office (GAO). (2008). *Combating gangs:
Better coordination and performance measurement would help clarify roles of federal
agencies and strengthen assessment of efforts.* Washington, DC: GAO.

131. Savelli, L. (December 14, 2011). "Gangs in the Military: A Dangerous Combination for America's Law Enforcement." Retrieved from http://www.gtitraining.
org/news_121411.htm.

132. WTOC (October 5, 2006). "Beaufort Marines Charged in Gang Activity."
Retrieved from http://www.wtoctv.com/Global/story.asp?S=5501411.

133. WLTX (September 14, 2006). "Richland County Sheriff—Marines Were
Here to Recruit Gang Members." Retrieved from http://www.firstcoastnews.com/
news/ usworld/news-article.aspx.

CHAPTER 3. CONTEMPORARY ISSUES
WITH MILITARY GANGS

1. Chávez, A. M. (February 26, 2013). "El Paso drug cartel killing: Victim was stalked." *El Paso Times.*

2. Chávez, A. M. (February 26, 2013). "El Paso drug cartel killing: Victim was stalked." *El Paso Times.*

3. Chávez, A. M. February 26, 2013). "El Paso drug cartel killing: Victim was stalked." *El Paso Times.*

4. Mercer, D. (September 6, 2007). "Guardsman gets jail for stealing, selling gear." Associated Press. Retrieved from http://www.armytimes.com/news/2007/09/ap_guardtheft_070905/.

5. Mercer, D. (September 6, 2007). "Guardsman gets jail for stealing, selling gear." Associated Press. Retrieved from http://www.armytimes.com/news/2007/09/ap_guardtheft_070905/.

6. U.S. Government Accountability Office (GAO). (2008). *Combating gangs: Better coordination and performance measurement would help clarify roles of federal agencies and strengthen assessment of efforts.* Washington, DC: GAO.

7. U.S. Government Accountability Office (GAO). (2008). *Combating gangs: Better coordination and performance measurement would help clarify roles of federal agencies and strengthen assessment of efforts.* Washington, DC: GAO.

8. National Gang Intelligence Center (NGIC). (2007). *Intelligence assessment: Gang-related activity in the US armed forces increasing.* Crystal City, VA: National Gang Intelligence Center.

9. Tan, M. (September 3, 2007). "Gangsters in the Ranks: Violence. Drugs. Weapons. Has the Army opened the door to a growing threat?" Retrieved from http://www.armytimes.com/news/2007/08/army_gangs_reports_070828w/.

10. Tan, M. (September 3, 2007). "Gangsters in the Ranks: Violence. Drugs. Weapons. Has the Army opened the door to a growing threat?" Retrieved from http://www.armytimes.com/news/2007/08/army_gangs_reports_070828w/.

11. Tan, M. (September 3, 2007). "Gangsters in the Ranks: Violence. Drugs. Weapons. Has the Army opened the door to a growing threat?" Retrieved from http://www.armytimes.com/news/2007/08/army_gangs_reports_070828w/.

12. Tan, M. (September 3, 2007). "Gangsters in the Ranks: Violence. Drugs. Weapons. Has the Army opened the door to a growing threat?" Retrieved from http://www.armytimes.com/news/2007/08/army_gangs_reports_070828w/.

13. Air Force Office of Special Investigations. (2007). *AFOSI criminal analysis assessment: The threat of street gangs on/near USAF installations.* Unclassified report.

14. Air Force Office of Special Investigations. (2007). *AFOSI criminal analysis assessment: The threat of street gangs on/near USAF installations.* Unclassified report.

15. Air Force Office of Special Investigations. (2007). *AFOSI criminal analysis assessment: The threat of street gangs on/near USAF installations.* Unclassified report.

16. Internet Movie Database (IMDB). (2008). "Basic Training." Retrieved from http://www.imdb.com/title/tt1262258/.

17. National Gang Intelligence Center (NGIC). (2007). *Intelligence assessment: Gang-related activity in the US armed forces increasing.* Crystal City, VA: National Gang Intelligence Center.

18. U.S. Department of Justice (DOJ). (2015). "About Violent Gangs." DOJ. Retrieved from https://www.justice.gov/criminal-ocgs/about-violent-gangs.

19. Johnson, J. (December 25, 2008). "Oklahoma City war veteran accused of selling bombs to gang members." *The Oklahoman.* http://newsok.com/article/3332977.

20. Chávez, A. M. (February 26, 2013). "El Paso drug cartel killing: Victim was stalked." *El Paso Times.*

21. Chávez, A. M. (February 26, 2013). "El Paso drug cartel killing: Victim was stalked." *El Paso Times.*

22. Hastings, D. (September 13, 2013). "U.S. soldiers accepting cash, drugs for Mexican drug cartel contract hits." *New York Daily News.* Retrieved from http://www.nydailynews.com/news/national/drug-cartels-mexico-hire-u-s-soldiers-assassins-article-1.1454851.

23. Chávez, A. M. (February 26, 2013). "El Paso drug cartel killing: Victim was stalked." *El Paso Times.*

24. Chávez, A. M. (February 26, 2013). "El Paso drug cartel killing: Victim was stalked." *El Paso Times.*

25. Main, F. (May 8, 2006). "Gangs claim their turf in Iraq and Beyond." *Chicago Sun-Times.* Retrieved from http://www.suntimes.com/output/news/cst-nws-gangs01.html.

26. Main, F. (May 8, 2006). "Gangs claim their turf in Iraq and Beyond." *Chicago Sun-Times.* Retrieved from http://www.suntimes.com/output/news/cst-nws-gangs01.html.

27. Main, F. (May 8, 2006). "Gangs claim their turf in Iraq and Beyond." *Chicago Sun-Times.* Retrieved from http://www.suntimes.com/output/news/cst-nws-gangs01.html.

28. U.S. Navy (2012). *Gang threat assessment 2011—Criminal intelligence brief.* Naval Criminal Investigative Service Multiple Threat Alert Center.

29. U.S. Navy (2012). *Gang threat assessment 2011—Criminal intelligence brief.* Naval Criminal Investigative Service Multiple Threat Alert Center.

30. U.S. Navy (2012). *Gang threat assessment 2011—Criminal intelligence brief.* Naval Criminal Investigative Service Multiple Threat Alert Center.

31. U.S. Navy (2012). *Gang threat assessment 2011—Criminal intelligence brief.* Naval Criminal Investigative Service Multiple Threat Alert Center.

32. Sazonov, S. A. (2011). "American Soldier: Gangs in the Military—A Preliminary Look at Active Gang Members in the U.S. Armed Forces." Unpublished Master's Thesis. John Jay College of Criminal Justice City, University of New York.

33. Sazonov, S. A. (2011). "American Soldier: Gangs in the Military—A Preliminary Look at Active Gang Members in the U.S. Armed Forces." Unpublished Master's Thesis. John Jay College of Criminal Justice City, University of New York.

34. Sazonov, S. A. (2011). "American Soldier: Gangs in the Military—A Preliminary Look at Active Gang Members in the U.S. Armed Forces." Unpublished Master's Thesis. John Jay College of Criminal Justice City, University of New York.

35. Sazonov, S. A. (2011). "American Soldier: Gangs in the Military—A Preliminary Look at Active Gang Members in the U.S. Armed Forces." Unpublished Master's Thesis. John Jay College of Criminal Justice City, University of New York.

36. Sazonov, S. A. (2011). "American Soldier: Gangs in the Military—A Preliminary Look at Active Gang Members in the U.S. Armed Forces." Unpublished Master's Thesis. John Jay College of Criminal Justice City, University of New York.

37. Sazonov, S. A. (2011). "American Soldier: Gangs in the Military—A Preliminary Look at Active Gang Members in the U.S. Armed Forces." Unpublished Master's Thesis. John Jay College of Criminal Justice City, University of New York.

38. Sazonov, S. A. (2011). "American Soldier: Gangs in the Military—A Preliminary Look at Active Gang Members in the U.S. Armed Forces." Unpublished Master's Thesis. John Jay College of Criminal Justice City, University of New York.

39. Romero, D. (March 5, 2014). "The Mysterious Case of L.A. Gangsters in Syria." Retrieved from http://www.laweekly.com/news/the-mysterious-case-of-la-gangsters-in-syria-4487924.

40. Romero, D. (March 5, 2014). "The Mysterious Case of L.A. Gangsters in Syria." Retrieved from http://www.laweekly.com/news/the-mysterious-case-of-la -gangsters-in-syria-4487924.

41. Davis, K. (April 15, 2015). "Feds: Guardsmen tried to sell guns to cartel." *San Diego Union Tribune.* Retrieved from http://www.sandiegouniontribune .com/news/2015/apr/15/army-reservists-arrested-in-gun-sale-scheme/.

42. Davis, K. (April 15, 2015). "Feds: Guardsmen tried to sell guns to cartel." *San Diego Union Tribune.* Retrieved from http://www.sandiegouniontribune .com/news/2015/apr/15/army-reservists-arrested-in-gun-sale-scheme/.

43. Davis, K. (February 3, 2015). "AF: Missileer who ran 'violent street gang' gets 25 years." Retrieved from http://www.airforcetimes.com/story/military/ crime/2015/02/02/minot-air-force-base-missileer-leon-brown-sentenced-25 -years/22753751/.

44. U.S. Department of Justice (DOJ) (2015). "About Violent Gangs." *DOJ.* Retrieved from https://www.justice.gov/criminal-ocgs/about-violent-gangs.

45. U.S. Department of Justice (DOJ). (2015). "About Violent Gangs." *DOJ.* Retrieved from https://www.justice.gov/criminal-ocgs/about-violent-gangs.

46. National Gang Intelligence Center (NGIC). (2015). "National gang report—2013." Washington, DC: National Gang Intelligence Center.

47. FoxNews.com. (October 15, 2014). "Dutch biker gang grabs rifles, joins Kurds in fight against ISIS." *FoxNews.com.* Retrieved from http://www.foxnews .com/world/2014/10/15/dutch-biker-gang-grabs-rifles-joins-kurds-in-fight-against -isis/?intcmp=HPBucket.

48. FoxNews.com. (October 15, 2014). "Dutch biker gang grabs rifles, joins Kurds in fight against ISIS." *FoxNews.com.* Retrieved from http://www.foxnews .com/world/2014/10/15/dutch-biker-gang-grabs-rifles-joins-kurds-in-fight-against -isis/?intcmp=HPBucket.

49. Bureau of Alcohol, Tobacco, Forearms, and Explosives. (2014). "OMGs and the Military 2014." U.S. Department of Justice. Retrieved from https://www.docu mentcloud.org/documents/2085684-omgs-july-2014-redacted.html.

50. National Gang Intelligence Center (NGIC). (2007). *Intelligence assessment: Gang-related activity in the US armed forces increasing.* Crystal City, VA: National Gang Intelligence Center.

51. Gunter, B. (November 11, 2012). "Extremists in the military a longstanding problem." Retrieved from https://www.splcenter.org/fighting-hate/intelligence -report/2012/extremists-military-longstanding-problem.

52. Gunter, B. (November 11, 2012). "Extremists in the military a longstanding problem." Retrieved from https://www.splcenter.org/fighting-hate/intelligence -report/2012/extremists-military-longstanding-problem.

53. Labi, N. (May 26, 2014). "Rogue Element: How an anti-government militia grew on a U.S. Army base." *The New Yorker.*

54. Labi, N. (May 26, 2014). "Rogue Element: How an anti-government militia grew on a U.S. Army base." *The New Yorker.*

55. Goose, E., and Kovaleski, S. F. (August 6, 2012). "Wisconsin Killer Fed and Was Fueled by Hate-Driven Music." *The New York Times.* Retrieved from http:// www.nytimes.com/2012/08/07/us/army-veteran-identified-as-suspect-in-wisconsin -shooting.html?_r=0.

56. Morlin, B. (December 12, 2013). "Minnesota Militia Leader Arrested in Military ID Ripoff." Retrieved from https://www.splcenter.org/hatewatch/2013/12/12/ minnesota-militia-leader-arrested-military-id-ripoff.

57. Morlin, B. (December 12, 2013). "Minnesota Militia Leader Arrested in Military ID Ripoff." Retrieved from https://www.splcenter.org/hatewatch/2013/12/12/ minnesota-militia-leader-arrested-military-id-ripoff.

58. Fernandez, M., Perez-Pena, R., and Bromwich, J. (July 8, 2016). "Five Dallas Officers Were Killed as Payback, Police Chief Says." *The New York Times.* Retrieved from http://www.nytimes.com/2016/07/09/us/dallas-police-shooting.html?.

59. Fernandez, M., Perez-Pena, R., and Bromwich, J. (July 8, 2016). "Five Dallas Officers Were Killed as Payback, Police Chief Says." *The New York Times.* Retrieved from http://www.nytimes.com/2016/07/09/us/dallas-police-shooting.html?.

60. Fernandez, M., Perez-Pena, R., and Bromwich, J. (July 8, 2016). "Five Dallas Officers Were Killed as Payback, Police Chief Says." *The New York Times.* Retrieved from http://www.nytimes.com/2016/07/09/us/dallas-police-shooting.html?.

61. Southern Poverty Law Center. (2016). "New Black Panther Party." Retrieved from https://www.splcenter.org/fighting-hate/extremist-files/group/new-black-panther -party.

62. Southern Poverty Law Center. (2016). "New Black Panther Party." Retrieved from https://www.splcenter.org/fighting-hate/extremist-files/group/new-black-panther -party.

63. Southern Poverty Law Center. (2016). "New Black Panther Party." Retrieved from https://www.splcenter.org/fighting-hate/extremist-files/group/new-black-panther -party.

CHAPTER 4. PROHIBITIONS AND PREVENTION MEASURES

1. H.R. 4986: National Defense Authorization Act for Fiscal Year 2008, Section 544, Public Law 110-181.

2. Curry, G. D., Decker, Scott H., and Pyrooz, D. C. (2014). *Confronting gangs: Crime and community* (3d ed.). New York, NY: Oxford University Press.

3. National Gang Intelligence Center [NGIC]. (2013). *National gang report, 2013.* Washington, DC: National Gang Intelligence Center.

4. Title 18, U.S. Code, Chapter 113B Section 2331(5 A-C)—Terrorism—Definitions.

5. U.S. Army CID. (January 1, 2001). "Criminal Investigations Command (CID) Regulation 195-1." Retrieved from http://www.governmentattic.org/6docs/USA -CID-Reg195-1ext.pdf.

6. Field Manual 3-39. (August 26, 201). "Military Police Operations." Headquarters Department of the Army, Washington, DC. Retrieved from http://armypubs .army.mil/doctrine/DR_pubs/dr_a/pdf/fm3_39.pdf.

7. Army Tactics, Techniques, and Procedures (ATTP) Manual 3-39.10 (FM 19-10). (June 2011). "Law and Order Operation." Headquarters, Department of the Army.

8. Army Techniques Publication (ATP). No. 3-39.12 (formerly FM 3-19.13/FM 19-25). (August 2013). "Law Enforcement Investigations." Headquarters, Department of the Army.

9. Army Techniques Publication (ATP). No. 3-39.12 (formerly FM 3-19.13/FM 19-25). (August 2013). "Law Enforcement Investigations." Headquarters, Department of the Army.

10. Army Tactics, Techniques, and Procedures (ATTP) Manual No. 3-39.20. (July 2010). "Police Intelligence Operations." Headquarters, Department of the Army.

11. U.S. Army (March 30, 2007). Army Regulation 190-45 (Law Enforcement Reporting). Retrieved from http://www.apd.army.mil/pdffiles/r190_45.pdf.

12. Army Regulation (November 2005). 190-30. "Military Police Investigations." Headquarters, Department of the Army, Washington, DC. Retrieved from http:// www.apd.army.mil/pdffiles/r190_30.pdf.

13. U.S. Army (June 2014). Army Regulation 195-2. "Criminal Investigation Activities." Headquarters, Department of the Army, Washington, DC. Retrieved from http://www.apd.army.mil/pdffiles/r195_2.pdf.

14. DoD Instruction (DoDI) 1325.6. "Guidelines for Handling Dissident and Protest Activities Among Members of the Armed Forces."

15. Reed, G. E. (2003). "Determining the scope and nature of racial and ethnic extremism in the United States Army." Unpublished doctoral dissertation, Saint Louis University.

16. DA PAM 600-15. (2000). "Extremist Activities." U.S. Army. Retrieved from http://www.apd.army.mil/pdffiles/p600_15.pdf.

17. Smith, C. F. (2011). "View from the field: The early days of military gang investigating." *Journal of Gang Research* (Summer 2011), 18(4), 46–52.

18. Smith, C. F. (2011). "View from the field: The early days of military gang investigating." *Journal of Gang Research* (Summer 2011), 18(4), 46–52.

19. *NAACP v. Patterson. 357 U.S. 449, 460* (1958).

20. Martin, G. (2013). *Understanding terrorism* (4th ed.). Thousand Oaks, CA: SAGE.

21. Southers, E. (2013). *Homegrown violent extremism.* Waltham, MA: Anderson Publishing.

22. Martin, G. (2013). *Understanding terrorism* (4th ed.). Thousand Oaks, CA: SAGE.

23. Federal Bureau of Investigation (December 16, 2010). "Domestic Terrorism: Anarchist Extremism, a Primer." Retrieved from http://www.fbi.gov/news/stories/2010/november/anarchist_111610/anarchist_111610.

24. Bjelopera, J. P. (May 15, 2012). "The Domestic Terrorist Threat: Background and Issues for Congress." 7-5700 Retrieved from www.crs.gov R42536. Congressional Research Service.

25. Borum, R. (2010). "Understanding Terrorist Psychology," in Silke, A. (ed.). *The Psychology of Counter-Terrorism.* Oxon, UK: Routledge.

26. Hudson, W. M. (March 1999). "Racial Extremism in the Army." *Military Law Review.* DA Pam 27-100-159.

27. Hudson, W. M. (March 1999). "Racial Extremism in the Army." *Military Law Review.* DA Pam 27-100-159.

28. Hudson, W. M. (March 1999). "Racial Extremism in the Army." *Military Law Review.* DA Pam 27-100-159.

29. Hudson, W. M. (March 1999). "Racial Extremism in the Army." *Military Law Review.* DA Pam 27-100-159.

30. Hudson, W. M. (March 1999). "Racial Extremism in the Army." *Military Law Review.* DA Pam 27-100-159.

31. Hudson, W. M. (March 1999). "Racial Extremism in the Army." *Military Law Review.* DA Pam 27-100-159.

32. U.S. Army CID. (2015). U.S. Army Criminal Investigation Command's Fiscal Year 2014 (FY 14) Gang and Domestic Extremist Activity Threat Assessment (GDEATA).

33. Department of Homeland Security (DHS). (2011). "Domestic Terrorism and Homegrown Violent Extremism Lexicon." Office of Intelligence and Analysis, Homeland Counterterrorism Division, Homegrown Violent Extremism Branch. DHS.

34. Department of Homeland Security (DHS). (2011). "Domestic Terrorism and Homegrown Violent Extremism Lexicon." Office of Intelligence and Analysis, Homeland Counterterrorism Division, Homegrown Violent Extremism Branch. DHS.

35. National Defense Authorization Act (NDAA) for 2008, SEC. 544. "Prohibition against members of the armed forces participating in criminal street gangs." Retrieved from http://thomas.loc.gov/cgi-bin/bdquery/z?D110:h4986.

36. Thompson, M. (May 17, 2007). "House Passes Thompson's Amendment to Prohibit Gang Members in the Military." Retrieved from https://mikethompson.house.gov/newsroom/press-releases/house-passes-thompsons-amendment-to-prohibit-gang-members-in-the-military.

37. National Defense Authorization Act (NDAA) for 2008, SEC. 544. "Prohibition against members of the armed forces participating in criminal street gangs." Retrieved from http://thomas.loc.gov/cgi-bin/bdquery/z?D110:h4986.

38. Smith, C. F. (2011). "View from the field: The early days of military gang investigating." *Journal of Gang Research* (Summer 2011), 18(4), 46–52.

39. Eiler, G. (2009). "Gangs in the Military." *The Yale Law Journal.* 118: 696–742.

40. Eiler, G. (2009). "Gangs in the Military." *The Yale Law Journal.* 118: 696–742.

41. National Gang Center (updated December 2015). "Highlights of Gang-Related Legislation." Retrieved from https://www.nationalgangcenter.gov/legislation/Highlights.

42. S.867 to the 112th Congress (2011–2012). Retrieved from https://www.congress.gov/bill/112th-congress/senate-bill/867.

43. Hattem, J. (June 2, 2015). "Obama signs NSA bill, renewing Patriot Act powers." *The Hill.* Retrieved from http://thehill.com/policy/national-security/243850-obama-signs-nsa-bill-renewing-patriot-act-powers.

44. Organized Crime (2015). "Glossary of Terms." *FBI.* Retrieved from https://www.fbi.gov/about-us/investigate/organizedcrime/glossary.

45. Organized Crime (2015). "Glossary of Terms." *FBI.* Retrieved from https://www.fbi.gov/about-us/investigate/organizedcrime/glossary.

46. Department of Justice (May 4, 2016). "Thirty-Two Gangster Disciples Members Federally Indicted on RICO Charges." U.S. Attorney's Office, Northern District of Georgia. Retrieved from https://www.justice.gov/usao-ndga/pr/thirty-one-gangster-disciples-members-federally-indicted-rico-charges.

47. Federal Bureau of Investigations (September 26, 2013). "Nine Alleged Members of Hobos Street Gang Indicted in RICO Conspiracy for Murders and Other Violent, Drug-Related Crimes." U.S. Attorney's Office. Northern District of Illinois. Retrieved from https://www.fbi.gov/chicago/press-releases/2013/nine-alleged-members-of-hobos-street-gang-indicted-in-rico-conspiracy-for-murders-and-other-violent-drug-related-crimes.

48. Federal Bureau of Investigations (May 2, 2015). "Thirty-Seven MS-13 Gang Members Indicted on Racketeering Conspiracy Charges; Some Also Charged with Murder, Attempted Murder, and Firearms Violations." U.S. Attorney's Office. Western District of North Carolina. Retrieved from https://www.fbi.gov/charlotte/press-releases/2015/thirty-seven-ms-13-gang-members-indicted-on-racketeering-conspiracy-charges-some-also-charged-with-murder-attempted-murder-and-firearms-violations.

49. Meltzer, G. R. (2001). "Evaluation of a probation department gang reduction and suppression program." Unpublished doctoral dissertation, Pepperdine University.

50. Meltzer, G. R. (2001). "Evaluation of a probation department gang reduction and suppression program." Unpublished doctoral dissertation, Pepperdine University.

51. Meltzer, G. R. (2001). "Evaluation of a probation department gang reduction and suppression program." Unpublished doctoral dissertation, Pepperdine University.

52. Di Placido, C., Simon, T. L., Witte, T. D., Gu, D., and Wong, S. C. P. (2006). "Treatment of Gang Members Can Reduce Recidivism and Institutional Misconduct." *Law and Human Behavior,* 30(1), 93–114.

53. Di Placido, C., Simon, T. L., Witte, T. D., Gu, D., and Wong, S. C. P. (2006). "Treatment of Gang Members Can Reduce Recidivism and Institutional Misconduct." *Law and Human Behavior,* 30(1), 93–114.

54. Di Placido, C., Simon, T. L., Witte, T. D., Gu, D., and Wong, S. C. P. (2006). "Treatment of Gang Members Can Reduce Recidivism and Institutional Misconduct." *Law and Human Behavior,* 30(1), 93–114.

55. Di Placido, C., Simon, T. L., Witte, T. D., Gu, D., and Wong, S. C. P. (2006). "Treatment of Gang Members Can Reduce Recidivism and Institutional Misconduct." *Law and Human Behavior,* 30(1), 93–114.

56. Klein, M. W. (1995). *The American street gang: Its nature, prevalence, and control.* New York: Oxford University Press.

57. Klein, M. W. (1995). *The American street gang: Its nature, prevalence, and control.* New York: Oxford University Press.

58. Maxson, C. L., Hennigan, K. M., and Sloane, D. C. (2005). "It's getting crazy out there: Can a civil gang injunction change a community?" *Criminology & Public Policy, 4*(3), 577–605.

59. Maxson, C. L., Hennigan, K. M., and Sloane, D. C. (2005). "It's getting crazy out there: Can a civil gang injunction change a community?" *Criminology & Public Policy, 4*(3), 577–605.

60. Klein, M. W., and Maxson, C. L. (2006). *Street gang patterns and policies.* New York, NY: Oxford University Press.

61. O'Deane, M. D. (2007). "Effectiveness of gang injunctions in California: A multicounty 25-year study." Unpublished doctoral dissertation, Walden University.

62. O'Deane, M. D. (2007). "Effectiveness of gang injunctions in California: A multicounty 25-year study." Unpublished doctoral dissertation, Walden University.

63. Fritsch, E. J., Caeti, T. J., and Taylor, R. W. (1999). "Gang suppression through saturation patrol, aggressive curfew, and truancy enforcement: A quasi-experimental test of the Dallas anti-gang initiative." *Crime & Delinquency*, 45(1) 122–39. doi:10. 1177/0011128799045001007.

64. Fritsch, E. J., Caeti, T. J., and Taylor, R. W. (1999). "Gang suppression through saturation patrol, aggressive curfew, and truancy enforcement: A quasi-experimental test of the Dallas anti-gang initiative." *Crime & Delinquency*, *45*(1) 122–39. doi:10. 1177/0011128799045001007.

65. Fritsch, E. J., Caeti, T. J., and Taylor, R. W. (1999). "Gang suppression through saturation patrol, aggressive curfew, and truancy enforcement: A quasi-experimental test of the Dallas anti-gang initiative." *Crime & Delinquency*, 45(1) 122–39. doi:10. 1177/0011128799045001007.

66. Smith, C. F. (2008). *Gang members in the military—Homeland security issue or hired guns?* Manuscript submitted for publication in the 2008 National Gang Crime Research Center Conference Proceedings.

67. Smith, C. F. (2008). *Gang members in the military—Homeland security issue or hired guns?* Manuscript submitted for publication in the 2008 National Gang Crime Research Center Conference Proceedings.

68. Huff, C. R., and McBride, W. D. (1993). "Gangs and the Police." *The gang intervention handbook*, Goldstein, A. P., and Huff, C. R., eds. Champaign, IL: Research Press.

69. Jankowski, M. S. (1991). *Islands in the street: Gangs and American urban society*. Los Angeles, CA: University of California Press.

70. National Alliance of Gang Investigator Associations (NAGIA). (2005). "National Gang Threat Assessment." Retrieved from http://www.nationalgangcenter.gov/threatassessments.cfm.

71. National Alliance of Gang Investigator Associations (NAGIA). (2005). "National Gang Threat Assessment." Retrieved from http://www.nationalgangcenter.gov/threatassessments.cfm.

72. Knox, G. W., McCurrie, T. F., Laskey, J. A., and Tromanhauser, E. D. (1996). "The 1996 National Law Enforcement Gang Analysis Survey: A Preliminary Report." NGCRC—National Gang Crime Research Center. Retrieved from http://www.ngcrc.com/ngcrc/page8.htm.

73. Knox, G. W., McCurrie, T. F., Laskey, J. A., and Tromanhauser, E. D. (1996). The 1996 National Law Enforcement Gang Analysis Survey: A Preliminary Report." NGCRC—National Gang Crime Research Center. "Retrieved from http://www.ngcrc.com/ngcrc/page8.htm.

74. Tornabene, R. (2005). *Gangs 101 for school personnel,* G.A.T.E. America Inc.

75. Main, F. (May 1, 2006). "Gangs claim their turf in Iraq." *Chicago Sun-Times.* Retrieved from www.freerepublic.com/focus/f-news/1624518/posts.

76. Ackman, D. (April 15, 2005). *McAmerica.Forbe*s [online edition]. Retrieved from http://www.forbes.com/2005/04/15/cx_da_0415topnews.html and Business.gov. (2009). *Pre-Employment Background Checks.* Retrieved from http://www.business.gov/business-law/employment/hiring/pre-employment.html.

77. U.S. Army CID. (2015). US Army Criminal Investigation Command's Fiscal Year 2014 (FY 14) Gang and Domestic Extremist Activity Threat Assessment (GDEATA).

78. Stabinsky, K. (September 25, 2009). "Home-grown gangs provide dangerous threat to local communities, service members." Retrieved from www.Army.Mil. The Official Homepage of the United States Army. Retrieved from https://www.army.mil/article/27866/Home_grown_gangs_provide_dangerous_threat_to_local_communities__servicemembers/.

79. Curry, G. D., and Decker, S. H. (2003). *Confronting gangs: Crime and community* (2d ed.). Los Angeles, CA: Roxbury Publishing.

80. Curry, G. D., and Decker, S. H. (2003*). Confronting gangs: Crime and community* (2d ed.). Los Angeles, CA: Roxbury Publishing.

81. Curry, G. D., Decker, Scott H., and Pyrooz, D. C. (2014). *Confronting gangs: Crime and community* (3d ed.). New York, NY: Oxford University Press.

82. Curry, G. D., Decker, Scott H., and Pyrooz, D. C. (2014). *Confronting gangs: Crime and community* (3d ed.). New York, NY: Oxford University Press.

83. Decker, S. H., Bynum, T., and Weisel, D. (1998). "A tale of two cities: Gangs as organized crime groups." *Justice Quarterly, 15*(3), 395; Allender, D. M., and

Marcell, F. (2003). "Career criminals, security threat groups, and prison gangs: An interrelated threat." *FBI Law Enforcement Bulletin*, 72(6), 8–12.

84. Allender, D. M., and Marcell, F. (2003). "Career criminals, security threat groups, and prison gangs: An interrelated threat." *FBI Law Enforcement Bulletin*, 72(6), 8–12.

85. Sheldon, R. G., Tracy, S. K., and Brown, W. B. (2001). *Youth gangs in American society* (2nd ed.). Stamford, CT: Wadsworth/Thomson Learning.

86. Di Placido, C. Simon, T. L., Witte, T. D., Gu, D., and Wong, S. C. P. (2006). "Treatment of Gang Members Can Reduce Recidivism and Institutional Misconduct." *Law and Human Behavior,* 30(1), 93–114.

87. Sanders, B. 2017. *Gangs: An introduction.* New York, NY: Oxford University Press.

88. Braga, A. A. (2003). "Responses to the Problem of Gun Violence Among Serious Young Offenders, Guide No. 23." Retrieved from http://www.popcenter.org/problems/gun_violence.

89. Howell, J. C. (2015). *The history of street gangs in the United States: Their origins and transformations.* Lanham, MD: Lexington Books.

90. Braga, A. A. (2003). "Responses to the Problem of Gun Violence Among Serious Young Offenders, Guide No. 23." Retrieved from http://www.popcenter.org/problems/gun_violence.

CHAPTER 5. GANGS WITH MEMBERS IN THE MILITARY

1. Labi, N. (May 26, 2014). "Rogue Element: How an anti-government militia grew on a U.S. Army base." *The New Yorker.*

2. Labi, N. (May 26, 2014). "Rogue Element: How an anti-government militia grew on a U.S. Army base." *The New Yorker.*

3. Hogg, D. R. (1993). "A Military Campaign Against Gangs: Internal Security Operations in the United States by Active Duty Forces." Retrieved from http://oai.dtic.mil/oai/oai?verb=getRecord&metadataPrefix=html&identifier=ADA274041.

4. Tomes, R. R. (2004). "Relearning Counterinsurgency Warfare," *Parameters* (Spring 2004), 16–28. Retrieved from http://strategicstudiesinstitute.army.mil/pubs/parameters/Articles/04spring/tomes.pdf.

5. Field Manual (FM) 3-24 MCWP 3-33.5 (May 2014). "Insurgencies and Countering Insurgencies." Headquarters, Department of the Army: Washington, DC. Retrieved from https://fas.org/irp/doddir/army/fm3-24.pdf.

6. Rothstein, M. D., LTC (September 29, 2006). "Fire, ready, aim: Developing intercultural skills during officer formal education." Air War College, Air University. Retrieved from http://www.au.af.mil/au/.../rothstein%20psp.doc.

7. Rothstein, M. D., LTC (September 29, 2006). "Fire, ready, aim: Developing intercultural skills during officer formal education." Air War College, Air University. Retrieved from http://www.au.af.mil/au/.../rothstein%20psp.doc.

8. Melillo, M. R. (2006). "Outfitting a Big-War Military with Small-War Capabilities." *Parameters* (Autumn, 2006), 22–35.

9. Manwaring, M. G. (2005). "Street Gangs: The new urban insurgency." Retrieved from http://www.strategicstudiesinstitute.army.mil/pubs/display.cfm?PubID=597.

10. Manwaring, M. G. (2005). "Street Gangs: The new urban insurgency." Retrieved from http://www.strategicstudiesinstitute.army.mil/pubs/display.cfm?PubID=597.

11. National Gang Intelligence Center [NGIC]. (2009). *National gang threat assessment, 2009.* Washington, DC: National Gang Intelligence Center.

12. National Gang Intelligence Center [NGIC]. (2009). *National gang threat assessment, 2009.* Washington, DC: National Gang Intelligence Center.

13. National Gang Intelligence Center [NGIC]. (2015). *National gang report, 2015.* Washington, DC: National Gang Intelligence Center.

14. McGoey, C. E. (2014). "Home Invasion Robbery: Protect Your Family with a Security Plan." Retrieved from http://www.crimedoctor.com/homeinvasion.htm and U.S. Army (1993, C1 1995). "Close Quarters Combat Techniques." Appendix K, Field Manual (FM) 19-10. Retrieved from http://www.globalsecurity.org/military/ library/ policy/ army/fm/90-10/90-10apg.htm.

15. U. S. Department of Defense. "Enlistment/reenlistment document." *Armed Forces of the United States: DD Form 4/1* (2007). Retrieved from http://www.dtic .mil/whs/directives/infomgt/forms/eforms/dd0004.pdf.

16. Knox, G. W. (2006). *An introduction to gangs* (6th ed.). Peotone, IL: New Chicago School Press.

17. National Gang Intelligence Center [NGIC]. (2007). *Intelligence assessment: Gang-related activity in the US armed forces increasing.* Crystal City, VA: National Gang Intelligence Center.

18. Alpert, G., Rojek. J., Hansen, A., Shannon, R. L., and Decker, S. H. (2011). *Examining the prevalence and impact of gangs in college athletic programs using multiple sources: A final report.* Bureau of Justice Assistance, the Office of Justice Programs, U.S. Department of Justice (2008-F3611-SC-DD).

19. Knox, G. W. (2006). *An introduction to gangs* (6th ed.). Peotone, IL: New Chicago School Press.

20. Galiani, S., Rossi, M. A., and Schargrodsky, E. (2009). "The effects of peacetime and wartime conscription on criminal activity." *Scandinavian Journal of Economics*, 119(3), April 2016.

21. Galiani, S., Rossi, M. A., and Schargrodsky, E. (2009). "The effects of peacetime and wartime conscription on criminal activity." *Scandinavian Journal of Economics*, 119(3), April 2016.

22. Galiani, S., Rossi, M. A., and Schargrodsky, E. (2009). "The effects of peacetime and wartime conscription on criminal activity." *Scandinavian Journal of Economics*, 119(3), April 2016.

23. Albaek, K., Leth-Petersen, S., le Maire, D., and Tranaes, T. *Does peacetime military service affect crime?* IZA Discussion Paper No. 7528. Retrieved from SSRN: http://ssrn.com/abstract=2314823.

24. Albaek, K., Leth-Petersen, S., le Maire, D., and Tranaes, T. *Does peacetime military service affect crime?* IZA Discussion Paper No. 7528. Retrieved from SSRN: http://ssrn.com/abstract=2314823.

25. Teachman, J., and Tedrow, L. (2015). "Military Service and Desistance from Contact with the Criminal Justice System." Unpublished paper. Research in support of National Institute of Child Health and Human Development grant R15 HD069968, accompanying Poster submission Poster Session on Demography of Crime. Population Association of America, 2015 Annual Meeting.

26. Teachman, J., and Tedrow, L. (2015). "Military Service and Desistance from Contact with the Criminal Justice System." Unpublished paper. Research in support of National Institute of Child Health and Human Development grant R15 HD069968, accompanying Poster submission Poster Session on Demography of Crime. Population Association of America, 2015 Annual Meeting.

27. Boucai, M. (2007). "Balancing your strengths against your felonies: Considerations for military recruitment of ex-offenders." 61 U. Miami L. Rev. 997.

28. Boucai, M. (2007). "Balancing your strengths against your felonies: Considerations for military recruitment of ex-offenders." 61 U. Miami L. Rev. 997.

29. Boucai, M. (2007). "Balancing your strengths against your felonies: Considerations for military recruitment of ex-offenders." 61 U. Miami L. Rev. 997.

30. Alpert, G., Rojek. J., Hansen, A., Shannon, R. L., and Decker, S. H. (2011). *Examining the prevalence and impact of gangs in college athletic programs using multiple sources: A final report.* Bureau of Justice Assistance, the Office of Justice Programs, U.S. Department of Justice (2008-F3611-SC-DD).

31. U.S. Department of Defense (January 2017). *Department of Defense (DoD) Personnel, Workforce Reports & Publications.* Retrieved from https://www.dmdc .osd.mil/appj/dwp/dwp_reports.jsp.

32. Knox, G. W. (2006). *An introduction to gangs* (6th ed.). Peotone, IL: New Chicago School Press.

33. Knox, G. W. (1992). "Gang Members Seeking Firearms and Ordnance from Friends in the American Military." *Gangs, Guerilla Warfare, and Social Conflict.* Available at http://www.ngcrc.com/introcha.html.

34. Knox, G. W. (1992). Gang Members Seeking Firearms and Ordnance from Friends in the American Military. *Gangs, Guerilla Warfare, and Social Conflict.* Available at http://www.ngcrc.com/introcha.html.

35. Jackson, J. (June 27, 2007). *Armed & Dangerous: How Extremists are Infiltrating the Military.* Retrieved from http://www.portfolioweekly.com/Pages/ InfoPage.php/iID/3028.

36. FBI Intelligence Assessment (2007). *Gang-related activity in the US armed forces increasing.* Retrieved from http://stripes.com/07/feb07/gangs/ncis_gangs.pdf.

37. FBI Intelligence Assessment (2007). *Gang-related activity in the US armed forces increasing.* Retrieved from http://stripes.com/07/feb07/gangs/ncis_gangs.pdf.

38. FBI Intelligence Assessment (2007). *Gang-related activity in the US armed forces increasing.* Retrieved from http://stripes.com/07/feb07/gangs/ncis_gangs.pdf.

39. Main, F. (2007). "FBI details threat from gangs in military: Says members of Illinois," *Chicago Sun-Times,* 2007-01-20.

40. Main, F. (2007). "FBI details threat from gangs in military: Says members of Illinois," *Chicago Sun-Times,* 2007-01-20.

41. FBI Intelligence Assessment (2007). *Gang-related activity in the US armed forces increasing.* Retrieved from http://stripes.com/07/feb07/gangs/ncis_gangs.pdf.

42. FBI Intelligence Assessment (2007). *Gang-related activity in the US armed forces increasing.* Retrieved from http://stripes.com/07/feb07/gangs/ncis_gangs.pdf.

43. FBI Intelligence Assessment (2007). *Gang-related activity in the US armed forces increasing.* Retrieved from http://stripes.com/07/feb07/gangs/ncis_gangs.pdf.

44. Knox, G. W. (1992). "Gang Members Seeking Firearms and Ordnance from Friends in the American Military." *Gangs, Guerilla Warfare, and Social Conflict.* Available at http://www.ngcrc.com/introcha.html.

45. FBI Intelligence Assessment (2007). *Gang-related activity in the US armed forces increasing.* Retrieved from http://stripes.com/07/feb07/gangs/ncis_gangs.pdf.

46. FBI Intelligence Assessment (2007). *Gang-related activity in the US armed forces increasing.* Retrieved from http://stripes.com/07/feb07/gangs/ncis_gangs.pdf.

47. Eyler, G. (2009). "Gangs in the Military." *The Yale Law Journal.* 118: 696–742.

48. Eyler, G. (2009). "Gangs in the Military." *The Yale Law Journal.* 118: 696–742.

49. Sazonov, S. A. (2011). "American soldier: Gangs in the military, a preliminary look at active gang members in the U.S. Armed Forces." Unpublished Master's Thesis. John Jay College of Criminal Justice, City University of New York.

50. Sazonov, S. A. (2011). "American soldier: Gangs in the military, a preliminary look at active gang members in the U.S. Armed Forces." Unpublished Master's Thesis. John Jay College of Criminal Justice, City University of New York.

51. Sazonov, S. A. (2011). "American soldier: Gangs in the military, a preliminary look at active gang members in the U.S. Armed Forces." Unpublished Master's Thesis. John Jay College of Criminal Justice, City University of New York.

52. Alvarez, L. (February 14, 2007). "Army Giving More Waivers in Recruiting." *New York Times.* Retrieved from http://www.nytimes.com/2007/02/14/us/14military.html?_r=0.

53. Alvarez, L. (February 14, 2007). "Army Giving More Waivers in Recruiting." *New York Times.* Retrieved from http://www.nytimes.com/2007/02/14/us/14military.html?_r=0.

54. Alvarez, L. (February 14, 2007). "Army Giving More Waivers in Recruiting." *New York Times.* Retrieved from http://www.nytimes.com/2007/02/14/us/14military.html?_r=0.

55. Klatell, J. (July 28, 2007). "Exclusive: Gangs spreading in the military." CBS. Retrieved from http://www.cbsnews.com/news/exclusive-gangs-spreading-in-the-military/.

56. Klatell, J. (July 28, 2007). "Exclusive: Gangs spreading in the military." CBS. Retrieved from http://www.cbsnews.com/news/exclusive-gangs-spreading-in-the-military/.

57. Eyler, G. (2009). "Gangs in the Military." *The Yale Law Journal.* 118: 696–742.

58. Eyler, G. (2009). "Gangs in the Military." *The Yale Law Journal.* 118: 696–742.

59. Eyler, G. (2009). "Gangs in the Military." *The Yale Law Journal.* 118: 696–742.

60. Sazonov, S. A. (2011). "American soldier: Gangs in the military, a preliminary look at active gang members in the U.S. Armed Forces." Unpublished Master's Thesis. John Jay College of Criminal Justice, City University of New York.

61. Sazonov, S. A. (2011). "American soldier: Gangs in the military, a preliminary look at active gang members in the U.S. Armed Forces." Unpublished Master's Thesis. John Jay College of Criminal Justice, City University of New York.

62. Alpert, G., Rojek. J., Hansen, A., Shannon, R. L., and Decker, S. H. (2011). *Examining the prevalence and impact of gangs in college athletic programs using multiple sources: A final report.* Bureau of Justice Assistance, the Office of Justice Programs, U.S. Department of Justice (2008-F3611-SC-DD).

63. Flacks, M., and Wiskoff, M. F. (1999). *Gangs, extremists groups, and the military: Screening for service.* Retrieved from http://stinet.dtic.mil/oai/oai?&verb=g etRecord&metadataPrefix=html&identifier=ADA359551.

64. Manwaring, M. G. (2005). *Street gangs: The new urban insurgency.* Retrieved from http://www.strategicstudiesinstitute.army.mil/pubs/display.cfm?PubID=597.

65. Manwaring, M. G. (2005). *Street gangs: The new urban insurgency.* Retrieved from http://www.strategicstudiesinstitute.army.mil/pubs/display.cfm?PubID=597.

66. National Gang Intelligence Center [NGIC]. (2013). *National gang report, 2013.* Washington, DC: National Gang Intelligence Center.

67. National Gang Intelligence Center [NGIC]. (2013). *National gang report, 2013.* Washington, DC: National Gang Intelligence Center.

68. U.S. Army Criminal Investigations Command (2006–2016). *Summary reports on gang and domestic extremist activity threat assessment fiscal years 2005–2015: A review of gang and extremist activity affecting the Army.*

69. U.S. Army Criminal Investigations Command (2006–2016). *Summary reports on gang and domestic extremist activity threat assessment fiscal years 2005–2015: A review of gang and extremist activity affecting the Army.*

70. U.S. Navy (2012). *Gang threat assessment 2011—Criminal intelligence brief.* Naval Criminal Investigative Service Multiple Threat Alert Center.

71. Air Force Office of Special Investigations (2007). *AFOSI criminal analysis assessment: The threat of street gangs on/near USAF installations.* Unclassified report.

72. U.S. Army Criminal Investigations Command (2011). *Summary report gang and extremist activity threat assessment fiscal year 2010: A review of gang and extremist activity affecting the Army.*

73. U.S. Army Criminal Investigations Command (2013–2016). *Summary reports on gang and domestic extremist activity threat assessment fiscal years 2012–2015: A review of gang and extremist activity affecting the Army.*

74. U.S. Army Criminal Investigations Command (2016). *Gang and domestic extremist activity threat assessment (GDEATA) fiscal year 2015.* U.S. Army Criminal Investigations Command.

75. National Gang Intelligence Center [NGIC]. (2015). *National gang report, 2015.* Washington, DC: National Gang Intelligence Center.

76. U.S. Army Criminal Investigations Command. (2013–2016). *Summary reports on gang and domestic extremist activity threat assessment fiscal years 2012–2015: A review of gang and extremist activity affecting the Army.*

77. Army CID. *Joint gangs in the military presentation,* Proposal draft 5-1-13.

78. U.S. Army Criminal Investigations Command. (2016). *Gang and domestic extremist activity threat assessment (GDEATA) fiscal year 2015.* U.S. Army Criminal Investigations Command.

79. U.S. Army Criminal Investigations Command (2016). *Gang and domestic extremist activity threat assessment (GDEATA) fiscal year 2015.* U.S. Army Criminal Investigations Command.

80. U.S. Army Criminal Investigations Command (2016). *Gang and domestic extremist activity threat assessment (GDEATA) fiscal year 2015.* U.S. Army Criminal Investigations Command.

81. Flacks, M., and Wiskoff, M. F. (1999). *Gangs, extremists groups, and the military: Screening for service.* Retrieved from http://stinet.dtic.mil/oai/oai?&verb=g etRecord&metadataPrefix=html&identifier=ADA359551.

82. Flacks, M., and Wiskoff, M. F. (1999). *Gangs, extremists groups, and the military: Screening for service.* Retrieved from http://stinet.dtic.mil/oai/oai?&verb=g etRecord&metadataPrefix=html&identifier=ADA359551.

CHAPTER 6. MILITARY-TRAINED GANG MEMBERS IN CIVILIAN COMMUNITIES

1. Southern Poverty Law Center (2016). "New Black Panther Party." Retrieved from https://www.splcenter.org/fighting-hate/extremist-files/group/new-black-panther -party.

2. Fernandez, M., Perez-Pena, R., and Bromwich, J. (July 8, 2016). "Five Dallas Officers Were Killed as Payback, Police Chief Says." *The New York Times.* Retrieved from http://www.nytimes.com/2016/07/09/us/dallas-police-shooting.html.

3. Egley, Jr., A., Howell, J. C., and Harris, M. (2014). *Highlights of the 2012 national youth gang survey.* Retrieved from http://www.ojjdp.gov/pubs/248025.pdf.

4. Pyrooz, D. C., and Sweeten, G. (2015). "Gang Membership Between Ages 5 and 17 Years in the United States," *Journal of Adolescent Health,* 1, 3.

5. National Youth Gang Survey Analysis (1996–2011). "Age of gang members." Retrieved from https://www.nationalgangcenter.gov/Survey-Analysis/Demographics.

6. Katz, C. M., and Webb, V. J. (2006). *Policing gangs in America.* New York: Cambridge University Press.

7. Katz, C. M., and Webb, V. J. (2006). *Policing gangs in America.* New York: Cambridge University Press.

8. New Jersey State Police. (2007). "Gangs in New Jersey: Municipal law enforcement response to the 2007 NJSP gang survey." New Jersey Department of Law & Public Safety Division of the New Jersey State Police Intelligence Section. Retrieved from http://www.state.nj.us/njsp/info/pdf/njgangsurvey-2007.pdf.

9. Florida Department of Law Enforcement. (2007). "2007 Statewide gang survey results." Retrieved from http://myfloridalegal.com/webfiles.nsf/WF/JFAO -789KGG/$file/2007GangSurvey.pdf.

10. Pyrooz, D. C., and Sweeten, G. (2015). "Gang Membership Between Ages 5 and 17 Years in the United States." *Journal of Adolescent Health, 56(4),* 414–19. DOI. Retrieved from http://dx.doi.org/10.1016/j.jadohealth.2014.11.018.

11. National Gang Intelligence Center (NGIC). (2011). *National gang threat assessment.* Washington, DC: National Gang Intelligence Center.

12. National Gang Intelligence Center (NGIC). (2013). *National gang report.* Washington, DC: National Gang Intelligence Center.

13. National Gang Intelligence Center (NGIC). (2015). *National gang report.* Washington, DC: National Gang Intelligence Center.

14. Pyrooz, D., LaFree, G., Decker, S., and James, P. (2017). "Cut from the Same Cloth? A Comparative Study of Domestic Extremists and Gang Members in the United States." *Justice Quarterly* (May 2017), http://dx.doi.org/10.1080/07418825.2017.1311357.

15. Potok, M. (2016). "The Year in Hate and Extremism." (2016). Spring Issue. Retrieved from https://www.splcenter.org/fighting-hate/intelligence-report/2016/year-hate-and-extremism.

16. Smith, C. F. (2011). "Documenting the pilot: The military gang perception questionnaire (MGPQ)." *Journal of Gang Research*, 18(4) 1–17 (Summer 2011).

17. Smith, C. F. (2011). "Documenting the pilot: The military gang perception questionnaire (MGPQ)." *Journal of Gang Research*, 18(4) 1–17 (Summer 2011).

18. National Gang Intelligence Center (NGIC). (2007). "Intelligence assessment: Gang-related activity in the U.S. armed forces increasing." Crystal City, VA: National Gang Intelligence Center.

19. National Gang Intelligence Center (NGIC). (2007). "Intelligence assessment: Gang-related activity in the U.S. armed forces increasing." Crystal City, VA: National Gang Intelligence Center.

20. National Gang Intelligence Center (NGIC). (2007). "Intelligence assessment: Gang-related activity in the U.S. armed forces increasing." Crystal City, VA: National Gang Intelligence Center.

21. National Gang Intelligence Center (NGIC). (2007). "Intelligence assessment: Gang-related activity in the U.S. armed forces increasing." Crystal City, VA: National Gang Intelligence Center.

22. McGoey, C. E. (2014). "Home Invasion Robbery: Protect Your Family with a Security Plan." Retrieved from http://www.crimedoctor.com/homeinvasion.htm and U.S. Army (1993, C1 1995). *Close Quarters Combat Techniques.* Appendix K, Field Manual (FM) 19-10. Retrieved from http://www.globalsecurity.org/military/library/policy/army/fm/90-10/90-10apg.htm.

23. Flacks, M., & Wiskoff, M. (1998). *Gangs, extremists groups, and the military: Screening for service.* Retrieved from www.dtic.mil/cgi-bin/GetTRDoc?AD=ADA359551.

24. Flacks, M., & Wiskoff, M. (1998). *Gangs, extremists groups, and the military: Screening for service.* Retrieved from www.dtic.mil/cgi-bin/GetTRDoc?AD=ADA359551.

25. U.S. Department of Defense (November 27, 2009). "Department of Defense Instruction," No. 1325.06: Handling Dissident and Protest Activities Among Members of the Armed Forces. Incorporating Change 1, February 22, 2012. Retrieved from http://www.dtic.mil/whs/directives/corres/pdf/132506p.pdf.

26. Pyrooz, D., LaFree, G., Decker, S., and James, P. (2017). "Cut from the Same Cloth? A Comparative Study of Domestic Extremists and Gang Members in the United States." *Justice Quarterly* (May 2017), http://dx.doi.org/10.1080/07418825 .2017.1311357.

27. National Gang Intelligence Center (NGIC). (2009). *National gang threat assessment.* Washington, DC: National Gang Intelligence Center.

28. National Gang Intelligence Center (NGIC). (2009). *National gang threat assessment.* Washington, DC: National Gang Intelligence Center.

29. National Gang Intelligence Center (NGIC). (2009). *National gang threat assessment.* Washington, DC: National Gang Intelligence Center.

30. Smith, C. F., and Doll, Y. (2012). "Gang investigators perceptions of military-trained gang members." *Critical Issues in Justice and Politics,* 5(1), 1–17 (May 2012). Retrieved from http://www.suu.edu/hss/polscj/journal/V5N1.pdf.

31. U.S. Army (2009). *Criminal Investigation Activities.* Army Regulation 195-2.

32. Tierney, K. E. (1998). *Study of Navy and Marine Corps prison inmates affiliated with gangs and extremist groups: Trends and issues for enlistment screening.* Retrieved from http://calhoun.nps.edu/bitstream/handle/10945/9029/studyofnavy marin00tier.pdf?sequence=1.

33. Tierney, K. E. (1998). *Study of Navy and Marine Corps prison inmates affiliated with gangs and extremist groups: Trends and issues for enlistment screening.* Retrieved from http://calhoun.nps.edu/bitstream/handle/10945/9029/studyofnavy marin00tier.pdf?sequence=1.

34. Tierney, K. E. (1998). *Study of Navy and Marine Corps prison inmates affiliated with gangs and extremist groups: Trends and issues for enlistment screening.* Retrieved from http://calhoun.nps.edu/bitstream/handle/10945/9029/studyofnavy marin00tier.pdf?sequence=1.

35. Tierney, K. E. (1998). *Study of Navy and Marine Corps prison inmates affiliated with gangs and extremist groups: Trends and issues for enlistment screening.* Retrieved from http://calhoun.nps.edu/bitstream/handle/10945/9029/studyofnavy marin00tier.pdf?sequence=1.

36. U.S. Army. (2009). *Criminal investigation activities.* Army Regulation 195-2.

37. National Gang Intelligence Center (NGIC). (2013). "National gang report." Washington, DC: National Gang Intelligence Center.

38. STG is a term adapted from Corrections, specifically prisons and jails, and identifies the subculture referred to in this report.

39. Knox, G. W. (2012). "The Problem of Gangs and Security Threat Groups (STG's) in American Prisons and Jails Today: Recent Findings from the 2012 NGCRC National Gang/STG Survey." National Gang Crime Research Center. Retrieved from http://www.ngcrc.com/corr2012.html.

40. Smith, C. F. (2015). "Military-Trained Gang Members—Two different perspectives." *Journal of Gang Research, 22*(2), 23–38.

41. Crawford v. Washington, 541 U.S. 36 (2004).

Index

Page references for figures are italicized.

251

About the Author

Dr. Carter F. Smith is a lecturer in the Department of Criminal Justice at Middle Tennessee State University in Murfreesboro, Tennessee. Smith is a retired Army Criminal Investigations Division (CID) Command special agent and was involved in military and federal law enforcement, both in the United States and abroad for over twenty-two years. His assignments included Karlsruhe, Germany; Camps Casey and Carroll, Korea; and Fort Campbell, Kentucky. He served fifteen years at Fort Campbell, where he was instrumental in identifying the growing gang problem that began affecting the military community in the early 1990s. In 1998, he became the inaugural team chief for the Army's first and most consistently operating Gang & Extremist investigations team. The team hosted the first "Gangs in the Military" conference and had the first Department of Defense prosecution involving a domestic terrorist extremist (hate group member) on active duty.

Smith has a bachelor of science degree in public management from Austin Peay State University in Clarksville, Tennessee, and a Juris Doctorate from Southern Illinois University in Carbondale. He received his PhD from Northcentral University in Prescott, Arizona, after completing his dissertation on the perceptions of law enforcement regarding military-trained gang members in the community.

In addition to the time he spent teaching while in the military and for the Federal Law Enforcement Training Center's Small Town and Rural Hate and Bias Crimes program, he has enjoyed teaching at the college level since 1990.

He has provided training and taught college courses on gangs since 1997. Carter has provided training on gangs and their impact on the community to many gatherings and conferences, including those sponsored by the Alabama, Arizona, Florida, Georgia, Mississippi, Northwest, Oklahoma, Southern Nevada, and Tennessee Gang Investigators Associations, the American Society of Criminology, the Academy of Criminal Justice Sciences, the National Crime Prevention Council, the Regional Organized Crime Information Center, the National Gang Crime Research Center, the Southern Criminal Justice Association, the Department of Justice, and the U.S. Army.

His academic publications include such topics as the dangers of spontaneous gang formation, military-trained gang members, gangs and their use of technology, and gang members in colleges and universities. He was a co-author of *Private Security Today*, *Gangs*, and *Introduction to Gangs*. He has been interviewed about gangs by several national as well as regional and local television, print, Internet and radio news sources, and has appeared twice in the History Channel's *Gangland* series.

He is a member of the American Society of Criminology, the Academy of Criminal Justice Sciences, the Southern Criminal Justice Association, the American Criminal Justice Association, the CID Special Agents' Association, and the Fraternal Order of Police. He was a founding (and still serving) board member of the Tennessee Gang Investigators Association, a member organization of the National Alliance of Gang Investigators Associations. In 1995, he was a recipient of the CID Command Special Agent of the Year Award and is also a three-time recipient of the Frederic Milton Thrasher Award of the National Gang Crime Research Center in Chicago, Illinois.